FATIGUE FREE
How to Revitalize Your Life

FATIGUE FREE
How to Revitalize Your Life

William J. Green

**With a Foreword by
Ralph N. Wharton, M.D.**

PLENUM PRESS • NEW YORK AND LONDON

Library of Congress Cataloging-in-Publication Data

Green, William J.
    Fatigue free : how to revitalize your life / William J. Green ;
  with a foreword by Ralph N. Wharton.
        p.   cm.
    Includes bibliographical references and index.
    ISBN 0-306-44120-9
    1. Health. 2. Vitality. 3. Fatigue--Prevention. 4. Fatigue,
  Mental--Prevention.   I. Title.
  RA776.5.G74   1992
  613--dc20   91-44235
                                                              CIP

ISBN 0-306-44120-9

© 1992 William J. Green
Plenum Press is a division of Plenum Publishing Corporation
233 Spring Street, New York, N.Y. 10013

Printed in the United States of America

For Ruth, Elizabeth, and Danny

FOREWORD

William Green's *Fatigue Free* is a crisply written, well-researched and well-documented text on an important and often neglected general health topic.

The baker's dozen plus one chapter include all the critical ingredients for thorough self-assessment of chronic fatigue states.

After the Introduction, which addresses the wisdom *and* necessity for a complete examination by a thoroughly meticulous physician, the first four chapters blend lively writing in a clear coherent style with necessary panels and tables of data on the specific amounts of caffeine in various drinks, nicotine and tar in cigarettes, an alcohol screening test, and sleep tips for shift workers.

The chapter on insomnia takes on a number of controversial issues with a particular viewpoint. Many may suffer jet lag generally longer than a day or two but it always recedes.

Appropriately, depression is the longest and most important subject in the book. The controversies about various treatments are addressed. The discussion of the most widely used drugs is up to date and generally on target. I cavil at undervaluing the role of psychoanalytic perspectives in therapy; I applaud the ten recommendations in choosing a therapist and the eleventh suggestion for consultation at the end of three months if there is no improvement.

The other issues of "burnout" and "supermom," of relevant concern to all citizens, are defined by Green in terms that go beyond cliché to clarification.

Chapters Seven, Eight, Nine, and Ten can make you well again with the programs of relaxation, exercise, weight loss, and a proper place for vitamins. Most stimulating is the exercise remedy chapter, which reviews current, valid hormonal links between mind and body. The psychological benefits of activity and a review of salutary styles that are advantageous at less cost than are the health spas is easily worth the price of the book. "Losing Weight To Beat Fatigue," Chapter Nine, points to the individuality of everyone who struggles with the panoply of new diet promotions. No single diet is a panacea nor are pills. Green properly advocates planning, long-term tenacity and a reasonable reward system of long-term restructuring.

Though William J. Green is not a physician or psychoanalyst, he is a comprehensive discussant of all pertinent issues for an "everyman's guide" to exercise fatigue.

The present boundaries of understanding are thoroughly examined in a language that is instructive to all concerned, both layman and professional.

The mirage of chronic fatigue as a "yuppie" syndrome is demystified to the present extent of our knowledge—still an enigma.

By Chapter Fourteen, the general practitioner, the psychologist in clinical practice, and the layperson is invigorated by the intellectual diet of a well-edited and understandable contribution to the social weal.

Ralph N. Wharton, M.D.

Columbia-Presbyterian Medical Center
New York

ACKNOWLEDGMENTS

It would be impossible to write a popular book on fatigue without the research of hundreds of physicians and scientists. The medical community has begun a diligent effort to address this phenomenon, especially as it relates to chronic fatigue syndrome, and its efforts are acknowledged throughout this book.

I offer my special thanks to some of the early reviewers: Joan Reen, Cynthia McGovern, and Douglas Post. Also, special thanks go to those who granted permissions to draw from their works: L. C. Lum, Alec MacKenzie, Irwin Kutash, Hans Selye, Thomas Holmes, Richard Rahe, Gary P. Holmes, Jonathan Kaplan, the American Psychiatric Association, National Academy Press, Martin Shaffer, the American Medical Association, C. Orian Truss, Oscar A. Hill, William G. Crook, Alcoholics Anonymous, Albert J. Stunkard, E. L. Wynder, M. L. Selzer, and the Metropolitan Life Insurance Company.

I also thank the staff of The Ohio State University Libraries, especially its Health Sciences Library, for its assistance in tracking down sources and for providing special interlibrary loan services.

My editor at Plenum, Linda Greenspan Regan, and her assistant, Naomi Brier, deserve special thanks for their careful editing of the manuscript and their professional guidance and support during the writing of the book.

To my parents, Jere and Priscilla Green, I offer my heartfelt thanks for their support of my early interests in science and writing. Finally, I thank my wife, Ruth, and our children, Elizabeth and Danny, for their devoted support of this project. Without their sacrifice, this book would never have been written.

CONTENTS

FATIGUE FREE
How to Revitalize Your Life

INTRODUCTION

Sometimes we feel energized, full of boundless vitality. Each step has a bounce in it. Anything we attempt is done tirelessly, effortlessly. From morning until night, we ride a crest of wonderful, invigorating energy. At such times of joy, all things seem possible.

For many of us, such exuberant feelings comprise only rare moments in our lives. Modern lifestyles tend to wear us down. We feel tired, drained, jaded, exhausted, and simply worn out. Work, play, and activities we used to enjoy lose their zest and we end up dragging ourselves through the days. Nothing seems to lift the veil of fatigue that clouds our happiness and makes us feel old before our time.

We feel as if we've lost something along the way. At some point, our enthusiasm gave way to boredom and disinterest. In solitary moments, we may ponder questions that probe the secrets of life itself. What went wrong? How can I change? How do I restore the zest in my life? This book seeks to help you find the answers to these meaningful questions.

There is nothing wrong with being tired once in a while. Occasional spells of fatigue are normal, but chronic, unremitting fatigue that does not improve with rest is something else. The whole body seems to ache. In time, the fatigue gives way to depression and inertia, which in turn creates boredom, deeper depression, and feelings of hopelessness.

Tired patients seek out their physicians to explain the symp-

1

toms, unaware that they are presenting the doctor with a challenging diagnostic problem. In some cases, he may discover a physical illness, prescribe treatment, and the patient will go on to recover health and former vigor. More frequently, however, the doctor returns with the "good" news. All tests show nothing is wrong. Sometimes he may write a prescription for sleeping pills or amphetamines as a temporary aid. More likely, however, the doctor will shrug his shoulders in sympathy, feeling satisfied that he has done his job by ruling out any serious disease.

Patients leave the doctor's office somewhat relieved, but also confused. Nothing wrong? Well, why do I feel so tired, then? Feelings of relief turn to frustration, even anger, and inevitably to greater fatigue.

In all fairness, we should not judge doctors too harshly. They have been trained to diagnose and treat the most dreadful diseases—cancers, tumors, heart attacks. In light of such potentially fatal diseases, it is no wonder that the medical community has given scant attention to fatigue.

The scarcity of information on fatigue for clinicians has been so noticeable that some doctors have complained about it themselves. Dr. Michael J. Halberstam, a Washington, D.C. physician, searched through the medical literature for information on fatigue during the period from 1966 to 1978. He did not find a single article he considered useful to the practicing physician. "There is no more telling indictment of academic medicine," Dr. Halberstam wrote. His search found "next to nothing on fatigue in clinical practice."[1]

The situation has improved since then but not by much. Fatigue receives relatively little attention from researchers. Many doctors view fatigue simply as a symptom of disease, leaving the patient to look elsewhere for a diagnosis. Unfortunately, their search may lead to unscrupulous charlatans, who make unorthodox medical claims and offer useless products or treatments. Although in most cases these treatments are harmless, they can be expensive and rarely bring relief.

The medical establishment has lately begun to come to grips with these problems. Family practitioners are demanding more information, particularly about chronic fatigue syndrome. More and more doctors are giving serious attention to the emotional and behavioral causes of fatigue, especially those doctors devoted to disease prevention. For the tired patient, the family doctor remains the most important link to solutions.

Some patients actually hope that their doctor will find a physical cause for what they feel. The debilitating effects of fatigue can be as bad as some serious physical diseases, which makes the patient's desperation understandable.

The patient who gets the "good" news and a clean bill of health may be surprised to hear the physician recommend some timeworn advice: Get more sleep, exercise regularly, and watch your diet. However correct it may be, such advice usually goes unheeded by the tired patient, who lacks the background knowledge to appreciate the doctor's prescription.

This book is designed to help the tired patient understand fatigue in its many guises. It is our hope that a greater awareness of the problem will facilitate better communication between patient and doctor and lead them both to reach the most effective remedies.

WHAT IS FATIGUE?

The physician's diagnosis is complicated by the many ways patients describe fatigue. Some say they feel "worn out," "disgusted," "overworked," "burned out," or "just don't care anymore." Others emphasize the physical symptoms, complaining that they are "weak all over" or "too tired to move."

These telltale signs will lead the doctor to one of four possible conclusions:

1. The fatigue is a normal response to something and there is no indication of a medical or emotional disorder.
2. A physical illness does exist and is causing the fatigue.
3. An emotional disorder—depression, anxiety, or stress—exists and requires psychological treatment.
4. No diagnosis can be made, but the patient has real symptoms and deserves further observation.[2]

In general, depending on the diagnosis, the cause of the fatigue will fall into one of three categories—physical, pathological, or psychological.

Physical fatigue is the tiredness that one feels after strenuous physical activity. Muscles ache, limbs feel heavy, and the person may be sleepy. Most people find this normal reaction to physical exercise to be pleasant and relaxing. It is the feeling one has an hour or so after jogging or swimming. This type of fatigue is nothing to worry about and will disappear with rest.

The second type, pathological fatigue, is more serious, but fortunately it is usually easy for doctors to diagnose. The fatigue is a result of some underlying disease or syndrome. When the body is sick, fatigue is a natural defense against further injury. It usually appears suddenly, often accompanied by muscle weakness, as an early sign of disease.

The third type of fatigue is psychological and is probably the most common. The stress of coping with day-to-day living takes a toll on people's emotions. Fatigue sets in as the mind ceaselessly attempts to resolve life's conflicts. The strain wears down a person emotionally and physically. But once the doubts, fears, and emotional troubles are resolved, the conflict eases and the accompanying fatigue disappears.

Emotional fatigue masquerades in many guises: job burnout, tired housewife syndrome, homesickness, depression, hysteria, stress, anxiety, resentment, frustration, and boredom. When this kind of emotional distress persists for weeks or months, a physician may refer his patient to a psychologist or psychiatrist for counseling. This is not always the case, however, and studies show many family doctors fail to make a psychiatric diagnosis, either due to lack of training or a natural hesitancy to intrude on their patients' privacy.

One might add a fourth type of fatigue that is caused by behavior and may include one or more of the other types. Behavioral fatigue is caused by unhealthy habits, such as smoking, alcoholism, drug abuse, overeating, an excess of caffeine, poor sleep habits, or nutritional deficiencies in the diet. Included here would also be fatigue caused by many prescription drugs or the interaction between various drugs. Fatigue caused by such things can be resolved only by eliminating the offending behavior, which is not always an easy matter.

HOW MANY ARE TIRED?

The age of anxiety has given way to the age of fatigue. The pace of life in the United States has never been quicker and the fast lane has never been more crowded. It is no wonder that more and more people are finding themselves in the breakdown lane, too tired to continue the journey.

Although the extent of the problem is difficult to measure, several authoritative studies indicate that millions of adults in the United States are tired a great deal of the time. In one of the largest national surveys of adults, the National Center for Health Statistics (NCHS) found that 14 percent of the men and 20 percent of the women experienced fatigue all the time, most of the time, or quite a bit of the time.[3]

As with other studies, the NCHS survey found that women were more likely to complain of fatigue, roughly 1.5 times as often as men. Other studies put this ratio as high as 2 to 1 among young adult populations.[4] People between the ages of 15 and 34 are most vulnerable, particularly those who are inactive. Sedentary individuals are twice as likely to suffer from fatigue as those who are physically active.[5]

Surveys of physicians consistently find that fatigue is a common symptom among their patients. One British survey found 80 to 85 percent of patients in general practice complained of fatigue as one of their symptoms. The survey found that about half of such patients suffer from psychosocial problems, specifically depression and anxiety.[6]

A study of patients in Denver, Colorado, indicated that single men and women were more likely to suffer fatigue than people with families. Single women tended to suffer from physical causes of fatigue, while women with families suffered from psychological causes. This study also found women more likely to seek treatment for fatigue than men by a ratio of 2 to 1. The researchers provided no theories that might explain these findings.[7]

Psychologists and sociologists have suggested several reasons why women seem to be more tired more often than men. First of all, women tend to see doctors more frequently than men and feel less inhibited about discussing their fatigue. Women are also more likely to suffer from depression, coincidentally by about the same margins. Furthermore, the social role of women has become much more demanding in the past 10 years. Many women are raising their children alone. Others work full-time jobs and then have to care for their children and husbands at home, not to mention that they still do most of the housework. Those who elect to stay home rather than work outside the home do not escape fatigue, since they are vulnerable to the so-called tired-housewife syndrome, a mixture of depression and anxiety that afflicts harried homemakers.

Men are not immune to fatigue either. They frequently experience fatigue caused by stress from their jobs, family responsibilities, or financial obligations. Because they are expected to be "strong," men are not as likely as women to discuss their stress or depression with a doctor or seek treatment in the first place, thus explaining the difference in the surveys.

Although the statistics differ on the extent of the problem, all surveys show that fatigue is a widespread problem and getting worse. At one time or another, men and women of all ages suffer fatigue for prolonged periods.

INSIGHT AND KNOWLEDGE

Identifying the cause or causes of fatigue is more than half the battle. Only after people understand the cause can they take the necessary steps to end the problem.

It is hoped that this book will provide new understanding that will lead to insight and self-awareness, which in turn will lead to solutions. A doctor can sometimes convey the insight that will convince a patient to change, but people have a better chance of lasting success if that deeper insight and conviction comes from within themselves.

When we say that people need to understand the causes of their fatigue, we recognize there are different degrees of understanding. One can comprehend at one level that smoking is bad for personal health, for example, but it is quite another to realize after a heart attack at age 50 that smoking has probably shortened your life by ten years. This book attempts to provide this deeper level of understanding and help people make the necessary connections. With proper insight, a person can gradually alter the offending behaviors and replace them with positive, healthy habits.

Once they understand the problem, people are prepared to take action. Each chapter in this book sets out specific steps for ending fatigue resulting from a specific cause or combination of causes. In some cases, a relatively simple solution may mean cutting back on coffee, while others may require modifying behavior in some other way.

NO EASY SOLUTION

There is no simple, quick and painless cure for fatigue. Neither is there a ten-point program that guarantees success for everyone. Fatigue is complex and highly individual. To regain their vitality, people may need to change fundamental aspects of their lives.

The old adage that "old habits are hard to break" was never more appropriate. Change requires determined commitment. Resistance to change comes from a fear of the unknown, producing that queasy feeling that accompanies visits to unfamiliar territory. Individuals face a natural inertia to move forward.

Any doctor can tell you stories of lung cancer patients who continued to smoke cigarettes until the end or alcoholics who continued to drink long after they were diagnosed as having cirrhosis of the liver. For these sad patients, the habits were just too hard to give up.

Techniques discussed in this book have proved effective in

treating causes of fatigue. The techniques are based on the latest scientific and medical evidence. In their broadest sense, the suggestions may seem simple at first. For example, the doctor's advice to get more sleep, exercise regularly, and watch your diet, seems easy, but *doing* it is something else. People know when something is good or bad for them. What they need to learn is not only *what* to do, but *how* and *why* to do it. The "how" provides the proper method and the "why" explains the underlying reasons that build motivation and enthusiasm.

Fatigue is rarely a matter of a single cause. Fatigue is homogeneous, a complex mixture of various elements. This means the best attack is usually waged on several fronts. One case, for example, might require quitting smoking, reducing caffeine, and losing excess weight. The person attacks one cause at a time in a methodical, systematic way. Once success is achieved over one problem, the person moves on to the next. Attacking all of the problems at once may overload one's capacity for change and result in a setback in the plan.

If the fatigue is caused by depression, the solution is more complicated. Psychotherapy may sound like an easy solution, but emotional change can be slow and painful, as well as expensive. In some cases, fatigue may disappear early in therapy, but full recovery for others may take years.

When all things are considered, patients with fatigue caused by a minor illness may be better off than others, since their problems are treatable and can be managed effectively. But, the overwhelming majority of tired people suffer from emotional and behavioral fatigue. For these people, the doctor's visit is only the first step in the process. The doctor is no less important to them, but these patients must realize they are responsible for their own recovery, and they must take decisive action to change.

As we said, there are no quick, painless solutions. The prescription only sounds easy, but the simplicity is deceptive. Effective measures take time and effort. Changing patterns of a lifetime in thinking, feeling, and acting are the hardest thing for people to do. Success takes knowledge, strength, patience, and perseverance.

PHYSICAL ILLNESS AND FATIGUE

Fatigue and similar complaints of exhaustion, tiredness, lethargy, or weakness can usually be explained by common factors, such as poor sleep, obesity, poor physical conditioning, inadequate nutrition, and/or emotional problems. A review of daily habits, work environment, and personal relationships will usually indicate one of these causes.

As a rule of thumb, fatigue is usually psychological in origin if it is most severe in the morning and lifts as the day progresses. On the other hand, if the fatigue worsens throughout the day, then a physical disorder is more likely.

If a physical disease is present, then symptoms other than fatigue will lead the diagnostician to the illness. Laboratory tests for diabetes mellitus, mononucleosis, hepatitis, human immunodeficiency virus (HIV) or other diseases may be ordered by a physician based on the symptoms.

Although many organic diseases cause fatigue, studies have shown that most tired patients do not suffer from any physical illness. A 1981 study, for example, found that nearly two thirds of the fatigued patients had no organic illness. Of the remaining one third, more than one in four had influenza or some other infection. Most cases were attributed to anxiety, depression, or psychosexual problems.[8]

Nevertheless, the Centers for Disease Control (CDC) recommends a thorough physical examination to exclude dozens of diseases. Based on inquiries from physicians about chronic fatigue syndrome, sometimes called the "yuppie flu," the CDC found many physicians in the 1980s were incorrectly diagnosing the disorder based on blood tests. The tests turned out to be a false indicator. As it turned out, chronic fatigue syndrome appears to be quite rare, certainly not the epidemic many feared in the 1980s.

Another false trail has been a diagnosis of hypoglycemia, a disease characterized by an abnormal decrease in sugar in the blood. Some physicians in the 1970s were diagnosing hypoglycemia when blood tests showed low sugar levels, but research has since discredited this procedure, since many normal subjects have comparable sugar levels with no hypoglycemia. Actual hypoglycemia does cause fatigue, of course, but this is not a common condition. Furthermore, the psychological states of anxiety and depression generally linked to this disorder are not, in fact, a part of the true syndrome. Patients who believe they have hypoglycemia when they do not are sometimes said to be suffering from "nonhypoglycemia" or "psychogenic hypoglycemia."

Physical Diseases with the Symptom of Fatigue[9]

The Centers for Disease Control recommends that physicians rule out the following conditions prior to making a diagnosis of chronic fatigue, since each of them also has fatigue as a symptom:

Autoimmune diseases, in which antibodies attack the body tissue, as in cases of rheumatoid arthritis
Malignant tumors
Localized infections, such as an abscess
Bacterial diseases, such as tuberculosis and Lyme disease
Fungal diseases, such as yeast infections
Parasitic diseases
Human immunodeficiency virus (HIV)
Chronic psychiatric disease, such as depression, hysteria, anxiety, or schizophrenia
Chronic inflammatory disease, such as hepatitis
Neuromuscular disease, such as multiple sclerosis
Chronic use of major tranquilizers, lithium, or antidepressive medications
Endocrine diseases, such as hypothyroidism, Addison's disease or diabetes mellitus
Drug dependency or abuse, including alcohol, controlled prescription, or illicit drugs
Environmental toxins
Hematologic disease, particularly anemia
Other known or defined chronic pulmonary, cardiac, gastrointestinal, hepatic, or renal disease.

Obviously, a complete examination by a physician is the first step in the search for the cause of fatigue. Because so many illnesses manifest themselves in the early stages with fatigue as a symptom, these diseases must be ruled out.

As part of the examination, your physician will want a careful, detailed history. You should review your past with your doctor for any clues to the onset of the fatigue. He will want to know what might have changed recently in your life. Such factors as increased physical activity, new medication, a change in jobs, a new member of the family, decreased sleep, or change in weight should be scrutinized carefully. Let him know the intensity and frequency of the fatigue and any other symptoms that might be associated with it, such as headaches or insomnia. You should also review the family history with the doctor for any occurrence of alcoholism, depression, anemia, or diabetes, since these conditions tend to run in families. A history of the use of medications, including over-the-counter, prescriptions, and illicit drugs, is usually requested by the physician. The amounts of caffeine and alcohol in the diet are especially important to his diagnosis.

Despite his best efforts, a doctor may not find a cause for the fatigue. This occurs in about 8 percent of the cases. When this happens, the physician will want to continue to monitor the patient and review the symptoms again later.

EMOTIONAL DISTRESS AND FATIGUE

Psychological causes are responsible for fatigue in the majority of cases. Stress, depression, and anxiety are most commonly at fault.

Stress from overwork, deteriorating relationships, or deep emotional conflicts causes wear and tear on the body and leads to exhaustion. Relaxation techniques and exercise will alleviate much of this sort of stress. Unless there is some intervention, especially if the fatigue is related to chronic stress, the person is susceptible to physical disease.

Depression is probably the most common cause of fatigue, especially the tiredness that lasts for weeks or months. Depression is closely associated with chronic fatigue syndrome (CFS), a condition with a specific set of symptoms we will discuss in Chapter Eleven. Whether or not the depression causes CFS or CFS causes the depression remains a point of debate among medical authorities.

As we will see later in Chapter Five, depression is a very complex condition affecting virtually all body systems. Often accompanied by anxiety, the depression may also be associated with paranoia, schizophrenia, or other mental illness. Depression responds well to treatment, either through antidepressants and/or psychotherapy.

Anxiety is closely related to stress, although it is a distinct emotional state. Acute anxiety may precipitate panic attacks or hyperventilation. About one third of those people who are depressed suffer such attacks. Anxiety leads to exhaustion and imbalances in the body's physiological systems. Treatment may include antidepressants or antianxiety medication in conjunction with psychotherapy or relaxation techniques.

Resolving emotional conflicts that cause stress, depression, or anxiety may be more difficult than overcoming some physical diseases. Because our emotional life is driven by subconscious forces, the underlying problems may not be readily identified. It is also difficult for some people to admit they have emotional problems. Much like the alcoholic who denies his drinking addiction, those who suffer from depression or other emotional troubles are reluctant to admit it. But, in many cases, just seeking help is in itself a significant step towards recovery.

No matter how established the fatigue may be in your life, the chances are good that you can overcome it with hard work. One thing is certain, more tools are available today to assist you than ever before. There is virtually no reason for anyone to suffer from fatigue.

If the task seems daunting at times, think of the days when you were full of that boundless energy. Remember the seemingly inexhaustible resources you poured into life and the things you accomplished. There is no reason why you can't recapture that tremendous vitality. Human beings have fantastic recuperative powers. With persistence, you can revitalize your life. It may not be easy, but the goal is worth all efforts.

CHAPTER ONE

CAFFEINE
STIMULATING FATIGUE

Caffeine, the most popular drug in the world, is consumed by millions of people every day. It can be found almost anywhere, anytime, and in a variety of foods, beverages, and medicines. Like cocaine, heroin, marijuana, and nicotine, caffeine stimulates the central nervous system and alters mood and behavior. Unlike these other drugs, however, caffeine is unencumbered by social stigma or legal restrictions.

The effects of caffeine were probably first experienced by humans during the Stone Age, when inhabitants of the Paleolithic period chewed plants containing the drug. Caffeine has been a part of the human diet ever since. Today the United States uses about 14 percent of the world's annual supply, consuming about 10,000 tons of the drug in coffee alone and an additional 3,000 tons each in tea and soft drinks. Worldwide consumption is tremendous. Even though Americans drink about 400 million cups of coffee every day, the United States consumption per capita ranks behind a dozen other countries (see Tables One and Two for additional information on consumption in the United States).

People suffering from fatigue often view coffee as a "good friend," something to boost their spirits and "get them through the day." The caffeine provides a quick lift, a pleasant sense of well-being, and enhanced mental alertness. With such side effects, it is

Table One.[a]   *Percentage of United States age groups drinking coffee*

	1962 (%)	1987 (%)
10–19 years old	25.1	5.3
20–29	81.0	33.1
30–59	90.8	67.2
60+	88.4	77.8
All ages	74.7	52.0

[a]From reference 1.

natural for people to turn to caffeine when they feel tired and depressed. The drug is ubiquitous, cheap, and convenient. Restaurants, coffee shops, office lunch rooms, convenience store counters, and even gas stations offer coffee, tea, and soft drinks containing caffeine.

Unlike amphetamines or other stimulants, caffeine is perfectly legal and heavily promoted as a social beverage for young and old. Coffee klatches and "tea for two" social gatherings make caffeinated beverages all the more popular and acceptable. And, despite a confused medical history, coffee and tea are widely viewed as natural beverages derived from coffee beans and tea leaves, another factor contributing to their appeal.

On the surface, at least, coffee would seem to be the perfect antidote to fatigue. It gives a kick to the nervous system, pushing the brain, muscles, kidneys, and adrenal glands into high gear.

Table Two.[a]   *Consumption of various beverages by percentage of United States population*

	1962 (%)	1987 (%)
Coffee	74.7	52.0
Tea	24.7	29.3
Milk	53.6	47.3
Soft drinks	32.6	58.1
Juices	41.4	42.8

[a]From reference 1.

Mental alertness and muscle coordination are quickly enhanced. These pleasant effects are short lived, however, and the body quickly pays a price. Rather than eliminating fatigue, caffeine is one of its most common *causes*. It is so common, in fact, that those who safely kick the habit may experience an immediate end to their fatigue.

CAFFEINE: AN EMOTIONAL ROLLER COASTER

Caffeine causes fatigue in several ways: It disturbs our sleep and relaxation; overexcites the brain and central nervous system; stimulates the adrenal glands, releasing tension-producing adrenalin; elevates, then depresses, our emotions; and causes a variety of exhausting withdrawal symptoms when we stop using it. In short, caffeine puts us on a roller coaster, with all the highs and lows, thrills and chills, associated with the classic amusement park ride.

As tolerance develops, the user finds that caffeine becomes less effective in giving the customary lift. Over time, the effects wear off sooner and sooner, leaving the user tired and drained. To counter these lows, people tend to consume more and more caffeine. This increased consumption is usually triggered during the day, when they experience withdrawal symptoms—mild episodes of anxiety, depression, fatigue, headache—prompting them to take more of the drug to offset these effects. The problem is compounded by alcohol or sleeping pills used to relax after a full day of coffee jitters.

A flurry of medical reports in the 1970s on caffeine suggested that it causes a variety of diseases. Most alarmingly, it was linked to several types of cancers and fibrocystic breast disease, diabetes, and heart ailments. Most of these studies have since been contradicted or discredited, although some questions still remain. After reviewing dozens of studies, the Federal Drug Administration (FDA) in 1988 found "a basis for being less concerned about caffeine's impact on health."[1] At the same time, the FDA warned consumers that more research is needed and that moderation is advised. The dangers of caffeine appear to have been exaggerated, however, and except during pregnancy, caffeine used in moderate amounts—two 5-ounce cups a day—should pose little threat to health.

A SHORT HISTORY OF THE COFFEE BEAN

The scientific name for the common coffee tree is *Coffea arabica*. It is actually a shrub or tree with shiny, green leaves and grows to about 20 feet. Snow-white flowers blossom and then the berries develop, turning from green to yellow to red as they ripen. These berries are the future coffee beans that will be roasted, ground, and mixed into various blends.

Coffee is native to Ethiopia, where it has grown wild since the 1500s. It is grown in many countries today, including Brazil, the West Indies, India, Sumatra, Java, Mexico, Colombia, the United States (Hawaii) and others. For many nations, it is an important economic crop.

The discovery of the coffee bean is often credited to Kaldi, a goatherd in Abyssinia, ten centuries ago. Kaldi, as the story goes, found his goats dancing and jumping around the field one night after they had eaten berries from some coffee trees. The goatherd decided to try some of the berries himself and discovered their stimulating, mood-altering quality.

Two beans dominate the market in the U.S.—arabica and robusta. Arabica is characterized by green and yellowish beans. It is the most popular and is noted for its pleasant aroma and rich taste. Robusta is indigenous to Central Africa, but grown in Java and many other countries. Together the two beans comprise nearly 99 percent of the world market. In recent years, coffee manufacturers have imported more and more of the robusta variety, however, since it is easier to grow and costs less. Robusta beans have twice the caffeine of arabica beans. The coffee tastes slightly more bitter and lacks the deep aroma of the arabica coffee. In the United States, most coffees sold are a blend of the two.

CAFFEINE: WHAT DOES IT DO TO YOU?

Caffeine has both psychological and physiological effects on humans: the degree of the effects depends on the dose. Contrary to popular belief, these effects do not vary much between individuals if differences in body weight and acquired tolerance are taken into account.

Ill effects of caffeine have been described in psychiatric patients, generally associated with increasing anxiety and depression among these patients. In a 1978 study, caffeine was found to substantially increase levels of depression in such patients. Other studies have found improvement in both anxiety and depression in patients once regular coffee was replaced with decaffeinated.

Intake of caffeine stimulates the thought processing part of the brain as well as the area that controls heartbeat, muscle coordination, and breathing. Excessive amounts can cause irritability, headache, anxiety, and panic. It increases the heart rate and appears to influence blood pressure, circulation, and promotes secretion of gastric acids. Additionally, it relaxes the kidneys and muscles in the digestive tract, causing more frequent urination. Higher doses cause muscle twitching and shaking hands, the sort of stimulation that is experienced as the "coffee jitters."

Since caffeine raises the body's metabolism, it helps burn off additional calories, something that attracts dieters and explains its use in some diet pills. As a dietary aid, however, caffeine can be a mixed blessing because it causes a release of insulin, which lowers blood sugar and depresses the emotions, triggering a craving for food.

HOW MUCH IS TOO MUCH?

As with any other drug, caffeine's effects vary depending on dosage, a person's body weight, and acquired tolerance level. Depending on these variables, some people can consume substantial amounts of caffeine while others are extremely sensitive to it.

The most immediate effects start within 30 to 60 minutes after ingestion. Although about half the amount of caffeine consumed disappears in three hours, some of the caffeine in a morning cup of coffee will be present at midnight because caffeine affects mental functioning for up to 20 hours.

Habitual users build up a considerable tolerance to the drug and may experience few symptoms. The heavy coffee drinker, for instance, probably has no trouble falling asleep, even after drinking a cup or two near bedtime, but the quality of his sleep is still likely to suffer.

Since tolerance levels vary, so do the symptoms. For some people unaccustomed to its effects, 200 milligrams of caffeine or slightly less than three 5-ounce cups of percolated coffee can bring on symptoms of insomnia, flushed face, and nervousness. A person consuming 1,000 milligrams of caffeine might experience periods of inexhaustibility, ringing in the ears, flashes of light, and/or an irregular heartbeat. A dose of 10,000 milligrams could cause seizures and respiratory failure and death. Fatal doses of caffeine are rare and usually confined to mistaken injections in a hospital. The consensus of recent studies is that the threat to health begins with habitual use of 650 milligrams or eight 5-ounce cups of percolated coffee a day. At this level, studies have suggested that caffeine causes irregular heartbeat, bladder cancer in men, and behavioral problems.

Researchers have consistently found anxiety more evident in people after they have consumed 600 milligrams or more of caffeine. Lower doses seem to increase anxiety among those already prone to this complaint. A recent study at the University of London, for example, found increased anxiety among mental patients when they each consumed 250 milligrams of caffeine after abstaining from it for a week. In addition to the anxiety, these patients complained of insomnia, muscle twitching, frequent urination, and stomach disorders. For normal individuals, amounts of caffeine greater than 700 milligrams may lead to classic panic attacks. This phenomenon is sometimes referred to as caffeinism.

Acquired tolerance blunts effects from the stimulation of the adrenal glands, which secrete adrenalin. Adrenalin calls the body to action as the muscles tense, blood sugar rises, and the blood pressure and heartbeat increase. This state is commonly known as the "fight or flight" reaction and is a biological response to stress and danger. Artificial stimulation of this state on a routine basis can lead to exhaustion.

WHAT HAS IT AND HOW MUCH

Caffeine is not just in coffee and tea anymore. In fact, the soft drink industry is the largest user of caffeine in the United States, with colas and other soft drinks containing caffeine surpassing coffee as the most popular beverage in 1985. Caffeine is also used in drugs, baked goods, chocolate, candy, puddings, and frozen dairy products (see Table Three). The FDA estimates that caffeine is an ingredient in more than 1,000 over-the-counter drugs, among them cold pills, aspirin, and diet pills.

The caffeine content of soft drinks ranges from 32 to 65 milligrams for a 12-ounce serving, according to a study published in the

Table Three.[a]   *Caffeine content of beverages and foods*

	Milligrams of Caffeine		
	Average	Per Ounce	Range
Coffee (5-oz. cup)			
Brewed, drip method	115	23	60–180
Brewed, percolator	80	16	40–170
Instant	65	13	30–120
Decaffeinated, brewed	3	0.6	2–5
Decaffeinated, instant	2	0.2	1–5
Tea (5-oz. cup)			
Brewed, major U.S. brands	40	8	20–90
Brewed, imported brands	60	12	25–110
Instant	30	6	25–50
Ice Tea (12-oz. glass)	70	14	67–76
Chocolate			
Cocoa (5-oz. cup)	4	0.8	2–20
Chocolate milk (8 oz.)	5	1.6	2–7
Milk chocolate	6	6	1–15
Dark, semi-sweet (1 oz.)	20	20	5–35
Baker's chocolate (1 oz.)	26	26	26
Chocolate syrup (1 oz.)	4	4	4

[a]From reference 1: Food Additive Chemistry Evaluation Branch of FDA based on literature on caffeine content of foods.

Journal of the American Dietetic Association.[2] Among the major advertised brands, Coca-Cola® had the highest level of caffeine, about 65 milligrams in 12 ounces. Dr Pepper® had 61, Mountain Dew®, 55, and Pepsi-Cola®, 43. The study found the levels had increased over the years but were within government standards (see Table Four for additional information on soft drinks and caffeine).

Next to soft drinks, the most common use of caffeine is in medicines, such as weight-loss pills, headache and pain relief tablets, diuretics, cold remedies, and stay-awake pills such as No Doz® and Vivarin®. (See Tables Four and Five for specific amounts in these products.)

EFFECTS OF CAFFEINE ON SLEEP

Since people use caffeine to stay awake and alert, it is not surprising that the drug can disrupt sleep. Especially when it is taken late in the day, caffeine either postpones sleep or reduces its restfulness. The depth of sleep may not change, but the sleeper may wake up more often, particularly early in the morning. Light sleepers

Table Four.[a]   *Caffeine in sodas*

12-ounce serving	Caffeine (mg)	12-ounce serving	Caffeine (mg)
Regular		Diet Sodas	
Cola, Dr.Pepper	30–46	Diet cola, Dr.Pepper	0.6
Decaffeinated colas	0–0.18	Decaffeinated colas	0–0.2
Cherry cola	36–46	Diet cherry cola	0–46
Lemon-lime (clear)	0	Diet lemon-lime	0
Orange	0	Diet root beer	0
Other citrus	0–64	Other diets	0–70
Root beer	0	Club soda, seltzer	0
Ginger ale	0	Diet, juice added	less than 0.48
Tonic water	0		
Other regular	0–22		
Juice added	less than 0.48		

[a]From reference 1: National Soft Drink Association.

Table Five.[a]   *Caffeine content of selected drugs*

	Caffeine (mg. per pill)
Prescription Drugs	
Cafergot (migraine headaches)	100
Norgesic Forte (muscle relaxant)	60
Fiorinal (tension headaches)	40
Darvon (pain relief)	32.4
Synalgos-DC (pain relief)	30
Nonprescription Drugs	
Alertness Tables	
No Doz	100
Vivarin	200
Pain Relief	
Anacin, Maximum Strength Anacin	32
Vanquish	33
Excedrin	65
Midol	32.4
Diuretics	
Aqua Ban	100
Cold/Allergy Medicines	
Coryban-D capsules	30

[a]From reference 1: FDA's Center for Drugs and Biologics.

unaccustomed to caffeine may have trouble falling asleep at all, and noises are more likely to arouse caffeine-users than others.

People thrash and turn more while sleeping if they have had caffeine. Some researchers believe caffeine contributes to the "restless legs" phenomenon, a sensation of creeping or crawling in the lower legs occasionally marked by violent jerkings or twitchings during sleep. This problem is usually inherited or results from spinal abnormalities. Still, Elmar Lutz, a physician at St. Mary's Hospital in Passaic, New Jersey, found that some young people first developed the syndrome after they began drinking coffee or colas.

Studies have repeatedly shown that caffeine affects the sleep cycle. As we will learn in Chapter Four on sleep disorders, a person moves through several stages during normal sleep. In Stage 1, the sleeper is nearly awake. In Stage 2, sleep is light. By Stage 3, it is difficult to awaken the sleeper. Stage 4 is the heaviest and deepest sleep. Stages 3 and 4 are sometimes called "slow wave sleep," a reference to the delta brain waves that dominate during these phases. A person passes through each of these stages about every 90 minutes throughout the night. In a sense, the stages of sleep form something of a staircase that the sleeper ascends and descends several times during the night.

Most dreams occur during another phase known as the rapid eye movement (REM) stage. It occurs several times during the night at approximately 90-minute intervals and consumes 20 to 25 percent of the total night's sleep. REM almost always emerges after a return to Stage 2 from the slow wave phases of sleep.

If a person has had caffeine shortly before bedtime, the bulk of the REM sleep shifts to the first half of the night and most of the time in Stages 3 and 4 moves to the latter half. This is the reverse of normal sleep patterns, when REM occurs most consistently in the latter half and slow-wave sleep dominates the first half. The periods of both REM and Stage 4 are shortened by caffeine. This deprives the person of the most restful stages of sleep needed to avoid fatigue the next day.

CAFFEINISM AND CAFFEINE DEPENDENCE

Caffeine is the most commonly used psychoactive drug in the world. As many as 30 percent of all adult Americans consume more than 500 milligrams of caffeine every day and may be dependent on the drug.

This dependence or addiction is primarily physical, rather than psychological, and can be ended without the risks associated with quitting heroin or cocaine. Unlike these drugs, caffeine does not create feelings of euphoria, so it is easier to quit psychologically. The difficulty in quitting caffeine depends on two things: the amount consumed on a regular basis and the duration of the habit.

Withdrawal symptoms reported by heavy coffee-drinkers who abstain for a day usually include headache, increased fatigue, and irritability. The symptoms intensify the second day and then recede over the next five or six days. Heavy caffeine-drinkers should taper off their consumption, cutting back by a cup or two a day, to avoid the brunt of these unpleasant symptoms.

HOW MUCH CAFFEINE ARE YOU GETTING?

About 100 million Americans drink coffee, putting caffeine at the top of the list of the most widely used drugs in the country. By comparison, 80 million use alcohol and 57 million smoke cigarettes.

The National Coffee Association of the U.S.A., Inc. estimates that Americans drink 3.5 to 4 cups a day, on average, which is significantly more than the two cups a day most physicians consider safe.

The first thing you should do is determine how much caffeine you consume each day. This may be more difficult than you think. In terms of coffee and tea, the caffeine content depends on two factors: the blend and the method of preparation. Because of these two factors, caffeine content of coffee varies widely at home and in restaurants, according to a 1988 study by the Canadian Health Protection Branch. The study found that caffeine in coffee varied from even one day to the next at the same restaurant, apparently depending on the method of preparation. Surprisingly, the study found that some decaffeinated coffees served in the restaurants inexplicably contained substantial amounts of caffeine.

Blends

The type of coffee bean makes a big difference in the amount of caffeine in the blend. Brazilian coffees have more caffeine than beans from Colombia or Central America. Manufacturers use a blend of several kinds, sometimes altering the mix because of changing prices in various countries. This makes it virtually impossible to find a consistent amount of caffeine even in the same brand. Tea leaves also vary greatly in the amount of caffeine they contain. Green and black teas from Ceylon and India have the highest levels.

Scoop for Scoop

The volume, and thus the caffeine content, of coffee or tea depends on the grind. A scoop of finely ground coffee contains more caffeine than a rough grind. Directions on the amount to use often differ, as well. For instance, some manufacturers recommend a "rounded" tablespoon of coffee, others a level tablespoon, which is nearly a third less caffeine per cup.

Brewing Coffee

Most people prepare their coffee in one of two ways: percolation or the drip method. Caffeine in percolated coffee depends on the amount of time it is brewed. Coffee should be percolated no longer than six minutes. The drip method, which is the most popular method in American households, produces higher concentrations of caffeine. Average drip times should not exceed four or five minutes. Longer times add more caffeine.

The Canadian study of coffee brewed in the home found that percolated coffee had between 39 and 168 milligrams of caffeine per cup, whereas drip coffee had between 56 and 176 milligrams. Instant coffee was found to have between 29 and 117 milligrams per cup.

Teas

Cup for cup tea has less caffeine than coffee, but the type of tea and its strength can lessen the benefits of using tea as a coffee alternative. A cup of strongly steeped tea (brewed for five minutes or more) can have the same caffeine content as instant coffee or a can of cola. American brands tend to have less caffeine than stronger, imported brands. The average cup has about 40 milligrams—only a third of the caffeine found in a brewed cup of coffee. According to the Federal Drug Administration (FDA), brewed domestic tea has a range of 20 to 90 milligrams for a 5-ounce serving. Instant teas have less, about 25 to 50 milligrams.

The study published in the *Journal of the American Dietetic Association* found caffeine content of tea varied widely, depending on the strength created by brewing time. The mean caffeine contents for all brews of black tea were 28 mg. for 1-minute brews, 44 mg. for 3-minute, and 47 mg. for 5-minute brews. There was some increase in caffeine when loose tea leaves were used, but the differences were not significant.[3]

So What's in a Cup?

When figuring out your caffeine consumption, it is important to consider the size of the coffee or tea cup. Compute the number of ounces you drink, rather than the number of cups. A common coffee mug holds about 8 fluid ounces, equivalent to the traditional "cup" used for measurement. A cup at a restaurant or in a set of good china usually holds about 5 ounces, while large decorative mugs might hold up to 15 ounces. Since most Americans drink coffee from an 8- to 10-ounce mug, the caffeine in a single mug of drip-brewed coffee would average about 230 milligrams and range from 120 to 360 milligrams! The caffeine content as measured in Table Two is based on 5-ounce servings.

WHY QUIT?

Since most of the myths about the health hazards of caffeine have been disproved, why should anyone want to give up their favorite beverage? The most common reason given by people who decided to quit is the effect caffeine has on their nervous systems. Other reasons often cited are stomach ailments and a recognition of the addicting qualities of caffeine.

It is usually hard for long-term coffee drinkers to gauge their moods because of the effects of caffeine and chronic withdrawal symptoms if they are deprived of it for long. After quitting, however, caffeine drinkers find they are calmer, less irritable, and experience fewer mood swings. Perhaps the most significant change mentioned by those who quit caffeine is the improvement in their sleep. They report that sleep is deeper and they wake up feeling more refreshed and rested.

For people suffering from fatigue, these are all good reasons to stop drinking coffee, tea, and other caffeinated beverages. Not only can you expect to feel better and sleep better, but you should find yourself rejuvenated with new sources of energy and vitality that are no longer squandered on the caffeine roller coaster.

KICKING THE HABIT

If you feel that you are getting too much caffeine, you may want to kick the habit altogether or cut back to a level you feel is appropriate. Anyone drinking two cups or less a day, roughly 10 ounces, should be able to quit immediately. For others, it is best to taper off slowly. As we have noted, abrupt withdrawal among heavy caffeine consumers prompts a variety of symptoms: headache, tiredness, muscle aches, depression, irritability, sleeplessness, and sometimes a runny nose.

The first step in reducing your intake of caffeine is to determine how much you are getting. Keep track of the number of ounces of coffee, tea, or colas you drink, add up the milligrams and then set up a schedule for quitting.

Here are some other suggestions for cutting back:

1. Mix decaffeinated blends with regular ground coffees to reduce the amount of caffeine. Gradually increase the decaffeinated portion until you are drinking only decaffeinated coffee.
2. Start drinking decaffeinated colas, alternating between caffeinated sodas until you are drinking only caffeine-free soft drinks.
3. Drink more water to offset the water retention caused by the reduction in the diuretic properties of caffeine if you notice a slight weight gain.
4. One common suggestion for combatting a negative addiction is to replace it with a positive one. To get the lift or "high" you are missing from lack of caffeine, try increasing exercise—take a walk, go jogging, or ride a bicycle.

5. Some people suffer from what professionals call cross-addiction, which means a dependence on more than one drug. If you smoke or drink alcohol in addition to consuming significant amounts of caffeine, you may need professional help to quit.
6. Make your coffee weaker, either while brewing or by drinking it lighter. Meanwhile, swap your mug for a smaller cup.
7. Switch to herbal teas or decaffeinated teas if drinking decaffeinated coffee simply makes you crave regular coffee even more.

CHAPTER TWO

SMOKING AND FATIGUE
ONE MORE REASON TO QUIT

Compared to other health risks—cancer and heart disease, for instance—fatigue may seem a relatively small price to pay for those who smoke, but unlike serious organic diseases linked to tobacco, the loss of personal vitality is something that smokers deal with in the here and now. Heart attacks and lung cancer may be years away, but fatigue affects smokers' daily lives.

Fatigue ranks as one of the most common complaints of smokers. People who smoke are twice as likely as nonsmokers to report fatigue as a problem. Smokers are also more likely to suffer from insomnia, which aggravates their fatigue.

More than 50 million Americans smoke, roughly a third of the adult population. Although three million people are quitting each year, smoking remains a major health hazard and contributes to more than 300,000 deaths annually. This is clearly one reason why 70 percent of all smokers say they would like to quit.

One of the most satisfying results of quitting is the remarkable change it brings to personal energy. Ex-smokers feel rejuvenated— full of energy and renewed strength. They breathe easier, sleep better, and feel younger. In general, ex-smokers take better care of their health, watch their eating habits, exercise more often, and get physical examinations more frequently than those who continue to smoke.

Smoking is frequently one of several factors contributing to fatigue, because smokers are more likely to exercise less and drink more coffee and alcohol than nonsmokers. Smokers, especially men, are less likely to take vitamin supplements. People who abuse one drug tend to abuse others and anyone who abuses drugs is more likely to smoke. More than 90 percent of all alcoholics smoke cigarettes, for example.

Smokers take more medicines—prescription and nonprescription—than nonsmokers. Smokers use more cough medicines, aspirin, sleeping pills, barbiturates, tranquilizers, stomach medicines, laxatives, and pain medicines. The only drugs used more by nonsmokers are antihistamines for allergic conditions and drugs for asthma.

A decision to quit smoking often accompanies a willingness to improve one's health in general. For smokers, quitting can be a life-affirming statement that not only increases their vitality, but adds years to their lives.

Smoking may be the hardest habit to break, but it may also offer the most rewards. According to the U.S. Surgeon General, the life expectancy of a 30- to 35-year-old who smokes two packs a day is reduced by eight to nine years. The longer one smokes, the greater the risk.

The next best thing to quitting is cutting back or changing brands to reduce nicotine, tar, and carbon monoxide, since the health risks are dose related. Overall mortality rates for smokers of low tar and nicotine cigarettes are 15 to 20 percent less than rates for those who smoke regular cigarettes but are still 50 percent greater than for nonsmokers. Those who smoke low tar and nicotine cigarettes, however, are only better off if they do not increase the amount they smoke.

EFFECTS OF NICOTINE ON BODY AND MIND

Nicotine is a psychoactive drug that provides pleasurable, mood-altering effects. In many ways, the addiction to nicotine is similar to addiction to heroin and cocaine. All three drugs are quickly absorbed into the bloodstream and provide a feeling of euphoria.

Nicotine has a dual nature and acts as both a tranquilizer and a stimulant. Some studies have shown that smokers alter their smoking style to obtain either the depressant or stimulant effects depending on their mood.

Smokers are in a continuous state of nervous stimulation. The natural consequence of this excitement is lethargy and fatigue. To combat this tendency, the smoker smokes another cigarette. The effects on the body and mind occur almost immediately. When the nicotine enters the body through the lungs, blood vessels constrict, blood sugar increases, blood pressure goes up, heart rate increases, and a host of hormones and neurotransmitters are released into the bloodstream.

Two hormones appear to be particularly important in determining the psychological effects of nicotine—epinephrine (adrenaline) and norepinephrine (noradrenaline). Adrenaline is naturally triggered by the body when a person is under stress, anxious, or bored. It calls the body to action, stimulating activity or anger in a "fight or flight" reaction. Noradrenaline is released during periods of heightened arousal or excitement, such as during sex, exercise, or

---

Reducing the Risk if You Can't Quit

1. Cut back on the number of cigarettes you smoke.
2. Switch to a brand that has lower tar and nicotine.
3. Take shallow puffs, or better still, don't inhale at all.
4. Smoke only part of the cigarette and then put it out. The toxins become stronger as you smoke down the cigarette.
5. Keep the cigarette out of your mouth between puffs.
6. Take a vitamin and mineral supplement.
7. Set up an exercise program. Even light exercise can reduce health risks for smokers.
8. Reduce the stress in your life. Stress increases smoking rates.
9. If you are taking an oral contraceptive, switch to another means of birth control.
10. Avoid smoking at work if you are exposed to other risk factors, such as dust, smoke, or fumes. Cigarette smoke can be a transporter for worksite toxins.

use of illicit drugs. These hormones may explain why people say they smoke to "get a lift" or "calm nerves." Smokers regulate mood by precisely monitoring their inhalation of nicotine, taking quick, deeper puffs to gain a lift and slower, smaller puffs to relax.

The bored smoker is attracted by the stimulating effects of nicotine. The release of the adrenaline increases blood pressure and the heart rate, heightens alertness, and creates a feeling of excitement. These effects are similar to those of caffeine. The biochemical process burns up energy the body might use elsewhere. A nervous, overly excited smoker, on the other hand, would be attracted by the calming, pleasurable effects of noradrenaline. The smoker alternates between a high marked by heightened activity and vigilance and a low characterized by lethargy and inactivity, depending on the dose of nicotine in his bloodstream.

These and other effects of smoking wear down the immune system, lowering a person's resistance to common ailments, particularly respiratory illnesses. The result is more illness. The U.S. Surgeon General estimated that smokers account for 81 million lost work days and 145 million days of bed disability due to smoke-related ailments. Incidence of influenza is 20 percent higher among smokers, apparently the result of a decrease in antibodies in the blood.

Other effects on the body are:

- Smoking constricts the blood vessels in the skin and decreases the blood flow, making smokers more susceptible to facial wrinkles.
- Smoking increases the utilization of vitamin C for a variety of reasons, namely, a change of diet, differences in absorption of the vitamin, and use of the vitamin to detoxify components of the smoke and increased metabolism. On the basis of available studies, smokers should consume about 40 percent more in vitamin C daily than nonsmokers to maintain adequate levels. Smoking also lowers both blood and tissue levels of vitamin B-12, and reduces amounts of vitamin B-6.
- Vitamin C helps the body use folic acid and assists in providing iron to red blood cells; both functions are critical in averting anemia. B-12 is vital for cell growth and formation of

DNA. B-6 is probably the most important of the B vitamins and plays a role in the function of the brain and central nervous system. Since smoking poses risks of deficiency for these vitamins, smokers should make sure each is adequately present in their diets.

- Impotence among some men has been linked to a reduction of blood flow to male genitals caused by smoking.
- Women reduce their fertility by smoking and are nearly three times more likely to be infertile than nonsmokers. Female smokers also experience menopause earlier than nonsmokers.

WHAT'S IN TOBACCO SMOKE?

Nicotine, the primary addictive component of tobacco, is only one of 4,000 compounds in tobacco smoke. Some others are arsenic, alcohols, acetone, benzene, carbon dioxide, carbon monoxide, DDT, nitric oxide, vinyl chloride, and a variety of acids, phenols, and sulfur-containing compounds.

The damaging health effects of smoking are not the result of nicotine, but the combined effects of all the elements of smoke. Two primary elements—tar and carbon monoxide—are considered more hazardous to health than nicotine (see Table Six for information on the amounts of nicotine, tar, and carbon monoxide found in popular brands of cigarettes).

Tar is composed of all the particles in smoke, except water and nicotine. The tar is the sticky, gummy substance found in filters of cigarettes and has a consistency similar to road tar. It is the tar that adheres to the tiny air holes in the lungs, turning them black and contributing to a wide range of respiratory problems, including emphysema.

When tobacco burns, it creates carbon monoxide, the colorless, odorless, and deadly gas produced by automobiles and gas stoves. As the carbon monoxide enters the smoker's body, it replaces life-giving oxygen in the blood. As the carbon monoxide robs the body of oxygen, the nicotine increases the heart rate, causing the body

Table Six.[a]   *Nicotine, tar, and carbon monoxide content of selected brands*

Brand Name	Type	Nicotine (mg)	Tar (mg)	CO (mg)
Chesterfield	K-NF-SP	1.7	25	16
Lucky Strike	R-NF-SP	1.5	24	17
Pall Mall	K-NF-SP	1.5	24	16
Camel	R-NF-SP	1.4	22	14
Benson & Hedges	100-F-SP	1.2	17	17
Winston	K-F-SP	1.1	17	16
Marlboro	K-F-SP	1.1	17	16
Virginia Slims	100-F-SP	1.1	15	14
Lark	K-F-SP	1.0	13	12
Tareyton	K-F-SP	1.0	14	15
L&M	K-F-SP	1.0	13	13
Kent	K-F-SP	0.9	12	13
Doral Full Flavor	K-F-HP	0.8	15	18
Marlboro Lights	K-F-HP	0.8	11	12
Vantage	K-F-SP	0.7	11	14
Merit	K-F-SP	0.6	8	10
True	K-F-SP	0.5	5	6
Now	K-F-SP	0.1	1	2
Carlton 100s	100-F-HP	0.1	1	1
Carlton	K-F-SP	1.0	0.1	2
Kool	R-NF-SP	1.3	21	14
Newport	K-F-HP	1.3	17	17
Marlboro	K-F-SP	1.1	17	16
Alpine	K-F-SP	1.1	17	16
Virginia Slims	100-F-SP	1.1	15	13
Kool	K-F-SP	1.0	21	14
Salem	K-F-SP	1.0	16	18
Newport Lights	100-F-HP	0.8	9	10
Kent Golden Lights	K-F-SP	0.8	9	9
Kool Lights	K-F-SP	0.7	8	9
Belair	100-F-SP	0.7	9	9
Merit	K-F-SP	0.6	8	10
Salem Ultra Lights	K-F-SP	0.4	5	8
Merit Ultra Lights	K-F-SP	0.4	5	6
Carlton	100-F-HP	0.1	1	1

[a]Source: Federal Trade Commission Report, *"Tar"*, *Nicotine and Carbon Monoxide of the Smoke of 272 Varieties of Domestic Cigarettes*. December, 1988.
K = King Size, R = Regular, F = Filter, NF = NonFilter, HP = Hardpack, SP = Softpack.

to use more oxygen. This explains why smokers are often short of breath.

Oxygen supplies all of the body's organs with energy. Less oxygen means less energy. Most importantly, less oxygen is carried to the brain, which results in lethargy and fatigue.

WHY DO PEOPLE SMOKE?

If smoking poses such hazards, why do 50 million Americans continue to smoke? Their addiction to nicotine is only part of the answer. The truth is that there are some tangible benefits to smoking and smokers repeatedly refer to them.

Smokers commonly say that smoking helps them cope with stress, helps them concentrate, keeps them from feeling bored, and reduces feelings of loneliness, distress, and anxiety. Women often cite weight control as a benefit of smoking.

Let us examine the two most commonly perceived benefits of smoking—controlling mood and weight.

Mood Regulator

Smokers use tobacco as a powerful psychological tool to help regulate their emotions. Nicotine from tobacco gives smokers a means of medicating themselves with a legal drug sold just about anywhere. The dose can be regulated precisely and delivered to the bloodstream in seconds.

A study involving Navy officers in 1981 linked stress and smoking rates. Fatigue, anger, and fear were also significantly correlated to the amount smoked. The study also indicated that people smoke more when they are tired.

Some scientists have challenged the idea that smoking improves mood. They argue that the smoke may simply offset the negative feelings associated with nicotine withdrawal. Regular smokers suffer a variety of unpleasant symptoms when deprived of nicotine, such as irritability, restlessness, and sudden mood swings. People continue to smoke to ward off these negative feelings.

Weight Control

Nicotine helps control weight in at least three ways. First, the nicotine decreases the efficiency with which the body converts food into energy, so more food is eliminated before it is turned into fat. Second, nicotine suppresses appetite, particularly cravings for sweets. Third, smoking tends to alleviate stress, a common cause of overeating.

It is not surprising, therefore, that smokers generally weigh less (about 7 pounds on average) than nonsmokers. About a third of the smokers who quit do gain weight. Studies of males have reported gains of up to 12 pounds. Weight gain seems to be related to the amount smoked prior to quitting, so heavy smokers tend to gain more weight.

SPECIAL CONCERNS FOR WOMEN

Women may feel that they are less vulnerable to the health risks of smoking because the leading causes of smoke-related deaths—lung cancer, heart attack, and emphysema—are associated with men. Traditionally, adult women began smoking later in their lives than men, usually starting with low-tar filter cigarettes, and generally smoking less than men. The lower overall death rates for women reflect this lower exposure to tobacco smoke. When women's exposure is similar to men's exposure, however, mortality rates are virtually the same.

The number of women smokers has increased over the years but peaked in the 1970s and has been falling steadily. Young women are as likely today as men are to begin smoking. According to a Gallup poll, 28 percent of the women in the United States smoked in 1986, whereas about 35 percent of the men smoked. The following regional differences were reported for all smokers: east, 31 percent; midwest, 29 percent; south, 35 percent, and west, 29 percent.

Women smokers appear to have more trouble quitting than men do, but the reasons are not fully understood. Frequently, women report more severe withdrawal symptoms than men. When they do succeed in quitting, women are more apt to start up again. They also do not try to quit as often as men do.

The fear of gaining weight seems to be another reason women continue to smoke; at least women report this as a concern more often than men do.

Smoking poses special risks to women because of their reproductive systems. Women who use oral contraceptives and smoke, for example, are 22 times more likely to die from a stroke and 20 times more likely to die from a heart attack than nonsmokers are. Their menstrual cycles are also more apt to be irregular. Menopause occurs earlier among smokers, so their years of fertility are reduced.

Smoking during pregnancy significantly affects the mother, the unborn fetus, and newborn baby. Fetal growth is retarded among smoking mothers and problems with the baby's heart, lungs, and central nervous system are more common. Fetal and neonatal deaths are also higher for smokers.

The smoking mother also suffers more miscarriages than nonsmokers do. A study by New Zealand doctors found that women who smoked more than 20 cigarettes a day were twice as likely to have a spontaneous abortion.

The risks of smoking during pregnancy are often explained to the mother by her doctor, and many women choose this time to quit. As many as a third of all pregnant women who smoke quit during their pregnancy, whereas about the same number continue to smoke. Others either stop temporarily or cut down.

THE BENEFITS OF QUITTING

The most important reward for quitting is the likelihood of a longer, healthier, and more energetic life. Once the initial withdrawal period is over, personal vigor and energy will continue to increase for two or three months.

Quitting brings immediate health benefits, but it takes years for the body to repair itself. Overall, mortality rates for ex-smokers, after 15 years, approach those who never smoked. The risk for heart disease approaches that of nonsmokers after 10 years and for lung cancer, after 10 to 15 years.

Not only do former smokers enjoy a longer life expectancy, but the quality of their lives improves. They are not ill as often and they recover faster from illness than when they smoked.

Several benefits accrue from an improvement in circulation—skin tone is brighter and the senses of smell and taste are heightened. Increased oxygen in the brain promotes clearer thinking and problem solving capabilities. Physical activities, such as swimming, bicycling, or jogging, can be resumed without difficulties caused by shortness of breath or chest pain. Heart rate and blood pressure return to normal within hours after physical activity.

WITHDRAWAL SYMPTOMS

As with any other addictive drug, nicotine has a variety of withdrawal symptoms that present themselves when someone tries to quit. Surprisingly, the success rate for quitting smoking is not much different than for heroin or alcohol, even though both of these drugs have much more severe withdrawal symptoms.

For the smoker, quitting smoking abruptly or "cold turkey" has advantages. Withdrawal symptoms are no worse than those experienced by someone who quits gradually, and the symptoms subside more quickly. Cutting down or gradual abstinence puts the smoker in a chronic state of withdrawal and frequently causes him or her to revert to smoking.

The most intense symptom is the "craving" for tobacco. This is one of a cluster of symptoms that also include irritability, anxiety, restlessness, difficulty in concentrating, and an increase in appetite. Other less common symptoms include insomnia, headache, nausea, and lower tolerance of stress.

HOW TO QUIT SMOKING

Smoking is not an easy habit to break, but millions of smokers quit each year, proof enough that it can be done.

According to the U.S. Surgeon General's report, about 95 percent of the 29 million smokers who quit between 1964 and 1979 quit on their own without assistance from formal programs.

Most successful ex-smokers quit "cold turkey," but there is no best way for everyone. Slightly fewer than two out of three smokers have tried to quit at least once. It usually takes several attempts before someone can quit permanently.

The most difficult time is during the first week or two when the withdrawal symptoms are strongest, and most relapses occur in the first three months. Long-term success relies on social and psychological support.

Quitting regimens concentrate on two approaches: treating nicotine dependence by changing behavior or administering certain types of medicine. Some programs combine the two methods. The most successful programs employ several different procedures, which more effectively address the wide range of individual differences among smokers and the complex environmental, social, and psychological aspects of smoking. Everyone should assess his or her own resources, and then choose the method that seems best.

BEHAVIORAL METHODS USED TO QUIT SMOKING

Behavioral programs for smokers have been available for many years. Two approaches distinguish behavioral programs: One relies on punishment with aversion therapy, and the other uses positive reinforcement through self-control.

Although the vast majority of ex-smokers have quit on their own, it is likely that most of them have used some of these techniques. Those who go it alone often rely on magazine or newspaper articles, books and manuals, tapes, over-the-counter remedies, radio and television programs, or quit kits from nonprofit or public health agencies. These sources commonly highlight the behavioral methods.

If the smoker wants professional help or social support, he or she should consider one of dozens of organized programs, many of which are listed in local telephone books. The success rate of smoking clinics after one year follow-ups has been estimated at 25 to 35 percent. This is better than a general finding of 15 to 20 percent for those who try it on their own.

Although the success rate among organized programs may be

Tips to Help You Quit

1. Set a date and prepare yourself to quit when you get up in the morning on that day.
2. Avoid coffee, alcohol, and other smokers during the early days of withdrawal. All are known causes for relapse.
3. Try to quit if you have a cold or flu when smoking is not as pleasurable.
4. Switch brands frequently, consistently reducing the tar and nicotine content of your cigarettes to help ease withdrawal symptoms. Make sure not to smoke more cigarettes to compensate for the lower dose of nicotine.
5. Make a list of things you can buy with the money you save by quitting. Figure out the cost of your habit and plan to buy special gifts for yourself. Rewards are important to encourage you to continue not smoking.
6. Long-term abstinence from tobacco depends largely on your ability to resolve life conflicts. When tempted to smoke again, remember that smoking will not solve your problems.
7. Support from friends, family, and spouse are very important to maintain abstinence, so enlist their help by explaining why you want to quit.
8. Replace your negative smoking addiction with a positive addiction, such as jogging, tennis, bicycling, swimming, or other aerobic exercise. Deep breathing exercises are also good substitutes. Exercise reduces stress and provides a reminder that your body is on the mend.
9. Watch your eating habits to avoid weight gain. Exercise plays a double role here, reducing stress and helping you maintain weight.
10. When you get the urge to smoke, remember that the intensity of the feeling will pass in a few minutes. With each passing urge, the interval between cravings will increase while the intensity decreases. Some ex-smokers report cravings years after quitting, but these episodes are rare and relatively mild.
11. Make a list of the reasons you want to quit and refer to it frequently during withdrawal.
12. If you start smoking again, remember that most smokers who quit permanently tried more than once before they succeeded, so resolve to try again soon!

higher, only about half of the smokers who want to quit express an interest in formal programs. Only a small fraction of these smokers actually attend programs when they are offered.

The problems with assessing the success of smoking clinics is that most of the information is self-reported. Furthermore, studies have found that up to 25 percent of participants of organized programs may not be telling the truth in follow-up interviews.

The most successful plan for you may incorporate a number of methods. Each individual has a different habit and needs special attention. One thing is sure, no single program or method has been especially successful for large populations.

Satiation

This method requires people to double their smoking consumption in order to satiate any desire to smoke. Notwithstanding the potential harm to one's health, this technique has been shown to be quite effective if combined with other methods. Success rates as high as 50 percent after one year have been reported for some combination programs. However, excessive smoking by itself does not produce an aversion to cigarettes, and, if used alone, the satiation method is not effective.

Rapid Smoking

Smokers are asked to smoke quickly, inhaling every six or seven seconds until they feel themselves getting sick. As with satiation, the success of this method is greatly improved when used in a multicomponent program.

Nicotine Fading

This method uses commercial over-the-counter nicotine filters or urges smokers to switch brands to lower doses of tar and nicotine. The idea is to cut back the dose of nicotine to make quitting easier. Success rates have been variable, but tapering off is a good option for those who want to quit gradually since it allows a person to smoke the same number of cigarettes while reducing the amount of nicotine. Most people find it just as difficult to quit, however, since cravings are still intense once the smoker quits abruptly.

Self-Monitoring

The smoker pays very close attention to when, how, and the amount he or she smokes. The smoker writes down the time, place, mood, activity, and amount of the cigarette smoked in a daily log. The idea is to change behavior by making smokers more conscious of their habit.

Controlling Triggers

The smoker lists the cues that makes him or her reach for a cigarette—drinking coffee or alcohol, talking on the telephone, finishing a meal. After rating these triggers on an intensity scale, the smoker starts to eliminate them, beginning with the easiest. The smoker works to modify these triggers by setting up new situations or conditions when and where they habitually occur.

Relaxation Techniques

Various methods have utilized relaxation techniques to reduce anxiety that might trigger smoking, relieve stress during withdrawal, and provide an alternative to smoking. Hypnosis, meditation, and breathing exercises are the most common. These techniques are often used in concert with other behavioral programs.

The success of any of these methods depends in large part on the motivation of the participants. Obviously, smokers with a strong sense of purpose and commitment to quitting do better in any program.

ACUPUNCTURE AND HYPNOSIS

The yellow pages of just about any major city will list acupuncture and hypnosis as smoking cessation aids. Both these methods seem to work for some people, depending on the individual motivation and predilection to the techniques.

Acupuncture

This procedure involves putting pins or staples in the ear. Although it has grown in popularity in the past ten years, there is little evidence that acupuncture relieves withdrawal symptoms or contributes to quitting. Acupuncture appears to work best with those who are strongly motivated to quit and plays a supportive role for these people.

Hypnosis

This method relies on posthypnotic suggestions that tobacco is a poison and harmful to the body. Greater success is reported if the subject is highly susceptible to hypnotic suggestion. A series of sessions seems better than a single session, and it is best to use hypnosis in conjunction with other methods.

MEDICINAL AIDS

The medicinal approach seeks to replace the nicotine, reduce withdrawal, or treat the symptoms of withdrawal. By far, the most widely used aid is nicotine polacrilex gum, more commonly known as nicotine gum.

The chewing gum has been the subject of many scientific studies. Sold under the brand name Nicorette®, the gum reduces some withdrawal symptoms but does not significantly reduce the urge to smoke. A considerable number of users revert to smoking after giving up the gum. Each piece of gum contains 2 mg of nicotine.

Quit rates after one year range from 6 to 10 percent. The success rate for the gum increases substantially when it is used in conjunction with other procedures, such as behavioral programs.[1]

The gum consistently reduced irritability among those quitting cigarettes in several studies, but other symptoms, such as depression, restlessness, and weight gain were reduced for some people but not others. One of the drawbacks is that much of the nicotine ingested from the gum is metabolized and detoxified by the liver, which reduces its effectiveness.[2]

Merrell Dow Pharmaceuticals, which markets Nicorette® in the United States, has listed a variety of adverse reactions to the gum, including insomnia, headache, indigestion, mouth sores, anorexia, vomiting, and hiccups.

Some studies have found evidence that the gum may itself cause physical dependence and create withdrawal symptoms when stopped abruptly. For example, a study by A. I. Hjalmarson in 1984 found 3 percent of those in the study group developed a long-term dependence on the gum and were still chewing it after 2 years.

A relatively new entry to the United States market is the transdermal patch, a skin-patch system intended to reduce nicotine cravings by delivering a steady dose of nicotine through the skin.

Nicoderm®, marketed by the ALZA Corporation of Palo Alto, Calif., was approved by the Food and Drug Administration in 1991. The product consists of three patches designed to wean the smoker from nicotine over the course of 10 weeks. The first patch delivers 21 milligrams of nicotine a day over six weeks. The second patch, which is smaller, provides 14 milligrams and is worn for the next two weeks. The third delivers only 7 milligrams a day over the final two weeks.

The success of skin-patch systems in other countries has been encouraging. The patch may be more effective when used in combination with other smoking cessation methods, since it does reduce some withdrawal symptoms. Its major advantage is that it delivers a dose of nicotine automatically and directly to the bloodstream.

Treatment of withdrawal symptoms with other drugs has been tried in a variety of studies, but success has been limited. Attention has focused on a variety of prescription drugs, including tranquilizers. The intent is to relieve the anxiety, irritability, restlessness, and tension experienced by the smoker while trying to quit in the hope that he will not revert to smoking. Some success has been reported with clonidine, a drug used in treating high blood pressure, but its side effects include fatigue, nausea, and agitation. One study found the drug more effective for women than for men.

Tranquilizers and antidepressants have also been used to alleviate emotional symptoms of withdrawal because stress and mood are common causes of relapse. None of these drugs has shown the promise of clonidine and the possibility of dependence should be weighed against other quitting methods.

HOW YOUR DOCTOR CAN HELP

People are more likely to stop smoking if told to quit by their physician, and more and more physicians are advising their patients to quit. According to national surveys, one in four smokers has been told to quit by their physician. Because patients are influenced more by their physician's advice than by just about anything else, his or her medical advice can be an important factor in a person's efforts to quit.

Although some doctors have little confidence in their abilities to get patients to quit smoking, the National Cancer Institute has urged physicians to raise the issue with their patients at every opportunity, rather than wait until a serious health problem presents itself. Physicians can correlate a variety of symptoms to smoking, such as sore throat, gum disease, angina, or ulcers.

Physicians are in unique positions to counsel people about smoking but generally do not offer advice until a serious health problem presents itself. One reason is that physicians have little confidence in getting their patients to quit.

The timely intervention by a family physician can have positive results, especially with patients suffering from lung and heart disease. Another effective time is during a smoker's pregnancy, when women are statistically more apt to quit.

SMOKING AND FATIGUE

A cigarette, like coffee, offers temptations to those who are tired and want a lift to get them through the day. A few quick puffs on a cigarette can be exhilarating. Smokers report enhanced concentration, reduced stress, and bursts of energy from tobacco smoke.

For the smoker, the cigarette, pipe, cigar, or chewing tobacco provides a temporary relief from the negative effects of withdrawal. As these symptoms present themselves, the smoker lights up and inhales more smoke for yet another "lift."

One of the prices for this exhilaration is, of course, fatigue. As the old saying goes, "What goes up, must come down." Smokers are in a chronic state of overstimulation from the nicotine, which leaves them exhausted toward the end of a long, smoke-filled day.

The more tired people are, the more they smoke, and the more tired they become as a result. This vicious cycle means personal vitality becomes a candle burning at both ends. Smoking forces the body to work harder, while at the same time impairing its resources. As soon as the smoke hits the lungs, the heart speeds up by 10 to 25 beats a minute. Blood pressure increases by 10 to 15 percent. It depletes antibodies, leaving the smoker vulnerable to disease. At the same time, the carbon monoxide in the smoke lowers the body's ability to carry oxygen, depleting this life-sustaining substance when the body needs it most. Less oxygen means less energy and leads to fatigue.

All too often, smoking is just one of a set of habits that contributes to fatigue. Smokers are more apt to drink alcohol, coffee, and use illicit drugs. They are less fit, so they exercise less than non-smokers. Nicotine affects their sleep patterns and contributes to insomnia.

Smoking also depletes valuable vitamins in the body, particularly vitamins C, B_6, and B_{12}, all of which are vital for proper health. Deficiencies of one or more of these vitamins will cause fatigue and a host of other symptoms.

As if this weren't enough, the anxiety associated with the health risks of smoking is greater than ever and this contributes to fatigue. As more information becomes known, the smoker is likely to have more to worry about.

Besides these more immediate causes of fatigue, smokers must deal with more sickness in their lives and the inevitable fatigue that accompanies disease. Smokers have the flu more often and it lasts longer for them than for nonsmokers. Smokers have higher rates of heart disease, lung cancer, bronchitis, ulcers, allergies, and a variety of other diseases.

Smoking is linked to 280,000 heart disease cases each year alone and more than a million cases of lung cancer. Both of these illnesses can be severely debilitating and leave a person exhausted much of the time.

Compared to other risks, fatigue may seem a small price to pay for smoking. After all, fatigue isn't going to kill you, right? But this misses an important point. For those who suffer from fatigue due to smoking, the habit robs them of the vitality needed to enjoy a productive life. Not only must smokers deal with the threat of a shortened life, but also the real prospect of a life devalued by unremitting fatigue.

CHAPTER THREE

ALCOHOL
THE NIGHTCAP THAT KEEPS YOU AWAKE

INTRODUCTION

Like caffeine and nicotine, alcohol is a tempting, widely available drug for people who are tired, depressed, anxious, or under stress. A few drinks induce relaxation and mild sedation, followed by a feeling of tranquility. These mild, rather pleasant effects encourage more than 100 million Americans to drink alcoholic beverages on a regular basis.

The price for these few moments of relaxation, however, can be high. Millions in the United States have developed a dependence on alcohol at one time or another during their lifetimes. One in ten drinkers—about 11 million Americans—is an alcoholic, according to the National Institute on Alcohol Abuse and Alcoholism (NIAAA), although other estimates put the number as high as 14 million.

Troubles from alcohol come in a variety of forms—marital discord, failed careers, child abuse, crushing debts, accidents, and suicide. Alcohol-related problems account for 85,000 deaths a year in the U.S. alone.

Compared with these sorts of troubles, fatigue may seem like a harmless side effect of alcohol, but it is a great deal more than a minor irritant. Fatigue aggravates any problem associated with this drug. Alcohol robs people of their personal vitality—the one thing they need most to cope with declining health and disruptions in their personal and professional lives. If one defines alcoholism as any rate of consumption that interferes with social, family, or working life, then fatigue caused by alcohol is a key element in this personal deterioration. Exhausted physically and mentally by the drug, obsessed in his search for it, the alcoholic may lose his job, family, savings, and even his life, unless a full recovery is pursued actively.

The emotional distress and pain caused by alcoholism infects other people associated with the alcoholic, too. Children, spouses, co-workers, and others can become caught up in the alcoholic's chaotic lifestyle and succumb to the same numbing fatigue, depression, and guilt that afflicts the alcoholic.

It is not only the chronic alcoholic who suffers from alcohol-related fatigue. As we will see, even moderate drinkers pay a price for their alcohol consumption. For one thing, it interferes with sleep. Negative emotions, such as depression and anxiety, are also common by-products of drinking and contribute to chronic exhaustion.

Four factors related to alcohol consumption directly cause fatigue:

1. sedative effects on the body, particularly the brain and central nervous system
2. insomnia due to the disturbance of normal sleep patterns
3. emotional turmoil associated with alcohol dependence, specifically depression, anxiety, and stress
4. nutritional deficiencies caused by depletion of various vitamins

Any one of these factors, or a combination of two or more, will cause fatigue, at least temporarily. The effects are proportional to the amount of alcohol consumed as well as to individual tolerances to the drug.

DO YOU HAVE A DRINKING PROBLEM?

If a person has a "drinking problem," it may mean that he or she is dependent or becoming dependent on alcohol. Many types of problems are associated with drinking and may or may not indicate that a person is an alcoholic.

Alcoholism is sometimes defined as excessive drinking that affects one of five major areas of a person's life:

1. *Employment or school work*: Absenteeism, lower productivity and performance, job loss or job hopping, hangovers, and money problems.
2. *Family, marital, and romantic relationships*: Includes arguments over drinking, jealousy, resentment, separation, divorce, physical fights, emotional abuse, and paranoia.
3. *Motor vehicle and criminal charges*: Motor vehicle accidents, drunken driving charges with subsequent loss of license, or charges of disorderly conduct, assaults, child abuse, or assaults on a spouse.
4. *Friendships and socializing*: Heavy drinkers choose friends who drink and seek out social occasions or even jobs that facilitate drinking. They frequent bars and taverns and avoid social situations where no alcohol is served.
5. *Health*: Alcohol causes serious damage to the liver, pancreas, and cardiovascular system, leading to disease and disability or death.

Any one or all of these problems can develop in moderate to heavy drinkers. What distinguishes the alcoholic from the casual drinker is the inability or unwillingness to quit or cut down significantly when one or more of these problems arise.

Although there are a number of definitions for alcoholism, the simplest is probably the one suggested by the World Health Organization in 1969. The WHO defines alcoholism or alcohol dependence as the consumption of alcohol by a person that exceeds the limits accepted by his culture or that limits his health or social relationships.

The DSM-IIIR manual, the standard reference for psychiatric disorders, identifies three major patterns associated with alcoholism: 1. regular daily drinking of large amounts, 2. heavy drinking restricted to weekends, and 3. binges of heavy drinking for weeks or months followed by long periods of sobriety.

Another definition was proposed by E. M. Jellinek, perhaps the most prominent researcher on alcoholism of the 20th century. Jellinek defined alcoholism as "any use of alcoholic beverages that causes any damage to the individual or society or both."

Jellinek was not satisfied with his own broad definition, however, and sought to specify a number of categories of problem drinkers.[1]

1. *Alpha Alcoholism*: This type of alcoholic has a deep emotional dependence on alcohol to relieve psychological pain, depression, and distress. Drinking is heavy, but there is no loss of control. Nor is there any physical dependence that might lead to withdrawal symptoms.
2. *Beta Alcoholism*: Physical disease, such as cirrhosis of the liver, stomach problems, or alcoholic hepatitis, develops, but there is no physical dependence or subsequent withdrawal symptoms.
3. *Delta Alcoholism*: This type is marked by an inability to stop drinking, even for a day or two, without the appearance of withdrawal symptoms, although these alcoholics can control the quantity of alcohol they drink.
4. *Gamma Alcoholism*: This is the most serious type of alcoholism in terms of the damage to relationships, work, and families. This type develops a tolerance quickly, increases consumption, loses control, and has a physical dependence. There is a constant craving for alcohol and the person experiences withdrawal symptoms.
5. *Epsilon Alcoholism*: This is the binge drinker or weekender. The benders are spaced out between periods of complete abstinence. The binges can lead to serious disruptions in relationships and physical disease or injury for the drinker.

THEORIES OF THE CAUSE OF ALCOHOLISM

The cause or causes of alcoholism are not known. More likely than not, several factors contribute to alcoholism. The different types of alcoholics suggest different causes. There appear to be no clear or simple answers.

Although not all experts agree, the evidence suggests that certain types of people are prone to alcoholism. Such things as a family

Michigan Alcohol Screening Test[2]

Considered one of the best self-administered tests for alcoholics, the Michigan Alcohol Screening Test (MAST) was developed in 1971 by M. L. Selzer, an expert on alcohol addiction. Studies have proved the test extremely reliable and sensitive to diagnosis, with a misdiagnosis in less than 10 percent of the cases.

Points	Questions
(0)	1. Do you enjoy a drink now and then?
(2)	2. Do you feel you are a normal drinker?*
(2)	3. Have you ever awakened the morning after some drinking the night before and found that you could not remember a part of the evening before?
(1)	4. Does your spouse (or parents) ever worry or complain about your drinking?
(2)	5. Can you stop drinking without a struggle after one or two drinks?*
(1)	6. Do you ever feel bad about your drinking?
(2)	7. Do friends and relatives think you are a normal drinker?*
(0)	8. Do you ever try to limit your drinking to certain times of the day or to certain places?
(2)	9. Are you always able to stop drinking when you want to?*
(4)	10. Have you ever attended a meeting of Alcoholics Anonymous (AA)?
(1)	11. Have you gotten into fights when drinking?
(2)	12. Has drinking ever created problems between you and your spouse?
(2)	13. Has your spouse (or other family member) ever gone to anyone for help about your drinking?
(2)	14. Have you ever lost friends or girl/boyfriends because of drinking?
(2)	15. Have you ever gotten into trouble at work because of drinking?
(2)	16. Have you ever lost a job because of drinking?

Continued

Michigan Alcohol Screening Test   (*Continued*)

(2)   17. Have you ever neglected your obligations, your family, or your work for two or more days because you were drinking?

(1)   18. Do you ever drink before noon?

(2)   19. Have you ever been told you have liver trouble? Cirrhosis?

(2)   20. Have you ever had delirium tremens (DTs), severe shaking, heard voices, or seen things that weren't there after heavy drinking?

(4)   21. Have you ever gone to anyone for help about your drinking?

(4)   22. Have you ever been in a hospital because of drinking?

(0)   23. (a) Have you ever been a patient in a psychiatric hospital or on a psychiatric ward of a general hospital?

(2)   　　(b) Was drinking part of the problem that resulted in hospitalization?

(0)   24. (a) Have you ever been seen at a psychiatric or mental health clinic, or gone to any doctor, social worker, or clergyman for help with an emotional problem?

(2)   　　(b) Was drinking part of the problem?

(2)   25. Have you ever been arrested, even for a few hours, because of drunk behavior?

(2)   26. Have you ever been arrested for drunk driving after drinking?

*Negative answers to these questions are "alcoholic" responses.

Scoring: A total of four or more points is presumptive evidence of alcoholism. A 5-point total would make it extremely unlikely that the person was not an alcoholic. But, an affirmative answer to 10, 23b, or 24b would be diagnostic of alcoholism.

history of alcoholism or severe depression, a broken home, being the last child in a large family, having an alcoholic brother or sister, and heavy cigarette smoking have all been suggested as predisposing factors to alcoholism.[3]

Psychologists sometimes refer to a certain personality as the "alcoholic personality" or "addictive personality," but there is no general agreement on what characteristics make up this profile. In general, prealcoholics are said to be friendly, gregarious, and independent, but have trouble developing meaningful relationships. They tend to be impulsive, seek immediate gratification, and cannot deal with frustration. Theorists point out a variety of inner conflicts as culprits, such as self-destructive impulses, sexual immaturity, and self-hatred.

Despite these clusters of possible psychosocial factors, no single psychological trait has been found to explain alcoholism. In fact, much of the psychological evidence is contradictory. The problem is that many other people who have experienced the same childhood traumas, emotional deprivations, and unhappy home lives do not become alcoholics. Furthermore, many of the personality characteristics are more likely the result of alcoholism rather than the cause of it.

GENETIC THEORY

Other research has attempted to establish a biological connection to alcohol addiction, but so far no persuasive explanation has been found. The controversy over the genetic aspects of the disease has existed for more than three decades. The theories have been supported by evidence that certain minority groups—American Indians and Canadian Eskimos—seem to be more prone to alcoholism than others.

A gene has been identified as a likely suspect by Dr. Kenneth Blum of the University of Texas Health Sciences Center in San Antonio, and Dr. Ernest P. Noble of the University of California in Los Angeles. They found the same gene in the brains of ten people who died of alcoholism. The gene is a blueprint for a protein in the brain that latches on to dopamine, a chemical that transmits nerve impulses. Despite the promising nature of this study, more recent research by the National Institute of Alcohol Abuse and Alcoholism was unable to duplicate this research, raising doubts about the theory. Dopamine and its interaction with alcohol have been linked for years to alcoholism, and it has been suggested as an explanation as to why alcohol appears to be more of a stimulant for alcoholics than for other individuals.

The interest in genetic factors is based on the long established view that alcoholism runs in families. Some theories point to the influence of the family environment, suggesting that alcoholism is a reaction to stressful situations or simply a child's imitation of an alcoholic parent. A child with an alcoholic father or brother has a 25 percent chance of becoming an alcoholic, which is five to eight times greater than the chance in the general population.[4] Although most early research studied males, more recent studies indicate that females can also inherit a vulnerability to alcoholism.

Others suggest that alcoholism is caused by some physiological defect, an addiction to some X factor or a nutritional, hormonal, or metabolic defect, but there is no conclusive evidence to point to this sort of physiological cause.

Alcohol is not inherently addictive. If it were, then the people who drink the most or longest would be most likely to be alcoholics, which is not necessarily the case. Alcoholism is an addiction, but the cause of the addiction is not known. Some as yet unknown combination of factors in the interaction of the person and the drug is involved.

PHYSIOLOGICAL EFFECTS OF ALCOHOL

The main effects of alcohol are depression of the central nervous system and a slowdown in the functioning of the body and thought processes. In this regard, alcohol is a sedative whose effects are dose related, just like sleeping pills, tranquilizers, or any other depressant. The physical action of the alcohol typically makes a person tired, sleepy, and can even lead to coma and death in large amounts.

Any amount of alcohol will cause some level of intoxication, but the degree depends on the concentration of alcohol in the blood. Low alcohol blood levels produce a mild sedative reaction, resulting in relaxation and a feeling of peacefulness. Higher levels may promote emotional reactions, such as anger, hostility, congeniality, or boisterousness due to a lack of inhibition of these emotions.

When an alcoholic beverage is consumed, it first comes into contact with the mouth, throat, stomach, and intestines. Only about one fifth of the alcohol is absorbed through the stomach, however, and the rest passes through the lining of the intestines directly into the bloodstream. The alcohol is carried in the blood to the liver, where it is metabolized or broken down into carbon dioxide and water. In one hour, the liver can metabolize the equivalent of the alcohol in a can of beer. Any additional unmetabolized alcohol continues to circulate in the bloodstream and reaches the brain and other organs.

The cerebrum or cerebral cortex, which is the outside layer of the brain, is the first part of the brain to be affected by the alcohol. The cerebrum is the most highly developed area of the brain and coordinates perceptions, speech, and critical reasoning faculties. Slurred speech and flawed judgment result when alcohol interferes with cerebral cortex functioning.

The cerebellum at the back of the brain is the next to feel the effects of alcohol. Since the cerebellum is responsible for coordination of movement and balance, a person may stagger or fall down once alcohol affects this area.

The limbic system, which is beneath the cortex, controls memory and emotional behavior. When affected by alcohol, this system may cause exaggerated emotional responses, such as tearfulness or hostility. Emotional outbursts follow a loss of inhibition and may release repressed feelings that are normally kept in check. This reaction has led to the widespread, but false, belief that alcohol is a stimulant because the drinker may initially feel euphoria but does not recognize other symptoms, such as staggered movements, delayed reactions, and poor coordination.

Since alcohol flows through the bloodstream, it has the potential to damage virtually all organ systems in the body. The stomach, liver, heart, brain, pancreas, and nervous systems are all adversely affected by alcohol abuse. In most cases, the alcohol causes inflammation of the organ, because of its irritating effects. Prolonged, heavy alcohol abuse has been linked to a host of diseases affecting these organs.

PSYCHOLOGICAL EFFECTS OF ALCOHOL

Most people drink for psychological reasons. They want to sleep better, boost their confidence, or relieve depression or fatigue. These are not social drinkers but people who are medicating themselves to alter their emotional state. As alcohol becomes more important to them, it exerts subtle, but cumulative influences over their lives.

Drinkers are unaware that although alcohol may initially calm them, it soon increases tension and causes mood swings and insomnia—the very symptoms the drinker is seeking to reduce. These emotional effects are similar to sedatives and tranquilizers, which may explain the dual abuse of these drugs by many alcoholics.

In time, heavy drinking undermines the drinker's self-esteem. Consequently, alcoholics may feel worthless, impotent, depressed, anxious, and disconnected from the people around them. Their chemical dependence, hangovers, fatigue, and emotional distress undercut any efforts to solve the ongoing problems in their lives. As a result, personal problems accumulate and become overwhelming, deepening the alcoholic's general misery.

The prealcoholic shows no evidence of these negative emotions until after he or she begins drinking heavily. Psychological profiles show the future alcoholic to be self-confident, independent, and friendly. Once alcohol abuse begins, however, self-esteem suffers, most precipitously among women.

The initial "good" feeling gained from drinking gradually gives way to moodiness, depression, and anxiety. The degree of these negative emotions seems to be directly proportional to the degree of physical dependence on alcohol. The greater the dependence, the deeper the emotional troubles. As both anxiety and depression increase, the alcoholic drinks more and more to obscure these negative feelings. This creates a cycle of greater woe, more drink, and still deeper depression. He or she continues to suffer as alcohol undermines the positive supports in life—marriage, career, friend-ships, school—and the alcoholic faces loneliness and despair.

Although it is difficult to tell sometimes if the depression and anxiety caused the drinking or vice versa, the evidence suggests that the negative emotions are consequences of drinking. Even moderate drinking may cause chronic depression and anxiety, according to the National Institute on Alcohol Abuse and Alcoholism (NIAAA).[5] In an NIAAA study, social drinkers who abstained from alcohol for six weeks felt better emotionally than those who did not.

As we will see later, depression is one of the most common causes of fatigue. In the case of alcoholism, treating the depression is not the answer. To overcome emotional turmoil, the alcoholic must first come to grips with the drinking problem.

EFFECTS ON SLEEP

Drinking even a small amount of alcohol tends to alter sleep patterns. Alcohol increases drowsiness and decreases the time it takes to fall asleep but then interferes with sleep by altering sleep stages and increasing the number of nighttime awakenings. The net result is general weakness, fatigue, and lethargy upon arising in the morning.

Alcohol delays and suppresses the rapid eye movement (REM) stage of sleep. The effect seems to be dose related and even small doses can affect this aspect of sleep. The higher the dose, the longer the alcohol suppresses REM sleep. When a person is de-prived of adequate amounts of REM sleep, as he or she would be after heavy drinking, the person is likely to experience fatigue, irritability, and anxiety. Mental processes may also be disrupted, so the person may forget things or be unable to concentrate as well as previously.

Insomnia is commonly associated with alcohol withdrawal and some alcoholics have experienced insomnia for weeks or months after quitting. The insomnia in some cases is so severe that the person resumes drinking just to alleviate it. Because of the alcohol addiction, this type of insomnia is rarely treated with medications. To treat this sort of insomnia, one must first resolve the problem with alcohol.

The depression associated with chronic alcoholism will also cause sleeping problems. Insomnia-related depression is marked by early-morning awakening as well as changes in the sleep cycle. Anxiety caused by withdrawal from alcohol typically delays the onset of sleep. (Refer to Chapter Five on depression for more information on this type of insomnia.)

Because alcohol interferes with sleep, alcoholics frequently combine their drinking with sedatives to induce sleep. A 1977 study of insomniacs in Los Angeles found that one in five frequently took alcohol and sleeping pills together to aid sleep. The danger of overdose is clear. About a third of the patients admitted to hospitals for drug overdoses have taken benzodiazepine and alcohol together.[6]

VITAMIN DEFICIENCY

Alcoholics usually do not eat adequately because they consume most of their calories in alcoholic beverages and are, therefore, not hungry. The problem is that alcohol has virtually no vitamins, minerals, or proteins needed for a healthful diet and this leads to malnutrition. Additionally, alcohol abuse interferes with the normal absorption of vitamins and minerals because the drug irritates and inflames the lining of the stomach, intestine, and pancreas. Liver damage from alcohol also decreases the body's ability to process vitamins.[7]

The most common deficiencies seen among alcoholics are in the B vitamins, particularly B_1, B_{12}, and folic acid. The B vitamins are interdependent and a deficiency in any one may cause a relative deficiency in one or more of the others. The depletion of this class of vitamins leads to damage of the nervous system and various types of anemia.

Vitamin deficiencies among alcoholics are so common that alcohol treatment centers routinely administer a shot of 100 mg of vitamin B_1 (thiamine) to patients upon admission as well as oral doses of other B vitamins.

Severe deficiency of B_{12} and folic acid can cause severe anemia, since both are required for the formation and maturation of red blood cells. Anemia will lead to chronic fatigue, weakness, diarrhea, depression, and headaches.

Thiamine (B_1) deficiency is associated with beriberi, a rare disease involving the degeneration of nerve and muscle tissues. Severe vitamin B_1 deficiency is also responsible for the Wernicke stage of Wernicke-Korsakoff, which is characterized by mental confusion, disorientation, and incoherence. Victims often cannot recognize family or friends during this stage of the disease. With thiamine treatment, the patient greatly improves within a few weeks, but in cases caused by alcohol abuse, the patient rarely recovers fully.

A deficiency in vitamin B_3 (niacin) is another common medical problem for alcoholics because this vitamin is absorbed in the upper intestine, a process disturbed by alcohol abuse. Pellagra is caused by a severe deficiency in this vitamin. Pellagra victims develop dermatitis, diarrhea, and mental illness associated with insomnia, depression, delusions, and hallucinations.

It is clear from the medical evidence that anyone who drinks alcohol regularly should make a sustained effort to eat a balanced diet. In some cases, physicians may also recommend special vitamin supplements, but megadoses of vitamins should not be seen as offering protection against the ravages of alcohol abuse.

WOMEN AND ALCOHOL

If fully reported, the number of women alcoholics would equal that of men.[8] If this comes as a surprise, it is another indication that the myths about women alcoholics die hard. The social stigma for a woman with a drinking problem persists, despite advances in many other women's issues.

More freedom for women in business and society has translated to greater freedom to drink. The rate of drinking by women has increased considerably since World War II. The added pressures on women from work and family have driven the problem of female alcoholism.

A drunken woman elicits disgust and revulsion from men and women alike, even from other alcoholic women. Trained physicians tend to take a negative view of them as well and consider them sicker than male alcoholics.[9] Female drunkenness continues to be equated with moral weakness and sexual promiscuity.

Women drink differently from men and alcohol affects them differently. Rather than beer, women prefer wine and hard liquor as a matter of taste and both have higher alcohol content. Women diet more, so they are more apt to drink on an empty stomach. This increases blood alcohol content and accelerates malnutrition. Menstruation lowers a woman's tolerance to alcohol, but increases tension and depression, which encourages heavier drinking.

Psychologically, alcoholic women have a harder time of it. They experience a higher rate of divorce than alcoholic men do. Even discounting alcohol abuse, women are statistically nearly twice as likely to suffer from depression than men do. Alcoholic women have a higher suicide rate than alcoholic men do.

Even if they do not drink alcohol themselves, women tend to be victims of abuse by males who do drink. Alcohol is a factor in many sexual assaults and domestic beatings. Despite abuse at home, nonalcoholic women are more likely than nonalcoholic men to stay with an alcoholic spouse.

Women alcoholics are frequently addicted to other drugs, compounding an already complex problem. The drugs of choice, usually tranquilizers or sleeping pills, make rehabilitation more difficult and sometimes facilitate suicide.

Pregnancy is another concern for alcoholic women. Heavy drinking can cause stillbirths, low birth weight, and a number of birth defects. The risk to the fetus posed by alcohol abuse is even higher than cigarette smoking. Other problems are infertility, miscarriages, and hysterectomies, all of which are special problems for women alcoholics.

Women alcoholics respond best in a treatment setting specifically focused on women. Female therapy or support groups offer a more sympathetic forum for issues such as extramarital affairs, battering, child abuse, and abortion.

Treatment of women alcoholics has grown in recent years and

many programs take their different problems into account. As more and more women come forward for treatment, this situation should continue to improve in the years ahead.

EFFECTS OF ALCOHOLISM ON FAMILIES

Alcoholics are not the only victims of alcoholism. Family members of alcoholics suffer severe emotional harm from years of abuse from the alcoholics living with them. Children may be deeply scarred by divorce, beatings, incest, abusive language, sexual abuse, and neglect.

Children raised by an alcoholic mother suffer greater harm than those raised in a home with an alcoholic father. This is due to the more intimate relationship between the child and mother and the fact that the mother usually spends more time caring for the child.

Spouses and children both suffer guilt, shame, anxiety, depression, and fear from the relationships with alcoholics. These feelings lead to emotional exhaustion and fatigue. Because the symptoms are fairly consistent and identifiable, psychologists have coined the term "co-alcoholic" to describe the patients with these traits. The term has been changed to co-dependent to include families of other kinds of addicts.

Co-dependents typically suffer many of the same psychological problems as their alcoholic parent or spouse and often repeat the same dysfunctional patterns in their own lives. They may become alcoholics or chemically dependent themselves or get entangled in other relationships with alcoholics. Others may live their lives without alcohol or drugs, but develop other addictions to careers, sex, gambling, or something else.

Children of alcoholics are obsessed with meeting others' needs, but fail to take care of their own. Co-dependents neglect and abuse themselves in the same way that others have. They grow up without many of the coping skills or self-care skills that help others deal with the disappointments and hardships of life.

Several groups have formed to offer co-dependents support and treatment. Some of these groups are Children of Alcoholics (CoA),

Adult Children of Alcoholics (ACoA), Al-Anon for spouses and other family members of alcoholics, and Al-Ateen for teenagers of alcoholics. Hundreds of chapters of these groups meet regularly.

Children typically deny their parents are alcoholics, or if they recognize the disease, they deny its impact on the family. Others deny the impact on their own emotional health, refusing to come to grips with their intense inner conflicts. Support groups can help these people work through the stages of denial and resolve the underlying problems.

Families tend to keep alcoholism a family secret and project a facade of normalcy to the outside world. Feelings are hidden, parents use children as confidants, and the children consequently grow up to feel responsible for other people's problems.

The alcoholic parent is not emotionally available to tend to the child's needs or even able to insure the child's physical safety. Life with an alcoholic is chaotic and unpredictable. Family attention is focused not on the children but on the alcoholic, whose disease determines the family's fate.

TREATMENT OF ALCOHOLISM

The fatigue associated with alcohol can be relieved only by treating the drinking problem first. It would do little good, for example, to treat alcoholic insomnia with barbiturates without reducing the drinking. Similarly, the depression, anxiety, and low self-esteem of an alcoholic will improve only if the drinking ceases.

The first step in treatment is diagnosis. It is surprising how many physicians fail to diagnose alcoholism. It is estimated that more than half the men and three quarters of the women alcoholics who visit physicians are not diagnosed.[10] Part of the reason is that an alcoholic is very clever at concealing the habit and very convincing in denying the problem. However, a careful interview can usually reveal the disease based on the disruption alcohol has caused in the patient's life.

Any treatment strategy must remain focused on alcohol as the problem. Without correcting the drinking problem, attempts to change other problems in the alcoholic's life will be virtually impossible.

Any treatment modality generally has four aims:

1. to provide an alternative behavior or nonchemical substitute for the alcohol addiction
2. to prevent relapse, either through prescription of Antabuse®, a drug that causes vomiting when taken with alcohol, or by some other means, such as peer support or counseling
3. to rebuild the alcoholic's social supports from family and friends and repair his or her physical health
4. to restore the patient's mental health and self-esteem.[11]

These goals are pursued in three different stages: detoxification, rehabilitation, and outpatient therapy. Despite many advances in medical treatment of alcoholism, there are still no easy or quick cures.

Detoxification and Withdrawal

The symptoms of withdrawal vary widely among individuals, depending on the nature and degree of the addiction. A "hangover" is actually withdrawal, but it is a relatively minor symptom. The first signs will usually show up within 8 hours of the last drink, most frequently as shakes or tremors in the morning.

Typical withdrawal symptoms are sweating, rapid heartbeat, disorientation, insomnia, agitation, elevated blood pressure, a fever, and hyperventilation. In severe cases, hallucinations may occur, usually within 24 hours of the last drink, and may persist intermittently for days. Mild dementia, seizures, and delirium tremens are also associated with severe cases of alcohol withdrawal. Delirium tremens, also known as D.T.s, occurs between 50 to 100 hours after drinking has ceased and should always be treated in a hospital.

Detoxification takes between four to six days and is usually done at an inpatient detoxification center, where tranquilizers, usually benzodiazepine, are administered to ease the discomfort of withdrawal symptoms. Most physicians advise against tranquilizers to control anxiety after this stage.

Rehabilitation

Once the patient leaves the detoxification center, he or she may enter a halfway house or some other type of center for alcoholics. The person lives in a residential setting among people with similar problems. The alcoholic attends therapy sessions, learns to develop relationships with others, and gains support for his or her return to work and society.

An alternative to inpatient centers is an intensive rehabilitation program run from hospitals, mental health clinics, or alcohol rehabilitation facilities. These programs permit the recovering alcoholic to continue ongoing relationships at home, work, or school, but attend therapy sessions three or four nights a week.

Sometimes physicians will prescribe Antabuse®, also known by its generic name disulfiram, during this stage of the recovery, since it makes individuals sick if they drink alcohol. This discourages drinking, but usually does not offer enough incentive to insure sobriety by itself. The benefits of psychological support from others cannot be overstated.

Alcoholics Anonymous and Outpatient Therapy

One of the chief resources for alcoholism in the community is Alcoholics Anonymous (AA), an independent self-help group formed in 1935 that now has 1.8 million members in 87,000 local chapters around the world. The AA has had a tremendous impact on alcoholism treatment in the United States and Canada.

Because attendance at AA meetings is free and sessions are available just about anywhere in the United States, many professional alcohol rehabilitation programs routinely recommend its meetings to their clients. The AA offers long-term support among a setting of peers who can share experiences.

The AA is not, and has never claimed to be, the only successful outpatient therapy available to the alcoholic. Many different programs are offered by hospitals, clinics, churches, or private institutions. Therapies include individual, group, or family psychotherapy, art therapy, occupational therapy, assertiveness training, relaxation techniques, and acupuncture. The choice is really up to the patient.

The importance of AA, however, cannot be stressed enough. It goes beyond the therapy it offers members at meetings and its principles become a way of life to many recovering alcoholics. Over the years, AA is estimated to have had tens of millions of members. The main idea behind AA, as well as any of the other rehabilitation programs, is to prevent relapse.

Although most medical professionals involved in the treatment of alcoholism believe AA works, there have been no scientific studies done on the group because of the anonymity provided its members. In controlled studies of other programs, the average rate of success is no better than 20 percent.[12] One estimate puts the AA success rate as high as 75 to 89 percent, with one relapse per person for about half of these.[13]

The AA was started in 1935 in Akron, Ohio, when an alcoholic stockbroker from New York, Bill Wilson, discovered that he could stay sober by helping other alcoholics. He and Dr. Bob, an alcoholic surgeon, teamed up with Sister Ignatia of St. Thomas Hospital in Akron. From their experiences, they devised the essential program as it stands now. The governing ideas are incorporated in the Twelve Steps in Chapter 5 of the book, *Alcoholics Anonymous*, first published in 1939.

Meetings of AA members are held in church basements, municipal buildings, clinics, schools, and storefronts. The AA provides an alternative social group to compete with the former camaraderie the alcoholic may have sought in bars. Parties, picnics, dances, and other social gatherings are scheduled around the holidays, when alcohol may prove too tempting at other functions.

Each AA group is autonomous and runs its own operation, creating great diversity among the groups. There are no dues and the group declines outside contributions. Members sometimes pass the

The Twelve Steps of Alcoholics Anonymous

1. We admitted we were powerless over alcohol—that our lives had become unmanageable.
2. Came to believe that a Power greater than ourselves could restore us to sanity.
3. Made a decision to turn our will and our lives over to the care of God as we understood Him.
4. Made a searching and fearless moral inventory of ourselves.
5. Admitted to God, to ourselves, and to another human being the exact nature of our wrongs.
6. Were entirely ready to have God remove all these defects of character.
7. Humbly asked Him to remove our shortcomings.
8. Made a list of all persons we had harmed and became willing to make amends to them all.
9. Made direct amends to such people wherever possible, except when to do so would injure them or others.
10. Continued to take personal inventory and, when we were wrong, promptly admitted it.
11. Sought, through prayer and meditation, to improve our conscious contact with God as we understood Him, praying only for knowledge of His will for us and the power to carry that out.
12. Having had a spiritual awakening as the result of these steps, we tried to carry this message to alcoholics and to practice these principles in all our affairs.

hat for donations at meetings to pay rent, buy coffee, or support activities. The groups refuse to become involved in controversy and shun endorsements of policy or social issues. The only requirement for AA membership is the desire to stop drinking.

Samplings from groups have found that many members are referred by professionals. A high number of members utilize several treatment modalities and come to AA for long-term follow-up and support. The AA is especially helpful for those who have made a break with the habit, overcome withdrawal symptoms, and achieved some level of sobriety by attending a detoxification center or other programs.

The AA has been sensitive to the religious overtones of the program and some of its groups are specifically designed for agnostics.

CONCLUSION

Anyone who suspects that he or she may be addicted to alcohol or may have a drinking problem might try to limit his drinking to a certain amount each day—two or three ounces of hard liquor or two or three beers, for example. If he cannot maintain this restricted level for two months or more, it indicates a problem with control that may require help to overcome.

Alcohol has been linked to many serious organic diseases, including liver damage, degenerative brain disorders, chronic pulmonary infection, hypoglycemia, a variety of anemias, ulcers, pancreatitis, gastritis, and heart disease.

Fatigue caused by alcohol abuse seems to pale in comparison to these serious and sometimes life-threatening diseases. But the impact of chronic, unremitting fatigue in an alcoholic's life should not be trivialized. The promise of a vigorous, revitalized life, free of fatigue, may offer a strong incentive to the chronic alcoholic to quit. As he or she recovers from the misery that alcohol has caused, the alcoholic may view this renewal of energy as a beacon of hope in rebuilding his or her life.

SOURCES FOR MORE INFORMATION ON ALCOHOL ABUSE

Alcoholics Anonymous World Services, Inc.
Box 459
Grand Central Station
New York, NY 10163

National Council on Alcoholism
12 West 21st St., 7th Floor
New York, NY 10010

National Institute on Alcohol Abuse and Alcoholism (NIAAA)
5600 Fishers Lane
Rockville, MD 20857

CHAPTER FOUR

GET A GOOD NIGHT'S SLEEP

INTRODUCTION

Common sense tells us that if we don't sleep well, we'll be tired. Sound sleep restores our vitality, while troubled sleep frustrates and exhausts us. Understanding our sleep habits and making adjustments to get a good night's sleep will go a long way towards ending fatigue.

For millions of people, however, a good night's sleep remains an elusive dream. As many as a third of all Americans—about 80 million people—suffer from insomnia or some other sleep disturbance during the year. For these insomniacs, nights are a lonely vigil. These victims of sleeplessness toss and turn in their beds, stare at the dim lights of the bedside clock, or watch the gray bedroom shadows lengthen as night gives way to dawn, and finally, after another sleepless night, they arise, tired, frustrated, and depressed, to face another day.

The mysteries of sleep have fascinated humans for centuries. In the last 30 or 40 years, research in dozens of sleep clinics has helped uncover many of these secrets. This new understanding has provided insomniacs with their best chances in years of overcoming their exhaustion.

WHAT IS SLEEP?

Strange as it may seem, scientists have had a hard time deciding upon a good definition for sleep. Properly speaking, sleep is a natural state of consciousness that is temporarily, but regularly, suspended while the powers of the body and mind are restored. Such a simple definition, however, does not address the complex activities underway in our bodies and minds as we sleep.

We spend roughly a third of each day and ultimately a third of our lives in sleep. What happens during this time determines our waking hours, how we feel, and what we are able to do.

Contrary to our general impression, sleep is not a passive activity. A night's sleep can be likened to climbing up and down stairs, each step representing one of five stages, and a person goes down and then up the staircase three or four times during the night. As the sleeper passes through the various stages, changes occur in his or her body—mental, physical, chemical, hormonal, and muscular changes.

Most people spend about 15 minutes in bed before falling asleep. This is the sleep latency period in which the body and mind relax before slipping into a twilight zone between wakefulness and sleep. Blood pressure, temperature, and heart rates decrease slightly.

This initial phase leads into Stage 1 sleep. The eyes roll slowly and body movements slow down. This is a light sleep and the person can be awakened easily. Thoughts drift and the body feels weightless, as if floating.

In Stage 2, a person may begin snoring as resistance in the airway increases. If the eyelids were opened at this point, the eyes would not see. The heartbeat slows and body temperature decreases further.

Stage 3 is a deep sleep and louder noises are required to awaken the person. This stage is marked by the appearance of delta waves, which are high amplitude electrical rhythms of the brain. These slow waves comprise 20 to 30 percent of the brain activity in this stage of sleep, but not more than 50 percent. Growth hormones are also secreted in Stage 3 sleep.

The deepest sleep occurs in Stage 4, which is sometimes classified with Stage 3 sleep because delta waves are present again, usually for more than 50 percent of the duration of this phase. In Stage 4, the sleeper has reached the bottom of the stairs and the brain is in its most restful period. After a variable amount of time, the sleeper makes a return trip and begins climbing back up through Stages 3, 2, and 1 to reach the first period of Rapid Eye Movement (REM) sleep.

The REM phase is characterized by violent movements of the eyeballs below the closed eyelid. This first REM phase lasts for 10 minutes or more. About 80 percent of REM sleep is spent in dreams usually marked by vivid images. When the REM ends, the sleeper once again ascends the stairs through Stages 1, 2, 3, and 4, only to return three or more times for increasingly longer periods of REM sleep.

One entire sleep cycle occurs in little more than 90 minutes. In general, the deeper, slow-wave sleep periods occur in the first third of the night and REM sleep occurs in the final two thirds. The usual portions of the night spent in various stages are: 50 percent in Stage 2; 25 percent in REM; 10 percent in Stage 3; 10 percent in Stage 4; and 5 percent in Stage 1.[1]

WHY DO WE SLEEP?

Common sense tells us that sleep is necessary to restore the body and mind from the ravages of a day's activities. This popular conception may be only partly true. Some researchers go so far as to argue that the absolute necessity for sleep has never been established, at least with scientific evidence.

Even though research has not yet determined the exact mechanism of sleep and the key to its restorative powers, most scientists agree that sleep is necessary for both physical and psychological well-being.

Social scientists believe sleep was necessary for our ancient ancestors to survive. Humans were more vulnerable to their predators at night, so they would hide and sleep to pass the time and save their energies for the daylight, when they needed strength to flee enemies. This explanation for sleep is an anachronism today, but the sleep cycle is firmly entrenched in our life cycle.

Other theories are based on the psychological aspects of sleep. Sigmund Freud believed sleep was a symbolic journey back to the womb. Others have seen it as a conditioned response derived from our evolution and that our need for sleep is rooted in the biological cycle we share with all other animals.

Whatever the reason for it, humans need sleep and display odd behavior when deprived of it. Case studies abound with strange happenings when disc jockeys, college students, and research subjects have gone many hours without sleep. Usually, a person deprived of sleep for long periods of time requires only a fraction of the sleep lost to return to normal. Even after one disc jockey stayed awake for 200 hours, he slept for only 14 hours.

Sleep deprivation studies may not have resolved the question of why we need to sleep, but they have demonstrated that we are quite unhappy and do not function well without it. REM sleep presents a special mystery for researchers. Scientists don't know why it is important or what function it serves, but it seems to be necessary.

If a person is deprived of REM sleep, for example, by taking brief naps of fewer than 90 minutes, after which REM sleep would normally begin, then the REM sleep shows up earlier in the cycle. Studies show we cannot function well if deprived of this type of sleep. Most of our dreaming occurs in the REM phase, although dreams do appear in other stages, too.

HOW MUCH SLEEP DO YOU NEED?

Most people would sleep more if they were given the chance, but there seems to be no optimum amount of time people require. When a Gallup poll questioned 1,550 adults in 1979, it found that about 60 percent slept less than 8 hours and only 26 percent slept 8 to 8.5 hours.

The need for sleep is highest at birth and drops dramatically by age 20. Newborns sleep 12 hours a day or more. By age 20, sleep time levels off to an average of seven hours and does not change very much thereafter. The sleep requirement is about the same for both men and women. The amount of sleep an individual requires to feel refreshed is determined by several factors, including personality, age, and general health. Transient occurrences in a person's life, such as a loss of job or a death in the family, may force a temporary increase in the daily sleep requirement.

The most important factor regarding sleep time is whether or not the person functions well on the amount of sleep he or she is getting. If a person feels tired after 6 hours of sleep, he should try sleeping 7 or 8 hours. On the other hand, there is no reason to be concerned if you are sleeping only 6 hours, as long as you feel rested in the morning. Those who are apt to be worriers or introverted tend to sleep more, while outgoing, extroverted people generally require less sleep.

Troubles with sleep tend to increase with age. The sleep patterns of the elderly, for example, are quite different from those of young people. Generally, the research shows elderly people spend more time getting to sleep, awaken more times during the night and for longer periods, and spend less time in REM and the deeper stages of sleep.

It is a myth that older people require less sleep, although certain stages of sleep diminish significantly with advancing age. The sleep of the elderly, for instance, is marked by the virtual absence of Stage 4 sleep, with apparently no psychological consequences.

Nightly awakenings increase after age 35. Young adults wake up one to three times a night, whereas older people wake up five to seven times. The length of waking time in bed also increases with age.

Besides these changes in sleep cycles, the elderly experience more physical diseases that have insomnia as a secondary symptom. Arthritis, diabetes, heart disease, respiratory problems, and many other illnesses interfere with proper sleep and are more likely to afflict the elderly. Additionally, depression is common among older populations, particularly among those who have recently experi-- enced the death of a spouse, and depression disturbs sleep.

TO NAP OR NOT TO NAP?

As anyone who has caught a few winks after lunch knows, a nap at midday can be quite restful. Some research indicates that humans prefer to sleep twice a day: eight hours at night and one hour in the middle of the day. In tropical climates, many societies encourage afternoon naps, a tradition encouraged by hot, humid weather.

More than one nap a day should be avoided, however, since they are more apt to interfere with getting to sleep at night. The length of time you are awake before going to bed is a crucial determinant in falling asleep and naps shorten this time.

Even though naps can be restful during the day, they usually reduce the quality of sleep at night. An afternoon nap decreases the amount of REM sleep at night, for example. Eliminating naps may help a person get to sleep faster at night and sleep longer. Most people who take regular naps do so to replace lost sleep. Workers on the night shift—nurses, factory workers, journalists, policemen—often take long naps to compensate for lost sleep.

If you have trouble sleeping at night, naps could make matters worse. Nap time should be subtracted from the next night's sleep, so if you nap an hour, go to bed an hour later or get up an hour earlier the next day. This will mean less disruption to your sleep cycle.

ASSESSING SLEEP HABITS

You may be sleeping better than you think. People who have trouble falling asleep, or getting back to sleep when awakened, often believe they are sleeping less than they really are. If you are not keeping track, you may be surprised by the number of hours you are sleeping. So keep track of your sleeping hours. Note the time you go to bed, the time lying awake, and the time you get up. Compare your findings and look for patterns after two or three weeks.

The first step in improving your sleep is to assess your sleeping habits and to become more aware of how you sleep. You can't change or improve something until you understand it better. Ask yourself the following questions:

1. What drugs, if any, are you taking? Do you use prescription drugs such as barbiturates, sedatives, tranquilizers, antidepressants, or over-the-counter drugs such as Sominex®, Nytol®, cold remedies, or allergy medications? Do you use

illegal drugs, such as marijuana, hashish, or cocaine? Do you smoke tobacco? Do you often drink alcohol or caffeinated beverages before going to bed? Any of these drugs or beverages have the potential to interfere with your sleep.

2. Do you snore, grind your teeth, kick your legs, or walk in your sleep? These are all specific symptoms of certain sleep disorders we will discuss in more detail later.

3. How long does it take for you to fall asleep? How many times do you wake up during the night? How much total sleep time do you get each night? Do you wake up to an alarm clock? Do you take a nap? Log your sleep time to determine if you are actually losing sleep. Many people who sleep poorly mistakenly believe they are sleeping less. First determine whether it is the quality or quantity of sleep that is suffering.

4. What is your dominant mood? Do you tend to worry a lot? Are you depressed, restless, irritable? Do you cry easily or lose your temper frequently? A heightened state of arousal will delay onset of sleep and cause frequent awakenings.

5. Are there noises that awaken you during the night—a snoring bed partner, barking dog, train whistle, traffic? Is it cool in your bedroom? Are your mattress, pillow, and bedcovers comfortable? Some things that disturb sleep are so obvious we overlook them. Any intermittent noise will disturb your sleep. Even though you may not awaken to trains or car noises, the sounds will alter your level of sleep.

The answers to these questions may prompt you to make adjustments based on good sleep habits (see Panel on page 88).

INSOMNIA—THE MOST COMMON SLEEP DISORDER

Insomnia is a symptom, not a disease. It is caused by a variety of factors, both psychological and physical, and it is ubiquitous. National surveys have found that one third of the American population at any given time suffers from insomnia: about 25 percent women and 12 percent men.

Literally speaking, insomnia means not being able to sleep at all.

In practical terms, insomnia is defined as not getting enough sleep over a prolonged period of time. Although the causes of insomnia are almost as varied as the people who suffer from it, insomniacs are typically plagued by depression, self-doubt, and worry. They are generally the type of people who keep their emotions bottled up inside and have trouble with personal relationships.

People living in disadvantaged socioeconomic conditions are more likely to suffer from insomnia, perhaps because they are more vulnerable to stress from low-income jobs, alcohol, financial problems, and crowded living quarters.

Causes of Insomnia

Several factors are usually working together simultaneously to cause a person's insomnia. A winning strategy will attack each of these factors successively until normal sleep returns. Psychological problems brought on by family and marital troubles, stress from work, chemical abuse, or physical illness are frequent contributors. Sometimes worry about not sleeping can keep people awake.

Depression

Virtually all depressed people suffer from insomnia. They often awake early in the morning, usually between 3 and 4 a.m. Depression upsets the normal sleep cycle and causes the first REM period to occur sooner in the night and last longer than normal. The amount of REM sleep is unchanged, but there is a loss of the deep sleep in Stages 3 and 4.

As we noted in Chapter Five, psychotherapy can be very effective in treating depression and there are many effective medicines available. If depression is causing the insomnia, it will need to be treated first, before normal sleep will return.

Anxiety

Depression-caused insomnia may be accompanied by anxiety. Unlike depression, anxiety tends to keep a person awake as he or she tosses and turns. Typically, the anxiety is free floating and the person is not aware of any specific reason for worrying. Once the anxiety is treated, normal sleep routines return quickly. Refer to Chapter Six for causes and treatment of anxiety.

Physical Illness

A variety of illnesses and the medications prescribed to ease their symptoms contribute to insomnia. More than 30 million Americans are seriously ill. A great many illnesses affect the quality of sleep, especially those associated with pain—arthritis, angina, ulcers, lower back injury, asthma, migraine headaches, and multiple sclerosis. If you are being treated for an illness, you should confer with your doctor about side effects from medications that may be disturbing your sleep. Your physician may be able to prescribe a different drug or lower the dose to enable you to sleep better. When taking over-the-counter medicines, you should be careful to avoid those containing caffeine.

Teeth Grinding

If you clench or grind your teeth, you probably wake up with sore jaws in the morning. This condition, also known as bruxism, will be quite evident to your dentist, as well as to a sleeping partner. Dentists report that 20 percent of their patients are teeth-grinders. If bruxism is caused by poor fillings, your dentist should be able to resolve the problem. Biofeedback, a relaxation technique that uses monitoring equipment to measure and report stress, and hypnosis have helped some people overcome this habit.

Sleep Apnea

If you have awakened at night fighting for breath, you may have sleep apnea. It is found almost entirely among middle-aged men between the ages of 40 and 60. There are two broad types: obstructive apnea, in which upper airways are temporarily blocked, and central apnea, which occurs when the brain fails to send the proper signals to the diaphragm regulating respiration.

Heavy snoring may have been present for many years before

apnea develops. Symptoms may worsen with alcohol or the benzo-diazepine drugs. Obesity, and possibly depression, are also associated with sleep apnea, but not every sufferer is overweight or depressed.

Patients complain of daytime drowsiness, repeated nighttime awakenings, unrefreshing naps, and morning headaches. Sleeping on the side or losing weight may help. Sometimes surgery is recommended for those patients with the obstructive form of apnea, and some drugs are being investigated to treat this disorder.

The treatment of any of these forms of insomnia should include various approaches to the problem, beginning with common sense changes in life-style and sleep habits. Psychological counseling may be necessary if depression or stress are factors. Your physician may recommend medication to induce sleep or counter depression in such cases.

NARCOLEPSY: DAYTIME SLEEP ATTACKS

When people have trouble staying awake, rather than sleeping, they are suffering from a disease of excessive sleepiness distinguished by daytime sleep attacks. The disease has two forms: narcolepsy and hypersomnia. The two forms are distinguished only by the nature and duration of the sleep attacks. In narcolepsy, the attacks are irresistible and last from one to 15 minutes. Hypersomnia is a chronic state of daytime drowsiness with longer-lasting attacks, some lasting for weeks.

The cause of narcolepsy is not known and there is no cure, although symptoms sometimes respond to stimulants. Recent sleep research has focused on an imbalance between the patient's REM and non-REM sleep systems so that the REM stage is always near the surface, ready to emerge without warning.

The narcoleptic suffers a deteriorated state of alertness throughout the day and may be overcome by sleep at almost any time in any situation—driving, working, walking, or sitting. Besides the sleep attacks, the disease has a group of other symptoms:

1. Cataplexy, a sudden loss of muscle tone, is triggered by a sudden emotional change, such as laughter, fear, anger, or surprise. The loss of muscle tension lasts only a few seconds or a couple of minutes.
2. Sleep paralysis, which is similar to cataplexy, occurs less frequently, perhaps only two times a month. The paralysis appears suddenly and muscles become very rigid, making it impossible for the person to move. Attacks may last 30 seconds or more and the patient will be fully conscious of what is happening. The paralysis might occur just as the person is about to fall asleep or awake.
3. Vivid hallucinations occur between the state of sleep and wakefulness. They resemble dreams and are sometimes accompanied by sleep paralysis and intense anxiety.

Several scientific approaches are underway to find the cause of narcolepsy and hypersomnia, but it may be many years before they are fully understood. Because these patients usually develop insomnia, proper sleep hygiene should be followed. Since there is no cure, physicians generally prescribe the lowest possible dose of any stimulants or antidepressants to forestall the development of tolerance to or adverse side effects from the drug.[2]

SHIFT WORK

Many people—as many as one in five workers in the industrialized world—work for businesses or institutions that operate around the clock. Hospitals, airports, newspaper offices, power plants, military bases, police and fire departments, and many manufacturing plants employ millions of workers who report to their jobs at all hours of the day and night. The result is occupational sleep loss that may cause insomnia and other sleep disorders.

Many rhythmic processes occur in human beings, but none is as important as the sleep-wake cycle of the circadian rhythm, which refers to the physiological cycle we humans experience over the 24-hour period we know as a day. The major problem with working shifts is that it disrupts this delicate bodily rhythm or biological clock.

Once the circadian rhythm is disrupted, sleep onset is delayed and the sleep-wake pattern is altered. Insomnia, chronic fatigue, and daytime sleepiness follow. These disorders will not only affect the person's job, but create various emotional problems, disrupt family life, and interfere with recreational and leisure activities. The result may be depression, anxiety, and stress, all of which aggravate the worker's fatigue.

The most disruptive schedules are weekly shift rotations, in which a person works one shift one week and another the next week. Repeated over months and years, this rotation causes a chronic interference with the circadian rhythm. These workers on rotating shifts tend to consult physicians, develop serious illnesses, and require hospitalization more often than their fixed-schedule counterparts.[3]

The central problem is that the worker's rhythms are out of step with the environment around him. Subjective stress is higher, problems mount, and sleep loss inevitably results in daytime sleepiness. Sleeping pills or alcohol are ineffective and may add to the problem.

Because night work disrupts normal sleeping hours, a person on rotating shifts develops trouble getting to sleep and usually sleeps less—usually only 5 or 6 hours. Some workers sleep twice, once after work and again briefly before returning to work. Besides less sleep, some studies indicate that shift workers experience less REM sleep, when most dreams occur.

Despite a good deal of research, nothing promises a solution to the sleep problems associated with shift work. Some improvement may be gained by scheduling the direction of rotation clockwise from day to swing to night shift rather than against the clock. Other possible solutions have focused on drugs to reset the biological clock or modify the circadian rhythm, but more research in this area is needed before hope can be offered.

Other than regular daytime shifts, afternoon and evening shifts appear to be the least disruptive to sleep patterns. Workers may not get to bed until 2 or 3 a.m., but they can sleep late the next morning and get normal amounts of sleep. The circadian rhythm peaks in the early evening, so these workers will be alert during the shift. By contrast, night shift workers complain of sleepiness during work hours, which may pose safety problems.

Another way to combat disruption to sleep due to shiftwork is assignment to permanent shifts. Most people, however, do not want to work the graveyard shift or other night shifts permanently, but a steady shift is better than rotation. Even with permanent night shifts, workers tend to revert to normal schedules on weekends and vacations, forcing their bodies to readapt when they return to work.

Contrary to popular belief, people do not get used to night shift work. It never gets easier. The difficulty of adapting to night work increases with age. Young people seem to adapt more readily.

Many of those who appear at sleep clinics with sleep disorders are shift workers. Rather than prescribing medication, most sleep specialists recommend changing jobs. This is the best solution in most cases because medical problems are more apt to appear in persons who have a low tolerance for rotating shifts.

Sleep Tips for Shift Workers

In the booklet, "Shiftwork and Your Health,"[4] M. Moore-Ede offers the following helpful suggestions for those who work nights and rotating shifts:

1. Keep to a regular schedule as much as possible. Go to bed at the same time each day and don't give in to the temptation to take random naps.
2. Eat your regular meals at the normal times. Choose light snacks at night to avoid stomach and digestive problems.
3. Use light to reset your biological clock. Keep your bedroom as dark as possible during daytime sleeping hours, but make things as bright as possible when you are awake during the night.
4. Follow good sleep hygiene. Daytime noises can be troublesome, so make sure your bedroom is quiet. Wear ear plugs if necessary to keep out the noise.
5. Don't drink coffee for a minimum of three hours before you go to bed.

JET LAG

Jet lag disrupts the circadian rhythm much like shift work, causing insomnia and fatigue. Diplomats, labor negotiators, professional athletes, journalists, and others who must perform at peak levels immediately upon arrival at distant destinations are especially concerned about jet lag. These flyers usually try to arrive at least a day ahead of the scheduled event to insure top performance.

Everybody seems to have a different tolerance to jet lag. The most frequent and usually the first symptom to appear is an ever-growing sense of fatigue that affects sense of time, concentration, memory, and overall effectiveness. Other symptoms begin to appear a few hours after arrival and include greater fatigue, insomnia, headache, loss of appetite, and stomach problems.

The degree of jet lag depends on several factors. The number of time zones through which you pass is the most crucial factor, but direction of travel plays a significant role. It is much easier to recover from a westbound than an eastbound trip because one has the feeling of gaining time. Eastbound flights, on the other hand, shorten the day and tend to cause greater disruptions in the circadian rhythm.

The traveler can take actions to minimize jet lag, but nothing will eliminate its effects altogether. The general idea is to get in step with the locals at the destination as quickly as possible. This will take the edge off jet lag symptoms and resynchronize your own daily time clock.

Arrival times play a role in ameliorating jet lag. If possible, plan to arrive in the morning by local time. You may be able to sleep on the plane the night before and the morning rush will get you in step with the locals immediately.

In terms of departure times, choose flights that depart as early as reasonable if flying east and as late as feasible when flying west. This will enable you to arrive either late enough local time to go to bed or early enough in the day to synchronize yourself to local time.

Sleep after a long flight is fragmented and unsatisfying. Some of the relaxation techniques described in a later chapter can help ease the tension. Sleeping pills and alcohol should be avoided. They may facilitate the onset of sleep, but they can exacerbate the symptoms of jet lag, leaving a person groggy and disoriented upon awakening.

Jet lag is a transient and temporary condition. It can be unpleasant and frustrating, especially when it occurs on vacation, but the most adverse effects generally recede in a day or two.

SLEEPING PILLS

In 1971, doctors wrote a record-breaking 42 million prescriptions for sleeping pills. The number has fallen significantly every year since then, but sleeping pills remain one of the drugs prescribed most often in America.

Since insomnia is a complex disorder with many causes, sleeping pills alone will not cure sleeplessness, especially if the underlying causes go unrecognized and untreated. Used correctly over short periods of time, however, sleeping pills can be effective for people suffering from short-term insomnia caused by temporary disruptions in their sleep.

The treatment of insomnia should begin with a complete assessment of sleep habits and hygiene. Sleeping pills should be used appropriately, but only as part of an overall strategy aimed at treating the underlying problems.

In many cases, particularly among the elderly, sleeping pills are prescribed when alternative types of treatment, such as psychotherapy, relaxation techniques, or a nutritional program, would be more effective. Adverse side effects are more likely among the elderly because they suffer more frequently from other health problems and may also be taking other medications.

EFFECTS OF SLEEPING PILLS

Sleeping pills belong to a classification of drugs known as hypnotics and central nervous system (CNS) depressants. Two primary groups, the barbiturates and benzodiazepines, are among the most widely prescribed as sleeping pills and are sold under many brand names.

Barbiturates were once the most popular kind of sleeping pill, but the problems of addiction, withdrawal, and overdose associated with these drugs have prompted today's doctors to recommend the benzodiazepines. The barbiturates include such brand names as Seconal®, Luminal®, Amytal®, and Nembutal®. The benzodiazepines have a greater margin of safety for overdose and act more quickly than the barbiturates, but there is also growing concern over a tendency for these drugs to cause dependence.[5] The benzodiazepines are sold under such brand names as Dalmane®, Valium®, Librium®, and Centrax®.

Some sleeping pills build up in the body and are eliminated more slowly than others. The result is daytime sleepiness and fatigue, sometimes accompanied by increased tension and anxiety. Morning grogginess and memory lapses are also associated with some sleeping medications.

Besides the prescription drugs, there are a host of over-the-counter sleeping pills on the market. Most of these drugs contain antihistamines, which cause drowsiness and are commonly found in cold remedies.

Among other things you should know about sleeping pills:

1. Tolerance develops more quickly with the benzodiazepines, so they are not effective for more than a couple of weeks. Users should avoid taking higher doses once tolerance develops because of the risks of dependence. Withdrawal symptoms among those who have taken the drug over a long period of time are just the opposite of those for which the drug was taken in the first place—agitation, insomnia, anxiety and even convulsive seizures.

2. People generally fall asleep within 15 to 20 minutes after taking a sleeping pill and may sleep 30 to 40 minutes longer than normal. Sleeping pills reduce the amount of deep sleep in Stages 3, 4, and REM, but this has not been found to be harmful.

3. It is critical to note that most studies of the side effects of sleeping pills are done with young healthy adults, although most prescriptions are written for the elderly.

4. The duration of the effects varies for different sleeping pills. Short-acting drugs should be used for those having trouble

falling asleep. Longer-lasting drugs will reduce nighttime awakenings but are a problem for people who must get up to tend to a small child or need to go to the bathroom during the night.

5. Side effects of the benzodiazepines include such things as confusion, drowsiness, shakiness, slurred speech, staggering, and weakness. Less common effects are nervousness, irritability, skin rashes, and depression. Barbiturates may cause anxiety, dizziness, vision problems, trembling of hands, clumsiness, and a "hangover" effect, in addition to addiction. Furthermore, an overdose of barbiturates or dual abuse with alcohol can be lethal.[6]

6. Sleeping pills pose a potential danger to pregnant women. An unborn child may become dependent on the drugs in their mother's womb and women who breastfeed their newborns may pass the drug to the child through the milk.

7. When a person stops taking sleeping pills, he or she may experience anxiety dreams and a resurgence of insomnia that can be worse than the insomnia experienced prior to taking the pills. This is why physicians recommend patients reduce their use of sleeping pills slowly over time.

8. Many people with insomnia are suffering from depression masked by anxiety. Once a sedative eases the anxiety, the depression reasserts itself. In such cases, physicians usually prescribe an antidepressant.

CONCLUSION

Many things interfere with a good night's sleep. The more we understand about this human mystery, the better we can cope with its disorders. Sleep research centers around the world are continually investigating new avenues toward greater knowledge about sleep.

Modern civilization continually puts obstacles in our paths to good sleeping habits. The environment in our cities overstimulates our senses, creates anxiety, and undermines our sleep. We encounter drugs of all types (over-the-counter, prescription, and illegal) as well as stimulants like caffeine, nicotine, or depressants like alcohol. All of these aspects of modern life can interfere with sleep.

Maybe, instead of wondering why millions of Americans suffer from insomnia, it would be better to ask why some people don't. What distinguishes these good sleepers from millions of insomniacs? The next time you meet someone who says "I sleep like a baby," ask them what the secret is.

For people suffering from fatigue, nothing seems to help like a good night's sleep. Getting that type of sleep, however, will probably require some adjustments in lifestyle. It is a safe bet that whatever is interfering with their sleep is also causing their fatigue.

Good Sleep Habits

1. Avoid caffeine, tobacco, and alcohol prior to bedtime. While caffeine and tobacco postpone sleep, alcohol helps a person fall asleep, but disturbs restfulness.
2. Avoid drinking liquids before turning in for the night. Awakening to make a trip to the bathroom during the night is a frequent cause of poor sleeping.
3. Regular exercise during the day will help you sleep soundly at night. Vigorous exercise late in the day is not recommended, since it speeds up the body's metabolism and will disturb sleep.
4. Go to bed the same time each night and get up at the same time every morning, even on the weekends. If you go to bed late, arise at the regular time anyway. The established rhythm will help you fall asleep easier.
5. When you awaken during the night, remain calm and avoid thoughts that may cause excitement or worry.
6. A quiet bedroom is crucial to good sleep. If necessary, wear earplugs or soundproof the windows. You may never get used to noise from motor vehicle traffic, airplanes, or trains. Even when these noises do not wake you up, they disturb the quality of your sleep.
7. Use sleeping pills only when necessary to overcome a severe problem and follow your physician's instructions carefully. Continued use should be avoided, since it will soon become ineffective.

8. Don't nap during the day. For most people a nap decreases the quality of sleep at night.

9. Get out of bed when you have awoken during the night and have not been able to get back to sleep after 15 or 20 minutes. Return to bed when you feel sleepy.

10. Keep the bedroom cool but not cold. In terms of sleep, it is better for the room to be cold than hot. Sleep studies have found that sleep is disturbed when room temperatures exceed 75 degrees.

11. Start winding down about an hour before bedtime so that you are relaxed and ready to sleep. Avoid intense mental activity prior to bed.

12. Engaging in sexual activity can be relaxing and restful if satisfying, but other forms of exercise are apt to be counterproductive.

13. Avoid using your bedroom for anything but sleep and sex. Using the room to watch television, study, or do homework or other work will distract your attention when you want to sleep.

14. Keep a sleep diary if you often have sleepless nights. Write down the time you went to bed, the number of nighttime awakenings, amount of coffee or alcohol consumed, exercise taken during the day, and other things that might affect your sleep. After a week or two, analyze your notes and look for any patterns.

CHAPTER FIVE

DEPRESSION
THE MOST COMMON CAUSE OF FATIGUE?

INTRODUCTION

Depression—sometimes called the "common cold" of mental illness—strikes 20 million Americans a year and can be a serious, even deadly, illness. Whether the depression is mild or severe, fatigue is almost always a dominant symptom. When a depressed person says "I'm too tired," he or she really means "I'm too depressed."

Serious depression destroys careers, marriages, family relationships, and can even lead to suicide. Commonly defined as a feeling of despair, sadness, or discouragement, depression can be a normal reaction to loss or failure. While occasional sadness is normal and inevitable, it can develop into a chronic state of intense misery and deep depression. This can occur if a person is predisposed to the illness or lacks the skills to cope with it.

Some people experience only one major depressive episode in a lifetime, but more than half will have at least one more. Sometimes the episodes are separated by years of normal functioning, but in other cases people have increasingly frequent bouts of depression as they grow older.

We have all had experience with mild depression. People have described the feeling in a variety of terms, such as "down," "unhappy," "blue," or "feeling low." In most cases, the mood passes in a few hours or days. When the depression lingers more than two weeks, occurring most of the day nearly every day, it is considered a major depressive episode and it could persist for six months or longer without treatment.

The family physician is usually the first one to see the depressed patient. A patient may visit the doctor's office complaining of fatigue or some other vague physical symptom, such as lower back or chest pain, stomach problems, or headaches. Once a physical cause has been ruled out, diagnosis of depression can usually be made by careful interviews with the patient.

A study of family practices in Colorado in 1980 found that, out of 176 patients diagnosed with fatigue, 22 percent were depressed. An additional 23 percent suffered from anxiety or stress.[1]

Not only is depression one of the most common causes of fatigue, but fatigue is one of the most common and most obvious symptoms of depression. Generally, the person feels especially tired and depressed in the morning, but his mood picks up as the day wears on, and he may feel almost normal by evening.

The degree of fatigue varies with the degree of depression. According to a study by Aaron T. Beck, a psychiatrist at the University of Pennsylvania, fatigue is most common among people with moderate depression (89 percent) and is ironically less frequent (84 percent) among the severely depressed. Only about 40 percent of nondepressed people report fatigue, whereas 62 percent of the mildly depressed report it as a symptom.[2]

Depressed patients refer to their fatigue in a variety of ways. Some emphasize the physical weakness, while others refer to a loss of mental vitality and acuity. Depression is almost always accompanied by insomnia or some other sleep disturbance, which only makes matters worse.

FATIGUE AND DEPRESSION

Since fatigue is such a prominent symptom of depression, some investigators theorize that a person may deplete his physical and emotional energy prior to becoming depressed because of some prolonged stress, either physical or mental. The depression thus represents something of a dormant period in which the person is rebuilding his energies like a battery being recharged.

The fatigue that is experienced from depression does not disappear with rest. After a night's sleep, a depressed person feels just as tired and low, or possibly worse. Unlike the normal fatigue that results from physical or concentrated mental efforts, the fatigue of depression is caused by tumultuous and exhausting unconscious conflicts.

Fatigue tends to perpetuate inaction and depression. People who are depressed don't want to do anything, and then they blame themselves for being lazy or worthless. Action is the best antidote. Activity improves mood, counterbalances the fatigue, and builds motivation and enthusiasm for activities that make the depressed person feel better. This is particularly true of physical tasks, like gardening, bicycling, swimming, or some daily exercise regimen. Even seemingly simple things like making a phone call or visiting a neighbor can help fight fatigue and depression.

The type of fatigue varies depending on the degree of depression. For a mildly depressed person, a nap may restore vitality, even though any real change in mood will be short lived. The mildly depressed person tires easily and recognizes a significant difference in the loss of personal energy compared to his predepressed state.

Fatigue caused by moderate depression tends to increase with any kind of physical activity. The fatigue is more stubborn than in milder depression and will not likely respond to any amount of relaxation or rest.

The most severe depression brings a virtual paralysis of will and motivation. Since lack of interest is also pronounced in such cases, it is sometimes difficult to separate fatigue from boredom. In many cases, the fatigue is so pervasive that the patient lies in bed for at least part of the day.

ARE YOU REALLY DEPRESSED?

One in five adults in the United States suffers major depression at least once in his or her lifetime. Although the reason is unclear, we know that this illness strikes women twice as frequently as it strikes men. Most sufferers never seek treatment and dismiss their depression as a character flaw or blame it on "life."

Dramatic progress has been made in recent years in the treatment of depression, both in terms of effective medication as well as new techniques in psychotherapy. As it stands today, there is no reason for most people to suffer from depression. Of all the emotional disorders, depression is the most responsive to treatment. Complete recovery may occur in a matter of weeks or a few months. Only a small percentage of depressed patients cannot be helped at all.

Sadness and depression are such a part of daily life that it is sometimes difficult to make a distinction between the two. Sadness is a normal and healthy emotion when it comes in response to a difficult life situation. Bereavement, divorce, failure, or other serious losses are situations that prompt normal feelings of unhappiness.

Depression is a different matter. It is not just a passing emotional response to a stressful situation but rather a persistent state of mind of indeterminate duration that has a specific set of identifiable symptoms. We know that major depressive illness is a heterogeneous problem. In other words, it is not composed of just one emotion, such as sadness. One or more other emotions usually coexist with depression, particularly anxiety, mania, or hostility.

Sometimes the depression is secondary to another underlying problem, such as a physical illness. Depression frequently appears along with other personal problems, such as alcoholism, drug abuse, insomnia, phobias, and marital strife.

Depression is not always a symptom of psychological illness. It may be a sign of organic disease. Indeed, several studies have shown between 10 and 50 percent of depressed psychiatric patients suffer from medical problems. Some common physical disorders include thyroid and adrenal diseases, anemia, cancer, epilepsy, viral infection, and vitamin deficiency.

Sorting all of this out requires a skilled clinician. Although a diagnosis may be challenging, and in fact the precise form of the depression may be impossible to identify, a diagnosis is important because it is the first step in the treatment process and will determine which specific type of therapy is best suited to cure the depression.

SYMPTOMS OF DEPRESSION

A host of physical and psychological symptoms characterize depression. Most of them are familiar and have been experienced by all of us at one time or another.

The American Psychiatric Association has set down a specific list of criteria for diagnosing major depression in the DSM-III-R, the standard reference manual for psychiatric diagnosticians.[3] At least five of the following symptoms must be present for two weeks and must include the first two for a patient to be categorized as experiencing a major depression:[4]

1. Depressed mood.—Sometimes described as "down in the dumps," "sad," "depressed," or "low" feelings, such as despair, discouragement, and hopelessness, are experienced as intense sadness and may be overwhelming.
2. Loss of interest or pleasure in activities.—The person has not necessarily lost *all* interest in *all* things, but his or her interest is noticeably *less* than it was prior to the depression.
3. Decrease or increase of appetite.—Loss or gain of more than 5 percent of a person's body weight within a month. Some people develop an increased appetite for chocolate or sweets, but about 70 percent experience a loss of appetite. Young people with milder depression eat more and gain weight.
4. Sleep disturbances.—Insomnia with early-morning or middle-of-the-night awakenings or trouble falling asleep is common. Hypersomnia is less common and appears as oversleeping by an hour or more than usual, apparently to avoid stressful situations.
5. Psychomotor agitation or retardation.—Psychomotor agitation is usually displayed as restlessness and pacing and is distinct from anxiety. It may involve increased smoking, hand wringing, or simply an inability to relax. Retardation is marked by reduced or slowed speech, a lack of facial expression, a fixed stare, and slowed movements.
6. Fatigue or loss of energy.—Daytime drowsiness and weakness are common and some people become so tired that they have to go back to bed during the day.

7. Feelings of worthlessness, self-reproach, or excessive and inappropriate guilt.—Sometimes these feelings are manifested in delusions and auditory hallucinations, solitary brooding, and ruminating. This is related to the low self-esteem and feelings of inadequacy common among those predisposed to depression.
8. Reduced ability to concentrate or indecisiveness.—Trouble with concentration is noticeable when reading, watching television, or in conversations with others. Slowed thinking, a blank mind, or poor memory may also be part of this symptom.
9. Repeated thoughts of one's own death, suicidal fantasies, wishes for death, or a suicide attempt.

The first two symptoms, depressed mood and loss of interest, are the most significant symptoms and are always present in any form of depression. The loss of interest in activities, especially hobbies, sex, and activities with family and friends, prevents the depressed person from experiencing any pleasure. Apathy, fatigue, and inactivity displace things that were previously enjoyable. Although depressed people have a decreased interest in sex, they are generally capable of performing physically.

Anxiety attacks accompany depression in about a third of the cases. Also known as panic attacks, these incidents activate a number of startling physical symptoms, including heart palpitations, rapid, shallow breathing, dizziness, and sometimes flushing, chest pain, and sweating. The attacks usually disappear once the depression passes.

Other less common physical symptoms reported by some depressed patients include dry mouth, constipation, blurred vision, dry skin, slurred speech, excessive salivation, difficulty in urination, and problems with sexual performance, such as impotency, loss of libido, premature ejaculation, and an inability to experience orgasm.[5]

Another frequent attribute of depression is a diurnal variation in mood, which, as we've noted, is worst in the morning and gradually improves over the course of the day. This is particularly common in the melancholic type of depression, a moderate form of depression.

Some Common Factors in Depression

1. Problems in relationships, either with a spouse or any other relative. Divorce or troubles with a teenaged son or daughter.
2. Grief that leads to a major depression following the death of a loved one.
3. Loss, change, or dissatisfaction in work leading to feelings of failure or loss of self-esteem.
4. A geographical move away from familiar surroundings or family and friends, requiring a change in social interactions.
5. Postpartum depression following childbirth.
6. A fear of obtaining self-esteem or pleasure from one's own efforts, rather than from those of someone or something else. For example, adhering to a rigid set of social standards rather than pursuing one's own inner goals.
7. Not expressing anger for fear it will damage a personal relationship and instead directing the anger at yourself, causing guilt, self-blame, and depression.
8. A feeling that others are overly conscious of your actions and behavior. You believe that your actions are the center of someone else's attention, when they are not.
9. An overwhelming feeling of helplessness or powerlessness to influence life in general or the immediate environment (marriage, job, school, etc.).

The person wakes up and feels depressed, moves and thinks slowly, but feels better by the evening. In these cases, fatigue is worse in the morning.

In severe cases of depression, sometimes referred to as psychotic depression, people may develop delusions and hallucinations. Delusions are false beliefs that are firmly held, despite obvious rational evidence to the contrary. Common delusions revolve around feelings of being controlled or persecuted. Hallucinations are imagined sensory perceptions. Hallucinations may involve any of the senses and may take the form of imaginary sounds, tastes, or sights.

Sometimes depression causes hypochondriasis, a preoccupation with fears of serious physical illness, even though exhaustive evaluations have found nothing physically wrong with the person. These patients usually have a long medical history and have had several unsatisfactory relationships with doctors. Fatigue is a common complaint along with psychosomatic ailments, such as back pain or headache. The hypochondriac refuses to be reassured, either by doctors or loved ones.

TYPES OF DEPRESSION

Depression appears in many forms. Mental health professionals have devised several categories and diagnostic procedures, tests, and interview techniques to identify the specific types and the severity of depression. The complexity of the human psyche, however, defies easy categorization, and a precise diagnosis may not be possible in all cases. Our emotional life is extraordinarily complicated and dynamic. We are constantly growing and changing, forever adapting to life around us. What we were yesterday is not what we are becoming or what we will be tomorrow.

Depression appears, recedes, and may never recur or may recur years later. In between, people can lead normal lives. For others, depression may appear and last for years. The severity and frequency of symptoms defines the depression, which usually falls within two broad categories: bipolar (manic–depressive) and unipolar (depressive disorders).

The usefulness of any classification system is problematic. Diagnosis of a specific type is particularly crucial if medication is prescribed since some drugs are effective only for certain types of depression, and not for others. For purposes of psychotherapy or "talk therapy," exact diagnosis is less important since the treatment can be tailored to the patient's individual needs and the same techniques seem to be effective for many types of depression.

In an effort to standardize the categories of depression, the American Psychiatric Association has classified types of depression in the DSM-III-R, a standard reference manual. All types share many of the symptoms already discussed, but some symptoms are more severe or more frequent in some types than in others.

MANIC–DEPRESSIVE ILLNESS

Manic–depressive or bipolar disorder is a form of depression distinguished by at least one manic episode, which is a period of extreme excitability, elation, and agitation that may last for a few days or a few months. Cyclothymia, a milder form, has similar symptoms, but the cycles of depression and hypomania, a mild form of mania, occur more frequently and are less severe.

The predominant mood of mania may be either euphoria and extreme sociability, or irritability. Euphoria, elation, and cheerfulness are the typical moods, but anger and irritability may dominate, especially if the person is feeling frustrated about a particular objective. One aspect of mania is an unceasing and enthusiastic interaction with people or activities. The manic is viewed as loud, gregarious, and bold, but he or she may be sent into a rage by a trifling slight. Hospitalization may be necessary in order to prevent harm to the patient or others.

Even though a person may suffer from mania alone, with no symptoms of depression, the condition is still considered a component of depressive illness. Mania represents the opposite or flip side of classic depression. Most manic–depressives experience both sides. When the mania is dominant, euphoria displaces sadness, inexhaustibility replaces fatigue, and inflated self-esteem contrasts with feelings of worthlessness. Sometimes the condition is mixed and both manic and depressive symptoms coexist in a single episode. Sometimes the mania and depression may alternate every few days.

Other symptoms of the manic cycle are decreased need for sleep, increased risk-taking, anger and irritability, increased sexual activity, rapid speech, distractibility, and psychomotor agitation. The manic is sociable, sometimes even charming, but in lacking judgment and restraint may make impulsive financial investments or engage in promiscuous sexual activity. In severe cases, delusions and hallucinations will occur and disrupt work, personal relationships, or schooling.

As noted before, cyclothymia has the same symptoms as mania, but they are milder and the cycle is repeated more frequently. Unlike mania, however, the mood disturbances are not severe enough to interfere with work, school, or relationships.

OTHER DEPRESSIVE TYPES

Although major depression may occur only once in a person's life, others may suffer several episodes, sometimes separated by years. As stated earlier, to meet the diagnostic criteria, a major depression must last for at least two weeks. Sometimes the episodes become more frequent as a person grows older. A loss of interest or pleasure in formerly enjoyable activities is almost always present. In severe cases, the patient may suffer from psychotic features, such as delusions and hallucinations. A major depression is chronic, with little relief for the patient. It can be either mild, moderate, or severe, and in chronic forms, it may persist at some degree for months or years.

According to statistics, nearly 25 percent of women in the United States have suffered a major depressive episode, compared to about 12 percent of all American men. At any given time, as many as 9 percent of women and 3 percent of all men suffer from this disorder.[6]

A persistent but less severe form of depression is called *dysthymia* or depressive neurosis. Dysthymia is also sometimes called endogenous depression or depressive personality. This form of depression is similar to mild depression, but the symptoms persist for at least two years and its onset is not associated with a precipitating event, such as a divorce or other personal tragedy. Dysthymia rarely requires hospitalization, and performance at work or school is not usually affected adversely. In some cases, however, a major depressive episode may strike simultaneously, a condition referred to as double depression, which is marked by a sudden worsening of symptoms. The patient will likely continue to suffer from dysthymia after recovery from the major episode.

Another subtype of typically severe major depression is *melancholia*, which the DSM-III-R manual identifies with symptoms that distinguish it from other types. The melancholic does not feel better even after good things happen and his depression is distinctly worse in the morning. Additionally, melancholics usually have a history of major depression from which they have recovered.

SEASONAL DEPRESSION

Seasonal depression has received considerable attention in the past decade. This condition plagues women far more frequently than men and typically develops during a person's 30s. The depression follows the pattern of the seasons, peaking in fall and winter, although the reverse condition has also been found. Hypomania, either euphoria or irritability, may also be part of the cycle. A diagnosis of seasonal depression is appropriate if a pattern of fall–winter depression has been traced for at least two consecutive winters. This type of depression is typically mild or moderate and disappears in spring and summer months.

The dominant symptoms of seasonal depression are fatigue and profound sadness. A study of 220 seasonally depressed patients found 94 percent reporting fatigue or lethargy as a symptom.[7] Other symptoms include overeating, the craving of carbohydrates, excessive sleeping, weight gain, anxiety, and difficulties with relationships and work.

A primary indicator of seasonal depression is the onset of symptoms as the days get shorter and bleaker. People who travel south toward the equator during the winter, where the light is stronger, have reported dramatic improvement.

Treatment requires light therapy for two hours or more a day during the fall and winter months. The patient sits in front of a bank of fluorescent lights and stares at them for a few seconds every minute. It is the effect of the lights on the eyes rather than on the skin that provides the therapeutic benefit. It is still not fully understood, however, why exposure to the lights decreases depression.

SOME POPULAR THEORIES OF DEPRESSION

Many theories attempt to explain the causes of depression, but the etiology of this illness remains only partially understood. Considerable attention has focused on four key areas: genetic, biochemical, hormonal, and environmental factors. Although most theories concentrate on one or another, in practical terms some combination of factors is usually involved when referring to specific cases.

An adverse event in a person's life can act as a trigger to depression—failure at work or school, death of a spouse, divorce, rejection by a lover, disease, or financial problems. People who are predisposed to depression—either biologically or psychologically—are more vulnerable when these events occur. For others, the onset of depression is more subtle with no ostensible precipitating event.

Most researchers believe that depression results from multiple causes. It would be impossible to review all the theories, but it may be useful to look at a few of them.

ENVIRONMENTAL FACTORS

Attachment and Loss

This theory advanced by J. Bowlby, a British psychiatrist, suggests that erratic relationships with parents may predispose people to depression. While stable attachments to parents lead to feelings of security, threats to attachment may cause anger and anxiety, and a complete loss of attachment may lead to depression. This pattern can be repeated in adult life when people form attachments to others.

According to Bowlby, disruptions in attachment may be caused by temporary separations of the child and parents, threats by parents to abandon the family, threats by one parent to desert or kill the other, threats of suicide by a parent, or inducing the child to think he or she is responsible for the parent's illness.[8] Such examples may occur if a couple is having marital difficulties or if one or both of the parents are depressed.

Loss of Dominant Other

Silvano Arieti and Jules Bemporad, authors of *Severe and Mild Depression*, believe people are vulnerable to depression when they suffer the loss of the dominant person in their lives, especially a parent or spouse, either through death, divorce, or any other major trauma.

Sometimes the loss comes as a result of a failure in an interpersonal relationship. A man or woman facing a divorce may feel betrayed, exploited, used, and abandoned. Feelings of anger, guilt, anxiety, sorrow, and finally depression result.

When the loss is due to death, the emotional reaction is complicated by grief. The sudden loss may lead to feelings of depression because the source of the person's self-esteem, security, and love is suddenly gone. Unlike a divorce, however, the loss is really beyond the control of the depressed person.

Another type of loss, mentioned by Arieti and Bemporad, relates to failure in the pursuit of a dominant goal. The impact of the loss depends on the significance of the goal in the person's inner life. This sort of depression may follow a midlife realization that he or she will not become a great singer, actor, politician, writer, musician, and so forth. The depression is, in a sense, grief over a large part of the person's life, which had been spent in the pursuit of the goal.[9]

Negative Thinking

Aaron T. Beck, a psychologist at the University of Pennsylvania, pioneered much of the work on a cognitive theory of depression that is based on distortions in thinking. This theory suggests that the way people think affects the way they feel—negative thinking breeds negative emotions. According to Beck, depression is caused by three major distortions:

1. The individual interprets events in his environment as pitted against him. He views these events as defeats, deprivations, disappointments, and discouragements. In his distorted view, the environment presents endless and impossible ob-

stacles to his goals. He tends to magnify the negative and minimize the positive things that happen to him.

2. The depressed person views himself in a negative way. He blames himself for everything that goes wrong in his life. He sees himself as inadequate, unworthy, lazy, "no good," undesirable, unlovable, and a person with a variety of defects.

3. He has a pessimistic attitude about the future. He always expects to fail. From his distorted perspective, both short-term and long-term goals are doomed to fail. He perceives future events in terms of his past failures, or in light of his present situation, which he considers unbearable.[10]

According to Beck, the treatment of depression must be targeted at altering these negative thinking processes since he believes that the way people think and perceive events affects the way they feel.

Learned Helplessness

Martin E. P. Seligman, a psychologist at the University of Pennsylvania, has advanced a theory of depression based on helplessness learned in childhood. The child "learns" that his response to traumatic events has no effect on his feelings, so he "learns" to believe that most or all events are uncontrollable. For instance, a child who is criticized by a parent no matter what he does learns that his actions make no difference. When a person feels that his actions are futile, feelings of helplessness and depression result. The depressed person believes that he cannot act to relieve his suffering. He develops the false idea that his actions are independent of the way he feels. To alleviate the depression, a person must realize that actions he or she takes will make a difference.

The concept central to this theory and to eventual recovery requires that the patient learn that his or her actions can influence events that are meaningful to him or her. A child who was exposed to uncontrollable events may be predisposed to depression, whereas an early mastery of events may make him or her immune. A child taught skills to cope with failure, such as trying alternatives until succeeding, for example, develops a sense of control over events that he or she perceives as dependent on his or her actions.[11]

Environment and Behavior

Depression and a lack of positive reinforcement in a person's environment are inextricably related, according to Peter M. Lewinsohn, a behavioral psychologist. A person becomes depressed if he or she does not receive positive reinforcement for his or her actions or if his or her efforts are punished. Discouraged by this response, the person does less, becomes passive, and reduces opportunities for future positive reinforcement. This pattern inevitably leads to more discouragement and depression.

Two factors are central to this theory—the immediate environment and personal coping skills. A person is prone to depression if the immediate environment at home, work, or school lacks positive reinforcement or if it becomes a source of punishment. If caught in such an environment without necessary coping skills, the person will become depressed.

The depressed person in general participates in fewer pleasant activities, which reduces positive reinforcement. To feel better, the depressed person must change his or her interaction with the environment by increasing positive and pleasant events as much as possible while decreasing negative influences.

Behavioral scientists like Peter Lewinsohn suggest making lists of activities, such as traveling, reading, camping, and so on, and then rating them for pleasure. By participating in the most pleasant things more often, a person should see an improvement in mood. Conversely, avoiding negative thinking and poor interpersonal relations can improve the outlook for depression.

HEREDITY AND GENETICS

Do people inherit a predisposition to depression? The answer increasingly seems to be yes.

The tendency of depression to run in families has been recognized for many years, but only recently have researchers begun to identify the genetic connections. The National Institute of Mental Health (NIMH) identified a specific gene in 1987 that triggers manic–depressive illness.

Although genetic vulnerability is an important factor, it is not enough in itself to cause depressive illness. The fact remains, however, that children whose parents have been diagnosed with a depressive illness are at a significantly higher risk of developing a depressive illness. Depending on the type of study, the risk ranges from 10 to 25 percent for offspring of such parents.[12]

The most convincing evidence of a genetic link to depression comes from studies of identical twins. If one twin suffers from depression or mania, the chances are significantly high that the other will also be ill. A Danish study of twins found a concordance rate of 74 percent for manic–depressive illness and 43 percent for unipolar depression.

In reviewing family studies, the risk of manic–depressive illness among children of parents with manic–depression runs between 15 and 35 percent, compared to 1 or 2 percent in the general population. The risk of unipolar depression among offspring of manic–depressive parents is also higher.[13]

Since the children of parents diagnosed with depressive illness face a greater risk of developing the disorder themselves, the people in this population group should be especially vigilant for symptoms of depression.

BIOLOGICAL THEORIES OF DEPRESSION

The search for a biochemical cause of depression has intrigued the medical world since the days of Hippocrates, when black bile was thought to cause melancholia. The biochemical theory enjoyed a resurgence with the discovery of antidepressant drugs in the 1950s, when it was found that the drugs had a variety of effects on catecholamines, a class of neurotransmitters in the brain that include norepinephrine, epinephrine, and dopamine.

Neurotransmitters provide the communication link between

neurons, which are the cells that transmit and receive nervous impulses. The neurons are separated in the brain by microscopic distances known as synapses. When an electrochemical impulse in the brain stimulates a neuron it releases a neurotransmitter, which travels across the synapse and attaches to a receptor on another neuron.

Scientists believe that antidepressant medicines provide their benefits by somehow altering the complex interaction between neurons. Antidepressants either allow the buildup of certain neurotransmitters or assist in their reabsorption by neurons in the brain. Until the mid-1980s, researchers believed that this was the reason antidepressants were effective. But they have since concluded that depression is not caused only by a simple lack or excess of one neurotransmitter or another, because drugs immediately alter the level of neurotransmitters, but depression lingers for several days or weeks before mood improves, indicating some other factor or factors are at work.

One of these other factors that has long been suspected as the culprit in depressive illness is some sort of imbalance in the endocrine system. The endocrine system includes several glands that maintain hormonal balance. Research has focused on the thyroid and adrenal glands and their function with two other important glands, the hypothalamus and pituitary. Since these endocrine glands secrete hormones, any disturbance in the integrated network of glands can create too many, too few, or no hormones at all. Some of these hormones affect the regulation of neurotransmitters in the brain.

A low functioning thyroid, a condition known as hypothyroidism, has long been known to cause depression.[14] Prescribed doses of the thyroid hormone have been used for years, either by itself or in combination with antidepressants, to treat this cause of depression. Some researchers believe low functioning thyroids may be a common factor in depression.

A great deal of new information is being developed on the biochemical aspects of depression. Several promising avenues of research have been opened, but the specific causes and effects of complicated biochemical processes largely remain a mystery.

THE SLEEP OF DEPRESSION

One reason depression causes fatigue is its disruption of sleep patterns. Insomnia is a common complaint of people who suffer from depression. Either they have trouble falling or staying asleep, or they awaken too early in the morning—generally one to two hours before normal. In other cases, the depressed person tends to sleep too much and complains of daytime sleepiness.

Researchers have discovered that depression actually causes no loss in the amount of sleep, but it does disturb the quality or restfulness of the sleep. Typically, a depressed person will sleep a normal 7 or 8 hours but will awaken tired in the morning and complain that he hardly slept at all.

Sleep patterns pass through four stages from light to deep sleep, plus brief periods of REM. The sleeper goes through these four stages every 90 minutes, with the deeper stages getting longer throughout the night. In depressed sleep, the pattern is reversed and REM periods are reduced.

In general, depressed sleepers are awake longer, spend more time in the lighter stages of sleep and less, if any, in the deepest and most restful periods. The reduction in these deeper levels of sleep is the most striking difference. It is interesting to note that the severity of the depression seems to have little influence on the sleep pattern, although there is slightly more wakefulness among the severely ill.[15]

Sleep patterns change as a person enters a depressive episode and can be an early warning of other symptoms. A common pattern is waking up more at night, waking early in the morning, an inability to get back to sleep, and waking up tired in the morning. If such people require medication, they will usually do better with anti-depressant medication than with sleeping pills.[16]

TREATMENT

Modern advances in medicine and therapeutic techniques mean that virtually no one needs to suffer from depression anymore. Either

Beck Depression Inventory

Read each question and circle the number next to the answer that best fits the way you feel at this moment. If more than one answer seems appropriate, circle the higher one. Be sure to read all statements in each group before making a choice.

A.   0   I do not feel sad.
      1   I feel sad.
      2a I am blue or sad all the time and I can't snap out of it.
      2b I am so sad or unhappy that it is quite painful.
      3   I am so sad or unhappy that I can't stand it.

B.   0   I am not particularly discouraged about the future.
      1   I feel discouraged about the future.
      2a I feel I have nothing to look forward to.
      2b I feel that I won't ever get over my troubles.
      3   I feel that the future is hopeless and that things cannot improve.

C.   0   I do not feel like a failure.
      1   I feel I have failed more than the average person.
      2a I feel I have accomplished very little that is worthwhile or that means anything.
      2b As I look back on my life, all I can see is a lot of failures.
      3   I feel I am a complete failure as a person (parent, husband, wife).

D.   0   I get as much satisfaction out of things as I used to.
      1a I feel bored most of the time.
      1b I don't enjoy things the way I used to.
      2   I don't get real satisfaction out of anything anymore.
      3   I am dissatisfied or bored with everything.

E.   0   I don't feel particularly guilty.
      1   I feel guilty a good part of the time.
      2a I feel quite guilty.
      2b I feel bad or unworthy practically all the time now.
      3   I feel as though I am very bad or worthless.

F.   0   I don't feel I am being punished.
      1   I have a feeling that something bad may happen to me.
      2   I feel I am being punished or will be punished.
      3a I feel I deserve to be punished.
      3b I want to be punished.

Continued

G.   0   I don't feel disappointed in myself.
       1a   I am disappointed in myself.
       1b   I don't like myself.
       2   I am disgusted with myself.
       3   I hate myself.

H.   0   I don't feel I am any worse than anybody else.
       1   I am critical of myself for my weaknesses or mistakes.
       2   I blame myself for my faults.
       3   I blame myself for everything bad that happens.

I.   0   I don't have any thoughts of harming myself.
       1   I have thoughts of harming myself, but I would not carry them out.
       2a   I feel I would be better off dead.
       2b   I feel my family would be better off if I were dead.
       3a   I have definite plans about committing suicide.
       3b   I would kill myself if I could.

J.   0   I don't cry any more than usual.
       1   I cry more now than I used to.
       2   I cry all the time now.
       3   I used to be able to cry, but now I can't cry even though I want to.

K.   0   I am no more irritated now than I ever am.
       1   I get annoyed or irritated more easily than I used to.
       2   I feel irritated all the time now.
       3   I don't get irritated at all at the things that used to irritate me.

L.   0   I have not lost interest in other people.
       1   I am less interested in other people than I used to be.
       2   I have lost most of my interest in other people and have little feeling for them.
       3   I have lost all of my interest in other people and don't care about them at all.

M.   0   I make decisions about as well as ever.
       1   I try to put off making decisions.
       2   I have great difficulty in making decisions.
       3   I can't make decisions at all anymore.

N.   0   I don't feel that I look any worse than I used to.
       1   I am worried that I am looking old or unattractive.
       2   I feel that there are permanent changes in my appearance that make me look unattractive.
       3   I believe that I am ugly or repulsive looking.

O.   0   I can work about as well as before.
     1a   It takes an extra effort to get started at doing something.
     1b   I don't work as well as I used to.
     2   I have to push myself very hard to do anything.
     3   I can't do any work at all.
P.   0   I can sleep as well as usual.
     1   I wake up more tired in the morning than I used to.
     2   I wake up 1–2 hours earlier than usual and find it hard to get back to sleep.
     3   I wake up early every day and can't get more than 5 hours sleep.
Q.   0   I don't get more tired than usual.
     1   I get tired more easily than I used to.
     2   I get tired from doing anything.
     3   I get too tired to do anything.
R.   0   My appetite is no worse than usual.
     1   My appetite is not as good as it used to be.
     2   My appetite is much worse now.
     3   I have no appetite at all anymore.
S.   0   I haven't lost much weight, if any, lately.
     1   I have lost more than five pounds.
     2   I have lost more than ten pounds.
     3   I have lost more than fifteen pounds.
T.   0   I am no more concerned about my health than usual.
     1   I am concerned about aches and pains or upset stomach or constipation.
     2   I am so concerned with how I feel or what I feel that it's hard to think of much else.
     3   I am completely absorbed in what I feel.
U.   0   I have not noticed any change in my interest in sex.
     1   I am less interested in sex than I used to be.
     2   I am much less interested in sex now.
     3   I have lost interest in sex completely.

To Score the Test: Ignore the letters after the numbers. Add the circled numbers from the 21 questions.

Scores: less than 14 (normal range); 14–20 (mild depression); 21–26 (moderate); greater than 26 (severe).

Professional counseling may be appropriate if a person scores 17 or more consistently.

Reproduced, with permission, from the Archives of General Psychiatry. (4) June, 1961, pp. 569–571. Copyright 1961, American Medical Association.

counseling, medication, or a combination of the two should resolve depression in the vast majority of cases.

Two questions are vital in terms of treatment. What type of depression is involved and which treatment is best indicated? There are basically three options: drugs, psychotherapy, or electro-convulsive treatment. These options can be used singly or in combination.

Therapists have debated theories of treatment for years, but they usually fall into two categories: those who believe depression is biological and should be treated with drugs and those who see depression as psychological and recommend psychotherapy.

To resolve this debate, the NIMH compared two popular types of psychotherapy with drug treatment in a 10-year study published in 1989. The project studied 250 patients being treated as outpatients at three clinics in Washington, D.C., Pittsburgh, and Oklahoma City. Each patient received one of four treatments: antidepressant medication (imipramine), cognitive behavioral therapy, interpersonal therapy, and a placebo (sugar pill) under physician supervision. Both the imipramine and placebo were administered by physicians with a minimum of supportive therapy.

The cognitive behavioral therapy concentrated on helping the patients correct negative, distorted views of themselves, the world, and the future. The interpersonal therapy concentrated on the patients' relationships with others, helping them identify and better understand their interpersonal problems.

The results of the study found that those taking the antidepressant medication responded best but that all showed some improvement. For patients with mild depression, neither the medication nor the psychotherapies finished significantly better than the placebo. In cases of severe depression, however, the medication did extremely well, interpersonal therapy did fairly well, but the cognitive behavioral therapy was not much better than the placebo.

Overall, of the subjects who completed the treatments in the study, the recovery rates were 57 percent for imipramine, 55 percent for interpersonal therapy, 51 percent for cognitive behavioral therapy, and 29 percent for the placebo. The general lack of difference between the psychotherapies was consistent with other studies that have found little or no significance between the outcomes of different forms of psychotherapies.[17]

PSYCHOTHERAPY FOR DEPRESSION

The most important aspect of psychotherapy is finding the right therapist. Most therapists are trained in a range of techniques and can adapt the therapy to the individual's needs. A family physician should be able to recommend a therapist. If not, a friend, clergyman, or relative may be able to recommend someone. After the first office visit, a patient should have a good idea whether or not the therapist is going to be helpful.

There are three types of professionals based on academic training: psychiatrists, psychologists, and psychiatric social workers. A psychiatrist holds a four-year medical degree and has served a residency in psychiatry. Of the three types, the psychiatrist is the only one licensed to prescribe medication or administer electroconvulsive therapy. A psychologist usually holds a doctoral degree in psychology, whereas the social worker usually has a master's degree in social work.

Psychotherapy is a general term that refers to a wide set of "talk" therapies. All forms fall under three broad categories: individual, family, and group. Within these groups are dozens of forms of therapy. Patients rarely know the type of therapy that is being used, unless they ask or are familiar with the specific techniques. Some therapists encourage their patients to read certain books to gain a better understanding of their problems and to facilitate the therapy sessions.

All therapies share some common techniques and processes. The dynamics vary, but the goal is the same—to provide relief of the patient's suffering, either with insight into a problem or by altering behavior to avoid harmful consequences.

Three types of therapy have been especially helpful in the treatment of depression: interpersonal, behavioral, and cognitive. Each uses concepts from the others, while concentrating on a cluster of principles central to itself. All three have been found effective by ongoing research like the NIMH study. Each may be used in either individual or group therapy.

Although these are generally considered short-term therapies, each can be used for extended treatment depending on the patient. If there is no noticeable improvement after three months, either the therapy or therapist should be changed.

Interpersonal

This sort of therapy is based on psychological theories related to the interaction between the patient and others. Sometimes called "supportive" therapy, interpersonal therapy concentrates on current issues and focuses on the significant others in the patient's life at the present time.

Depression can predispose a patient to problems in personal relationships, and problems in relationships can lead to greater depression. The therapist reviews current relationships in detail with the patient, helping him or her understand the dysfunctional patterns.

Interpersonal therapy is often used to treat life crises, such as grief over the death of a loved one, loss of a job, divorce, or serious illness. The therapy helps patients understand the nature of depression, encourages them to establish new interests and relationships, and eventually allows patients to free themselves from attachment to their loss.

The primary objective of the therapy is to renew the patient's self-esteem and assist in the transition to a new, healthier way of life, either with a new job, relationship, or different social role.

Behavioral

Behavioral therapy concentrates on changing impaired behavior, altering an adverse environment, and strengthening a patient's coping skills. The idea is to increase a person's pleasurable activities and decrease or eliminate the unpleasant ones.

Patients are encouraged to pursue the pleasurable, such as outdoor activities, rewarding friendships, positive sexual experiences, and a variety of other relaxing activities. At the same time, patients learn to cope better and avoid such punishing events as fights with a spouse, job difficulties, or discordant relationships with others.

Once the patient's depression has been diagnosed and the problem areas have been identified, the therapist can help the patient learn new social techniques that will change the dysfunctional behaviors that caused the depression. The tactics of behavioral therapy attempt to alter the environment, change distorted cognitive patterns and develop new coping skills.

Sometimes a complete change in environment—such as a job, marriage, or school—may be necessary, but other times, simply modifying the way the patient interacts with the environment is sufficient.

To help the patient increase his or her awareness of the pleasant and unpleasant factors in the environment, behavior therapy enlists the help of "activity schedules," which rate activities based on the amount of pleasure they provide. This list helps focus on events that contribute to a patient's depression.

Social skills such as time management, goal setting, assertiveness training, relaxation techniques, or stress management, are also employed in behavioral therapy.

Behavioral therapists have adopted many of the ideas of the cognitive school, since altering perceptions of the environment is just as important as changes in the environment itself.

Cognitive Behavioral

Rather than an activity schedule, cognitive therapists utilize a "daily record of dysfunctional thoughts." The negative thoughts are noted and then analyzed. The harmful, automatic thoughts are replaced by more valid and positive thoughts. For example, someone who habitually thinks "I'm a bad person" might change the thought to "I'm a good person most of the time."

The basis for this theory is that negative, dysfunctional thoughts cause depression by lowering self-esteem. By changing misconceptions caused by faulty thinking, the therapy hopes to resolve the

Negative or Distorted Thinking

Dr. Aaron T. Beck of the University of Pennsylvania has pioneered a theory of depression based on a variety of errors in the depressed person's perception of events. According to Dr. Beck, depressed people tend to make six kinds of errors:

1. *Arbitrary Inference*—Jumping to negative conclusions about things without sufficient supporting evidence. This is a distortion based upon negative assumptions that may or may not be true.
2. *Selective Abstraction*—Selecting a single detail out of context (usually a negative one) while ignoring other salient features. These people draw false conclusions of an entire experience based on one element.
3. *Overgeneralization*—drawing a sweeping, far-ranging, pessimistic conclusion about one's abilities, performance, or self-worth, based on a single incident.
4. *Magnification and Minimization*—This is an error in the evaluation of one's ability, achievement, and performance. The person tends to exaggerate the negative and discount the positive aspects of his life.
5. *Personalization*—relating negative external events to the self, when there is no connection between the two. A child, for instance, might blame himself for a fight between his parents.
6. *All or Nothing*—This cognitive error involves thinking in black and white terms. For example, something or someone is all good or all bad, when in fact most things and most people have components of each.

patient's depression. Cognitive therapy is most effective in the treatment of mild to moderate depression.

The role of the cognitive therapist is to help the patient understand how his perception is faulty and why it is based on illogical assumptions. (See table of cognitive distortions.) The therapist uses techniques developed by Dr. Aaron Beck of the University of Pennsylvania to help the patient correct distortions in perception and thinking. (Refer to the panel entitled "Negative or Distorted Thinking" above.) Patients are given "homework" by the therapist, such as lists of activities, automatic thoughts, pros and cons on issues, coping techniques that work, and charts of mood changes. These homework assignments help solidify the lessons of the therapy and make them part of the patient's self-awareness.

The therapist targets a specific problem and explores how and why the problem has led to depression. Cognitive therapists play an authoritative role, similar to a teacher who wants to educate students about misconceptions in their thinking. The therapist is friendly, supportive, helpful, and sympathetic.

Cognitive therapy techniques are used in a variety of settings, including group and family therapies.

A general knowledge of the various therapies will give a patient a greater understanding of the process. In a real sense, therapy is a learning process, with the therapist as teacher. The patient should take an active role in his own education, whether in terms of "homework" or recommended reading.

ANTIDEPRESSANT DRUGS

Sometimes prescription medicine as an adjunct to psychotherapy can be very effective. In these cases, a therapist, if he or she is not a psychiatrist, may refer a patient to a family doctor or psychiatrist to receive a prescription for one of a growing number of antidepressant drugs.

An important debate is raging over the benefits of psychotherapy versus medication, or a combination of the two approaches, and it is not likely to be resolved until many more studies are done. We saw before that medication in the NIMH study did slightly better than psychotherapy. In terms of costs, medication is much less expensive then psychotherapy, but there are always side effects and not everyone responds to medicine. Although drugs show results faster in most cases, the underlying psychosocial causes of the depression are not being treated. The question of who treats the patient on medication is also a matter of contention, since the prescribing physician or psychiatrist may have professional opinions at odds with the treating therapist.

In any case, the antidepressants have shown dramatic results in depressed patients. Most are inexpensive and bring relief in a matter of weeks. After the depression remits, a maintenance dose may be necessary for six months or longer to insure that the depression does not return. The drugs are widely prescribed by both general physicians and psychiatrists, but as all drugs do, they have side effects. If they appear, the side effects usually occur only in the early stage of treatment. None of these medicines should be stopped abruptly.

The four main categories of antidepressants are tricyclics, MAOIs, Prozac, and lithium salts.

Tricyclics

These antidepressants have been in use since the 1950s and are widely prescribed. The generic tricyclics are imipramine, amitriptylene, desipramine, nortriptylene, protriptylene, and trimipramine, which are all marketed under a number of trade names.

Studies have found improvement with the tricyclics to be in the range of 60 to 75 percent of cases. The tricyclics are useful in a wide range of depressions but are particularly effective for acute, major depressions of long duration. They are also useful for panic disorders and depression mixed with anxiety.

No completely reliable procedure or test exists to predict if a patient will respond to these drugs, but an improvement in the patient's sleep pattern after starting treatment is usually a good sign. On the other hand, failure of any improvement of activity, appetite, sleep, or social interest within a week or two is an unfavorable sign. Changes in mood will take at least a week and sometimes three or four weeks to appear.

Some of the common side effects of tricyclics are dry mouth, constipation, sweating, blurred vision, weight gain, and impaired bladder and sexual function. Some other undesirable side effects include dizziness, lightheadedness, fatigue, palpitations, restlessness, and insomnia. Most tricyclics cause postural hypotension (a decrease in blood pressure during change of position), which may cause dizziness when a person stands up quickly. These side effects ameliorate as the body adjusts to the drug. Outpatients are given low doses at first, perhaps as little as 25 mg a day, and slowly build to the therapeutic dose.

These antidepressants are highly toxic when taken in large doses. A dosage of more than 2,000 mg of imipramine is almost always fatal. Acute toxicity may induce agitation, confusion, seizures, and coma. One of the most dangerous toxic effects is cardiac toxicity, which can lead to heart irregularities or even cardiac arrest. For this reason, no more than a week's supply of the drug should be provided for suicidal patients.

To be effective, the level of the antidepressant in the bloodstream must be high enough to work but low enough not to cause adverse side effects. People tend to metabolize the drug differently, leading to a wide variation in the effective dose for individuals. Periodic blood tests are sometimes needed to determine the drug levels. The normal daily dose for an adult is 100 to 150 mg a day of imipramine, but some patients may require as much as 300 mg. This dose may be continued for several months or a year, depending on the severity of the illness. The dose is generally reduced to half six months after remission.

MAO Inhibitors

Another class of antidepressants, known as the enzyme monoamine oxidase inhibitors or MAOIs, are usually the second choice among physicians after a trial of the tricyclics has failed to show improvement.

Phenelzine has received the most clinical study and is marketed under the trade name of Nardil®. Use of phenelzine and other MAOI drugs, such as iproniazid, tranylcypromine, and isocarboxazid, has been limited because of their toxic effects and adverse interactions with other drugs and some foods.

In order to avoid potentially dangerous side effects, doctors require patients on MAOIs to adhere to a strict diet. Of particular concern are fermented foods, such as alcohol, yeast products, wine, pickled herring, sour cream, yogurt, and ripe cheeses. Other prohibited foods are bananas, sour cream, soy sauce, and meat tenderizers. Restrictions are also placed on cold remedies and other medications.

Because of these dietary restrictions, maintenance among undisciplined patients is difficult.

In the 1950s, when the MAOIs were used primarily to treat tubercular patients, it was discovered that people taking the drugs developed a hypertensive crisis if they ate ripened cheese, red wine, and other foods. Because this complication caused a few deaths from intracranial bleeding, physicians became very conservative in prescribing the MAOIs. Despite these risks, the drug appears to be effective in some patients who do not respond to the other antidepressants.

Some of the early side effects to phenelzine include dizziness, insomnia, sexual dysfunction, dry mouth, drowsiness, and an increase in appetite. Postural hypotension, which is common with tricyclics, is also present with the MAOIs.

The daily dose is based on body weight and ranges from 45 to 90 mg. A patient may not notice any improvement in mood for two weeks. The drug is prescribed for six months to a year.

If a patient can follow the strict diet and is not taking other medication that might interact with the MAOIs, these antidepressants can be a safe and effective treatment.

Prozac®

Known in the medical literature as fluoxetine, Prozac® was introduced into the United States market by the Eli Lilly Co. in 1988. It quickly became the most widely prescribed antidepressant drug, primarily because it does not have the toxic effects associated with the other antidepressants. An overdose of Prozac® is not fatal.

Within a year of its introduction, anecdotal reports began to appear that the drug may have caused suicidal thoughts and violent behavior among a small percentage of patients. A controversy developed and the popularity of the drug plummeted, even though no causal relationship has been established. The controversy was fueled by several highly publicized lawsuits filed against the drug.

According to Dr. Martin Teicher, of the McLean Hospital in Belmont, Mass., about 3.5 percent of the patients taking Prozac® have experienced suicidal thoughts.[18] Since similar effects have been seen in patients taking the other antidepressants, however, it is not known if Prozac® poses any greater risk in this area. Some physicians recommend careful supervision of patients beginning fluoxetine therapy if they have suicidal tendencies.

Monitoring is especially important during the early phase before the drug becomes effective, because as with the tricyclics, it takes time for Prozac® to act, usually between one and four weeks. The usual daily dose is about 40 mg, but not all patients respond effectively. In terms of side effects, patients may experience restlessness, nervousness, diarrhea, headache, insomnia, and develop severe fatigue. Rare adverse effects and signs of overdose are vomiting, hypomania, or agitation.

The controversy surrounding Prozac® may continue for some time, but it remains a drug with great potential for treatment of depression. The drug was thoroughly tested in clinical trials prior to its market release and the manufacturer considers it safe and effective.

Lithium

This drug is used to treat manic–depression and is effective in preventing recurrent manic episodes and in stabilizing mood. Lithium decreases irritability, hostility, and the rapid thoughts common to mania. It also reduces any psychotic features associated with manic–depression, such as paranoia, hallucinations, or delusions.

The daily dose varies from one patient to another, but ranges from 900 to 1200 mg. The therapeutic effects are noticed more quickly than other antidepressants, usually within two to six days. The lithium is so quickly absorbed that patients must take three or four doses a day.

A narrow margin exists between the proper dose and toxic effects, so most patients must receive periodic blood tests to measure the level of lithium. Toxic effects include nausea, diarrhea, and confusion.

Many manic–depressives take lithium all their lives and as long as the dose is monitored, the treatment is considered safe and effective. One of the problems reported by therapists treating patients with lithium is not the discomfort of side effects but convincing patients of the need to maintain the dose over such long periods.

CHARTING A NEW COURSE

Treatment of depression, whether by psychotherapy or drugs, is a complex task. The problems associated with the illness have not developed overnight and will take time to resolve no matter which treatment is chosen. The patient will need to change deeply rooted patterns, a difficult undertaking in the best of circumstances.

Fatigue is one of the most troublesome symptoms of depression, because it undermines a person's motivation and diminishes the prospects for recovery. The depressed person may perceive his fatigue as laziness, which makes him feel even more worthless and guilty. To break this cycle, a person must take action, either by getting professional treatment or by taking individual steps to deal with the problem.

Making a decision to seek professional treatment is a difficult step for someone to take, especially the first time. Discussing the decision with a spouse or friend or discussing the depression with a family doctor may make it easier to contact a therapist. Times have changed. In recent years, more and more people have been seeking treatment for depression and it no longer bears the social stigma it once did. The success of new medicines and therapeutic techniques makes it unnecessary for nearly anyone to suffer from depression and the fatigue it causes.

A few weeks or months after therapy or medication has been started, the depression will lift in the vast majority of cases and the fatigue will disappear. With renewed energy, a person can pursue more positive activities, build self-esteem, improve interpersonal relationships, and begin approaching life from a new, healthier perspective. By learning new behavioral techniques, a person who is predisposed to depression can avoid recurrent episodes in the future.

If the depression is relatively mild and professional help is not necessary or, in the case of private psychotherapy too expensive, an individual may seek counseling at a clinic or strive to make the appropriate changes themselves. Many people who become depressed use the episode to reorganize their lives, reexamine their goals, and make new plans for the future.

Hundreds of books and articles have been written about depression. Local libraries and bookstores offer many self-help resources on depression that will help mildly depressed people take stock of their lives and start the process of rebuilding. Just recognizing the problem and making the decision to do something about it is the first step to a more satisfying and fatigue-free life.

Choosing a Therapist

The decision to enter therapy can be disturbing and cause apprehension. Here are some points to consider that will help you choose the best therapist for you:

1. The first rule for any medical practitioner should always be: "Above all else, do no harm." The therapist should be warm, friendly, supportive, and relaxed. A tense, impatient, restless, or inattentive therapist is not likely to be helpful, and, in fact, may add to the depressed patient's troubles.
2. Avoid therapists who demand payment for missed meetings or want to be paid in advance. They are more interested in maintaining income than in improving your mental health.
3. You should feel comfortable with your therapist. The relationship should engender mutual trust and respect.
4. Avoid a therapist who uses technical jargon—"masochistic," "compulsive," or "paranoid"—to describe you or others. These labels are abusive, punitive, and indicate insensitivity and unprofessionalism.
5. A good therapist should be active in providing guidance and advice, although this help is usually indirect and subtle. The Hollywood stereotype of an aloof, insensitive practitioner who nods and murmurs "uh huh" or "I understand" is unlikely to be helpful.

Continued

Choosing a Therapist (*Continued*)

6. Sexual overtures by a therapist are highly unethical and can damage the patient. If the therapist gives indications along these lines, notify your family doctor and ask to be referred to someone else.
7. The idea that therapists should keep their distance—not touch the patient or display any emotion—is discounted by many researchers. A firm handshake on greeting, for example, can help establish a human bond and ease initial anxiety.
8. A good therapist knows how to strike a balance between a professional and social relationship. The professional relationship always focuses on the needs of the patient, not those of the therapist.
9. Mutual respect is integral to a productive relationship. If the therapist seems angry at criticism, or annoyed by personal mannerisms, it will inhibit free expression and impede therapeutic progress.
10. Most importantly, the therapist should present himself or herself to the patient as another human being. Sometimes therapists appear larger than life to their patients, fostering a dependency that is not healthy for the patient.
11. If a patient shows no improvement after three months, a change in therapists or therapies is recommended.

CHAPTER SIX

STRESS, ANXIETY, AND BURNOUT

INTRODUCTION

We live in an age of anxiety. The stresses of modern life are pervasive, inescapable, and cumulative. In modern society, if we live and breathe, we experience anxiety and stress. The way we cope determines whether or not the stress will rob us of energy, leaving us too tired to enjoy life or resilient enough to adjust and overcome our difficulties.

In our popular culture, stress goes by many names—anxiety, worry, tension, pressure, or distress. Without relief, they all lead to fatigue. Physical and emotional exhaustion are the first warnings of approaching disease. Unless something intervenes, any organism exposed to prolonged and unremitting stress will die.

The more stress we encounter, the more energy we need. Stress has a voracious appetite for the energy in our bodies and minds. It draws off vitamins, minerals, and other nutrients as well as all of our psychological resources. Gradually, the wear and tear on our systems takes its toll.

The fatigue from stress does not come out of the blue. It usually appears slowly, little by little, over weeks or months. Mixed with anxiety and depression, this fatigue rarely responds to sleep or rest and is pervaded by a sense of helplessness. Everything becomes a great effort. Nothing we do seems to make a difference.

The depression associated with stress is caused by exhaustion, not by a sense of loss or emotional conflict as we have seen in other cases. The depression seems to be nature's way of telling our bodies to slow down and take it easy.

Stress is part of life. We cannot expect to live without it. So, how should we deal with it? To cope better, we need to learn more about stress—what it is, what causes it, what it does to us, and finally, how to find relief.

WHAT ARE STRESS AND ANXIETY?

The word stress means different things to different people. The wide variety of uses of the term has led to confusion. The word "stress," like "pain" or "love," is virtually meaningless out of context.

Hans Selye, a pioneer in research on stress, defines stress as "the nonspecific response of the body to any demand" or more simply as "the rate of wear and tear in the body."[1] Selye called anything that prompted this response a stressor.

Stress is a response by the body to a perceived threat, either emotional or physical. The nature and degree of the threat determines the reaction. People usually respond with a strong emotion: anxiety, depression, anger, or fear.

Walter B. Cannon, a professor of physiology at Harvard University in the early 1900s, called this reaction the "fight or flight" syndrome and the "emergency response." As we will see later, the stress reaction prepares us to flee or fight in the face of danger.

Anxiety and stress are sometimes used interchangeably, but they are quite distinct. Anxiety is an emotion. Stress is a response that summons an emotion. Stress is the stimulus for the emotion, which may turn out to be anxiety or some other feeling, such as anger or fear. Stress refers only to the cause or stimulus, a perceived threat that can be physical or psychological.

Unlike stress, anxiety does not always have an easily decipherable cause. The origins of anxiety are imperceptible and based on shadowy fears and conflicts, not necessarily discernible external threats.

Despite their innate differences, stress and anxiety are inextricably linked. Anxiety coexists with some sort of stress, and the physical symptoms of both are almost indistinguishable. Anxiety represents the "flight" aspects of stress, a diffuse fear that readies the body to flee from the threat. A person who suffers from claustrophobia, for example, might have an intense anxiety attack during a business meeting in a small room, even though there is no tangible threat. The cause of the anxiety may be unconscious and lie in some early childhood trauma.

Like anxiety, anger is an immediate reaction to stress but comprises its "fight" aspects. Anger occurs when a person perceives some obstacle to a goal and summons the emotional power to remove it. Although anger is usually directed outward from the self, it can be aimed inward as self-blame and self-loathing. The intensity of anger varies and may range from mild irritation to rage. In its purest form, anger is short lived, but it can smoulder within us as frustration, hostility, or irritability. Like anxiety, anger saps our energy.

Depression develops later in the emotional cycle of stress and is caused by exhaustion from prolonged or intense anxiety. Depression is complex and heterogeneous, which means it is composed of more than one emotion. The dominant feeling is sadness, but the melancholy may coexist with a combination of anger, anxiety, fear, guilt, hostility, or shame.

Whatever the emotional reaction, fatigue is a common byproduct. Our response to stress devours a great deal of energy, both physiological and psychological, leaving us exhausted and unprepared to deal with events in our lives.

GENERAL ADAPTATION SYNDROME

When faced with a stressful event, the body summons its defenses to guard against the damaging effects. Hans Selye called this reaction the general adaptation syndrome or GAS. He said the syndrome has three stages:

1. **Alarm Reaction.** This is the initial reaction by a person who is suddenly exposed to a stressor. This stage has two phases:
   a. *Shock Phase.* The immediate reaction to the noxious stimulus. Typical symptoms are loss of muscle tone, decreased

body temperature, decline in blood pressure, and rapid heartbeat.

b. *Counterstroke Phase.* This phase marks a rebound brought about by the mobilization of defenses. The adrenal cortex pours hormones into the bloodstream.

2. **Stage of Resistance.** The person adapts to the stress and there is an improvement or disappearance of symptoms. In this stage, however, there is a decrease in the resistance to other stimuli.

3. **Stage of Exhaustion.** Since a person's ability to adapt to stress is limited, exhaustion inexorably follows if the stress is severe or prolonged. The earlier symptoms will reappear and if stress is unrelieved, death will result.[2]

Selye said exhaustion followed a depletion of "adaptation energy," the biological fuel used by the body to adapt to the stress. He said this energy is different from caloric energy derived from food, since, given enough food, the body would theoretically be able to adapt indefinitely. Selye believed this adaptation energy could not be renewed. Sleep and rest could restore most of one's energy following the exhaustion phase, he believed, but not completely to the previous level.

Stress-induced fatigue is almost always accompanied by a general, diffuse anxiety. The anxiety enhances vigilance and alertness to cope with the real or imagined danger, and drains the body's energy. Such a state is commonly referred to as "nervous exhaustion."

The anxiety level declines once the person enters the resistance or second stage of the GAS, but will reappear with depression in the final or exhaustion phase of the syndrome. Depression may be present in any stage, but it typically appears later when the person feels helpless and believes any effort to remedy the situation is useless.

PHYSIOLOGY OF STRESS

When faced with danger or a threat, whether real or imagined, the body shifts into high gear to deal with it. This reaction summons physical and emotional defenses to meet the perceived danger.

The "fight or flight" syndrome demands more blood, more oxygen, and more energy for the body. The energy enables the body to act above and beyond its normal limits to fight the threat or escape from it. During the stress response, several physiological changes occur: The heart beats faster, metabolism increases, perspiration increases to cool the body, muscles tense for action, sugars rush into the bloodstream to give quick energy, breathing accelerates to build the oxygen supply, blood circulation increases to the muscles, and several hormones are released.

Three hormones are especially important—norepinephrine, epinephrine (adrenalin), and cortisol. Norepinephrine increases heart rate and blood pressure, whereas epinephrine helps release stored sugar as fuel. Cortisol gets the body prepared for vigorous exercise.

The senses become more acute during this time. The pupils of the eyes dilate to increase visual perception. Hearing, taste, and smell are also intensified. At the same time, a person's pain threshold rises to dull the pain from any injury.

The activation of the stress response places burdens on major parts of the body, particularly lungs, heart, kidneys, and the endocrine and gastrointestinal systems. The overstimulation of organs of the body can lead to their exhaustion and even disease.

A number of organic diseases have been linked to stress—peptic ulcers, heart disease, colitis, hypertension, bronchial asthma, hyperventilation, allergies, and skin disorders. The mechanism for such illnesses is an excessive arousal of body systems. Peptic ulcers, for example, are caused by the excessive secretion of digestive acids.

Stress also undermines the immune system, making the body more vulnerable to infectious disease. Stress weakens antibodies that fight invading bacteria and viruses. Prolonged stress, depression, and bereavement have all been shown to weaken body defenses. A person under unusual stress can be expected to suffer more sore throats, influenza, colds, and other infectious diseases due to his or her inhibited immune system.

Although we associate negative emotions with stress, such as fear, anxiety, and depression, some positive emotions, such as excitement, joy, and exhilaration can also cause stress. Some people are surprised by the number of "pleasant" events that can be very stressful. Weddings, for example, may seem like wonderful events, but they can be very stressful, too. The Christmas holiday is another "pleasant" event that triggers stress for many people.

Dr. Thomas Holmes and Dr. Richard Rahe, two prominent psychologists, developed a scale in 1967 to measure stress based on life events. Their Social Readjustment Rating Scale includes both negative and positive events, based on the premise that any change produces stress. The scale lists 43 life events that contribute to stress. You can rate your own stress level by using the following panel.

Social Readjustment Scale[3]

Dr. Thomas H. Holmes and Dr. Richard H. Rahe of the University of Washington Medical School devised the following scale to rate stress based on changes in a person's life.

Instructions: Check the events that occurred during the past two years and circle the value. If an event occurred more than once, multiply the value by the number of times the event occurred. Thus, if you celebrated Christmas twice, multiply 12 by 2 = 24.

Rank	Life Event	Value
1	Death of a spouse	100
2	Divorce	73
3	Marital separation	65
4	Jail term	63
5	Death of a close family member	63
6	Personal injury or illness	53
7	Marriage	50
8	Fired at work	47
9	Marital reconciliation	45
10	Retirement	45
11	Change in health of a family member	44
12	Pregnancy (applies for both spouses)	40
13	Sexual difficulties	39
14	Gain of a new family member	39
15	Business readjustment	39
16	Change in financial state	38
17	Death of a close friend	37
18	Change to a different line of work	36

Rank	Life Event	Value
19	Change in a number of arguments with spouse	35
20	Mortgage over $100,000*	31
21	Foreclosure of mortgage or loan	30
22	Change in responsibilities at work	29
23	Son or daughter leaving home	29
24	Trouble with in-laws	29
25	Outstanding personal achievement	28
26	Spouse began or stopped work	26
27	Began or ended schooling	26
28	Change in living conditions	25
29	Revision of personal habits	24
30	Trouble with boss	23
31	Change in work hours or conditions	20
32	Change in residence	20
33	Change in schools	20
34	Change in recreation	19
35	Change in church activities	19
36	Change in social activities	18
37	Mortgage or loan less than $100,000*	17
38	Change in sleeping habits	16
39	Change in number of family get-togethers	15
40	Change in eating habits	15
41	Vacation	13
42	Christmas	12
43	Minor violations of the law	11
		Total LCU score: ___

If total score is	Chance of illness	Level of resistance
150–199	Low (9–33%)	High resistance
200–299	Moderate (30–52%)	Borderline resistance
300 or more	High (50–86%)	Low resistance, high vulnerability

*Figures adjusted for 1990s dollars.

Reprinted with permission from *Journal of Psychosomatic Research* vol. 11. Holmes, Thomas, and Richard Rahe, "The Social Readjustment Rating Scale." Copyright 1967, Pergamon Press, plc.

PERSONALITY AND STRESS

Stress is a response to something, but its effects can be mitigated or exaggerated by the way a person perceives that something. As we have seen in the Holmes scale in the preceding panel, many events can have stressful consequences. One deficiency of the Holmes scale, however, is that it fails to take into account individual differences that influence the degree of stress that events create.

What might be stressful for one person may not be as stressful to someone else. It is how that event or situation is interpreted and evaluated that determines the degree of stress experienced. A divorce, for example, although generally stressful for most people, might bring relief from stress for some individuals in some circumstances.

Positive thinking and an optimistic outlook on life can diminish stressful events. The well-known adage of the cup that is half full or half empty provides a good illustration. The person who sees the cup as half full is happy, encouraged, and optimistic. Those who see the cup as half empty are disappointed, discouraged, and pessimistic. The stimulus is the same in each case, but the interpretation and evaluation are different and have opposite emotional consequences.

Personality and individual traits that make up personality have a lot to do with the effect of stress. It is not necessarily the event itself, but the way a person perceives the event that results in activation of the stress response. People who tend to view themselves or events in a negative way are more prone to stress and anxiety, since they are more apt to interpret events as threats or exaggerate the events.

When one thinks of personality and stress, one immediately recalls the Type A behavior described by Drs. Myer Friedman and Ray Rosenman, two cardiologists. The doctors devised this personality model based on three factors: time, work, and ambition. The Type A personality feels an intense urgency about time and tries to do as much as possible in the shortest time period. This person is frequently hostile and may lose his temper easily, often in response to minor frustrations. At work, he is highly motivated, intensely competitive, very ambitious, and has a consuming desire to control his environment. Typically, he is involved in many projects simultaneously and consequently fails to complete all of his tasks satisfactorily.[4]

The Type A personality is just one model for the way an individual interacts with his environment and responds to stress. Each personality has its own coping strategies and unique ways of meeting the challenges of stress.

One personality trait that helps reduce stress is the ability to relate and identify constructively with others. A person who enjoys healthy relationships with others can call upon them for support in times of stress. People who fear rejection, humiliation, or failure avoid relationships that would otherwise help them cope. The constructive support of a spouse can help a person cope successfully with stressful life events. Others cling to relationships even after they deteriorate and become damaging and destructive, thereby perpetuating and aggravating the stress in their lives. These personal dynamics are most evident in marriages.

Stress is sometimes caused by a personality disorder or mental illness, such as paranoia, schizophrenia, obsessive–compulsive disorder, or hysteria. These personalities tend to exaggerate the danger from external events, perceiving threats where there are none. In these cases, psychiatric treatment is the appropriate course.

Psychotherapy is especially helpful for people who have distorted views of themselves and their world. Cognitive therapists, for example, concentrate on changing the way people think because they believe negative feelings are caused by negative thoughts. Cognitive therapy attempts to modify distorted thinking to promote self-esteem and more positive attitudes. Other types of therapy, such as interpersonal therapy, focus on a patient's personal relationships, helping to identify sources of conflict with others. (See Chapter Five on depression for more information about psychotherapy.)

COPING STRATEGIES

One can develop a number of skills and habits to cope with stress. Generally, coping strategies are either good or bad, positive or negative, depending on their long-term impact on health. Good skills, such as exercise, relaxation, and proper nutrition, promote health and vigor. Bad habits, such as smoking, alcohol, and drug abuse may reduce stress in the short term but undermine a person's health in the long run.

Suzanne C. Kobasa, a psychologist at the University of Chicago, has extensively studied the relationship of personality traits and stress. She believes that there is a "hardiness" factor in some people that acts as a buffer between them and the damaging aspects of stress. She identified three factors that make up this quality in individuals:

1. The "hardy" individuals believe they have control over their lives and can act to influence important life events. These people have a range of coping skills to respond to stressful events and are able to incorporate these events into an ongoing life plan. In effect, they can turn misfortune to their advantage.
2. They have a commitment to become actively involved in meaningful ways with life experiences, involving work, social institutions, interpersonal relationships, family, and self. A sense of purpose and a belief in oneself, founded on individual values, goals, and priorities, are especially important.
3. They view the changes in their lives as challenges rather than as threats. Unexpected changes act as catalysts that make life interesting and challenging for them. This attitude allows them to respond well to the unexpected.[5]

Control, or a perception of control, is crucial for the success of any coping strategy. If an individual feels he or she has a measure of control over events, that person is more encouraged to initiate action. On the other hand, a person with little faith in himself or herself to cope with events is more apt to withdraw, give up, and give in to the feelings of helplessness and hopelessness, which may lead to serious depression.

How does a person exert control? It is not necessarily the actual control of outcomes that is important, but the *feeling* that a person has control over the way he or she reacts that counts. Of course, nobody can control all events and an attempt at such control will definitely lead to stress, given its inevitable failure. A person has a much greater chance of success, nonetheless, in learning how to control emotional reaction. In this effort, a positive mental attitude is indispensable.

Ironically, control can sometimes be gained by relinquishing control, at least emotionally, by accepting the event and discounting its negative effects. For example, a person who loses money in the stock market may be able to accept the loss more easily by attributing it to a national economic downturn rather than to a poor investment

---

Are You Suffering from Stress? Table of Symptoms

A host of physical and psychological symptoms accompany the stress response. Some of the things that signal stress and burnout are:

1. Feeling tired most of the time and rarely feeling rested or refreshed after a night's sleep.
2. Never feeling relaxed. Always under a strain from excessive worry or too much work and responsibility.
3. A general lack of energy and motivation. No reserves to call upon when a situation arises that requires extra effort.
4. A host of complaints, such as frequent headaches, backaches, rapid heartbeat, perspiration, shaky hands, and insomnia with nightmares.
5. Irrational fears or panic attacks during situations that require performance, such as meetings or before presentations.
6. Hypersensitivity to criticism. Excessive ruminating about past slights or perceived failures.
7. Lack of enjoyment in your job or social role. Loss of interest in most things that were once pleasurable.
8. A habit of taking on responsibility for things over which you have little or no control, such as another person's feelings or financial setbacks caused by national economic conditions.
9. Plagued by worry, dread, distraction, absent-mindedness, and agitation.
10. Other physical symptoms, such as flushing, dry mouth, constipation, sighing, belching, chest tightness, shallow breathing, muscle tightness, tremors, tics, chills, and diarrhea.

decision, thus resolving negative feelings associated with self-blame, discouragement, and personal loss.

Self-confidence builds with each success scored in controlling the impact of life events. If results can't be controlled, a person can certainly shape events through verbal persuasion, problem solving, time management techniques, and other skills. People who believe they can influence their destinies inevitably cope better with adversity, recognizing that setbacks in life are unavoidable, and seeing these misfortunes as exceptions rather than the rule.

Besides a positive attitude, any strategy to combat stress and anxiety should include one of the relaxation techniques, such as autogenic training, progressive relaxation, meditation, hypnosis, or biofeedback discussed in the next chapter. Combined with an overall strategy, these techniques will bring a marked reduction in tension and the fatigue it causes.

ANXIETY AND SLEEP

Stress and anxiety interfere with sleep, depriving the body of the thing it needs most—deep, restorative rest. Unfortunately, anxious people tend to experience a variety of sleep disturbances.

Anxiety appears to cause a shorter than normal period of rapid eye movement (REM) sleep, when most dreams occur, and a greater percentage of light sleep, although the framework of the sleep cycle itself is relatively normal. The degree to which anxiety disrupts sleep is proportional to the level of anxiety.

Studies of insomnia patients have consistently found them to suffer from significant levels of anxiety. The Hamilton Anxiety Rating Scale, a standard psychological test, includes insomnia in one of 14 categories measuring a person's anxiety. Symptoms included in the insomnia category are broken sleep, difficulty in falling asleep, unsatisfying sleep, fatigue upon waking, nightmares, and night terrors.[6]

The agitation caused by anxiety delays the onset of sleep and prolongs the periods of nighttime awakenings. Anxious patients seem to experience more incidents of night terrors, sleepwalking, nightmares, sleeptalking, or teethgrinding.[7]

Nightmares and night terrors are two different things. Nightmares are frightening dreams and usually occur in the REM stage of sleep. Night terrors, on the other hand, are not dreams, but sudden, powerful and terrifying episodes, sometimes accompanied by sleepwalking. These terrors occur in Stage 4 of sleep, the deepest phase of sleep that occurs early in the night.

HYPERVENTILATION

Anxiety and stress may cause hyperventilation syndrome (HVS), a condition marked by rapid, shallow breathing that brings on a number of symptoms by increasing oxygen and depleting carbon dioxide in the blood. An individual is especially susceptible to HVS if his breathing is normally rapid, since it increases even more under stress.

Those who suffer from hyperventilation get caught up in a cycle of escalating anxiety. The original attack may be triggered by a stressful event, causing the depletion of CO_2 and the onset of symptoms, which in turn lead to more anxiety, greater hyperventilation, stronger symptoms, and so on, repeating the cycle.

The anxiety can be aggravated considerably by false medical diagnosis, which is not rare in such cases. If HVS is initially overlooked by the treating physician, the patient may face a frightening round of sophisticated diagnostic tests, since the symptoms may appear in any part of the body and involve several systems. When the tests turn up nothing, the patient is left even more anxious about his condition.

The symptoms of HVS appear in a collection of apparently unrelated and bizarre manifestations. The symptoms may be neurological, cardiovascular, psychological, gastrointestinal, respiratory, or general in nature. For example, the patient may suffer from rapid heartbeat or palpitations, shortness of breath and excessive sighing, as well as muscle pain, tremors, belching, flatulence, faintness,

Symptoms of Chronic Hyperventilation[9]

General: fatigue, weakness, exhaustion, sleep disturbance, and nightmares

Cardiovascular: palpitations, rapid heartbeat, and chest pain

Neurological: dizziness, disturbances of consciousness or vision

Respiratory: shortness of breath, asthma, and chest pain

Gastrointestinal: dry throat, unproductive cough, belching, difficulty in swallowing, flatulence

Musculoskeletal: muscle pains, tremors, and muscle spasms

Psychological: tension and anxiety

dizziness, and blurred vision. The psychological symptoms include fear and panic, anxiety, depersonalization, and disturbed memory and concentration.[8]

Overbreathing is a tiring exercise and many HVS patients complain of exhaustion and fatigue. The first signs of hyperventilation are usually tingling sensations in the hands, feet, or face and these are followed by dizziness, lightheadedness, giddiness, fainting, dryness of the mouth, and breathlessness.[10]

If a person has a tendency toward shallow, rapid, thoracic breathing rather than slow, steady abdominal breathing, then any increase in stress, anxiety, or tension could increase ventilation and cause HVS. People with a habit of sighing are especially prone, because this dramatically reduces carbon dioxide levels in the blood, the first step toward hyperventilation.

Although HVS has been known for many years, it is routinely misdiagnosed by physicians because of its vague, almost universal, symptoms. Some surgeons have operated on the abdomen, spine, and some organs under the mistaken belief they were responsible for the HVS symptoms. HVS may also be mistakenly diagnosed as epilepsy, cardiac infarction, and other illnesses.[11]

Physicians can diagnosis HVS by having the patient reproduce his symptoms by voluntarily hyperventilating. This quickly confirms the connection between symptoms and breathing. Another method is to test CO_2 levels in the blood by having a patient voluntarily hyperventilate into an infrared gas analyzer. This instrument measures the recovery rate of alveolar CO_2 to normal resting values after a few minutes of hyperventilation.[12] The combination of the two techniques should lead to the proper diagnosis of HVS.

Fortunately, hyperventilation is relatively easy to treat. If the symptoms are caused by habitually breathing incorrectly, i.e., shallow breaths and frequent sighing, the problem can be corrected by teaching the patient alternative breathing techniques. If anxiety is high and is exacerbating the problem, a physician may recommend psychotherapy, depending on the underlying problems.

Dr. L. C. Lum, a British physician, studied hyperventilation among 640 patients at the Papworth Hospital and found simple reeducation on breathing techniques was all that was necessary for full recovery in most cases. Dr. Lum found that anxiety was alleviated once the patient understood the physiology of hyperventilation and was told about the plan of treatment.

The majority of patients recover completely without medication or psychological counseling. Whether HVS is caused by or causes anxiety is a moot point in terms of treatment, since the therapy is the same.

MEDICATION FOR STRESS AND ANXIETY

At times of acute stress, medication can help reduce tension and anxiety and the resulting overstimulation and hyperactivity. Drugs are especially useful when the stress interferes with other forms of therapy, such as relaxation techniques or psychotherapy.

The drugs that are used to reduce anxiety are known as psychotropic drugs because they alter mood, thinking, and perception. They are effective by either stimulating or inhibiting the action of neurotransmitters, the chemical messengers in brain and nerve tissues.

All antianxiety drugs depress the central nervous system

and may cause drowsiness. Because tolerance to all the sedative-tranquilizers develops, they tend to be required in increasingly higher doses and can create dependence.

The most constructive use of antianxiety drugs is for short-term intervention and as part of an overall treatment program. The idea is to reduce symptoms to the point where other nonpharmacological approaches can be effective.

One of the oldest and still most widely used drugs for reducing stress is alcohol, but drunkenness and the possibility of addiction limits its usefulness. Nevertheless, a beer or glass of wine has depressant effects on the central nervous system and creates a feeling of relaxation.

Barbiturates

Barbiturates were used for many years to treat anxiety and some physicians still rely on them for this purpose, but most barbiturates are now prescribed only for insomnia. Common barbiturates are phenobarbital (Luminal®), amobarbital (Amytal®), pentobarbital (Nembutal®), and secobarbital (Seconal®).

One of the disadvantages of barbiturates for the fatigued patient is that they induce drowsiness. Additionally, a tolerance develops and higher doses are required to produce the desired effect. In treating stress, there is no advantage to barbiturates over other options.

A marked degree of physical and psychological dependence develops with use of barbiturates and a slight increase in the dosage can sometimes precipitate toxic symptoms. Barbiturates used with alcohol can be lethal. The drug may cause reduced mental activity, slurred speech, and unwanted drowsiness. Overdose can lead to coma and death. Barbiturates are the leading drugs used to commit suicide.[13]

Withdrawal symptoms for the barbiturates are decidedly unpleasant and patients should taper off their use. Such symptoms include anxiety, irritability, delirium, seizures, and insomnia, all of which the patient has probably taken the drug to remedy.

Benzodiazepines

Another group of drugs, the benzodiazepines, has found wider acceptance in treating anxiety and is considered very effective. The benzodiazepines, sometimes called minor tranquilizers, can cause fatigue and drowsiness, two of the most common side effects. The benzodiazepine group contains several generic forms, including chlordiazepoxide (Librium®), diazepam (Valium®), clorazepate (Tranxene®), oxazepam (Serax®), and alprazolam (Xanax®).

Their main advantage is that they do not reduce a person's ability to work or concentrate. Another advantage is that the margin of safety is much greater with benzodiazepines than with other tranquilizers. Although tolerance to and dependence on them can develop, the dose needed to produce dependence is at least five times the daily therapeutic dose. If used properly, the benzodiazepines are relatively safe and withdrawal symptoms are mild.

One of the major disadvantages to the benzodiazepines is that the half-life, the time the drug stays in the system, is fairly long— from 40 hours for Librium® to 96 hours for Valium®. With repeated daily doses, blood levels of the drug can increase and cause more sedation than the patient may want.[14] The treating physician should be told of any of these adverse effects so the dosage can be adjusted accordingly.

Propanolol

Propanolol is prescribed for patients suffering from some of the peripheral symptoms of stress, such as rapid heartbeat or general tension. Because this medication blocks the synaptic transmission to the beta group of adrenergic receptors in nerve tissue, it is commonly referred to as a "beta-blocker."

Propanolol, marketed by Wyeth-Ayerst Laboratories under the trade name Inderal®, is usually prescribed for high blood pressure, angina, or migraine headaches. The drug is not officially approved for treatment of anxiety, but is frequently prescribed for it, particularly for stage fright and performance anxiety.

The drug has few side effects and does not alter mood or thinking processes, so it is not a psychoactive like the sedative–hypnotic class of drugs.

Depression is a common side effect of propanolol, so the drug is not recommended in cases of anxiety mixed with depression. Other side effects are relatively mild, such as slow pulse, lightheadedness, insomnia, and cold hands and feet.

Buspirone

Buspirone hydrochloride is a relatively new antianxiety drug that is marketed under the trade name of BuSpar®. It has the advantage of reducing anxiety without sedation, so it is particularly appropriate for anxiety-induced fatigue.

The daily dose ranges from 20 to 30 mg. Treatment should continue for at least three to four weeks for full therapeutic effect.

The manufacturer, Mead/Johnson, indicates that there is no evidence that buspirone is addictive, either physically or psychologically. Side effects are mild and the most common symptoms of overdose are nausea, headache, and nervousness.

Antidepressants

As we learned in the previous chapter, the antidepressants can be effective for treating anxiety as well as depression. These drugs are especially helpful if the patient suffers panic attacks or a combination of anxiety and depression.

The two types of antidepressants are the tricyclics and the monoamine oxidase inhibitors (MAOIs). Both have some bothersome side effects, as we also pointed out in the chapter on depression.

Imipramine, one of the most popular tricyclics, has been found to be effective in countering panic attacks in doses as low as 10 mg a day compared with 100 to 200 mg a day for treatment of depression. As with other tricyclics, imipramine has sedative effects and can cause fatigue. These side effects usually disappear as the body adapts to the drug.

Although it may take weeks before the tricyclics reduce depression, they are effective against anxiety fairly soon after treatment begins. There is a possibility of a paradoxical reaction with increased anxiety, but this is not common.

OCCUPATIONAL STRESS AND JOB BURNOUT

Work dominates our lives. A preoccupation with money, possessions, and success seems at times to preclude happiness itself. The more people have, the more they seem to want, so they work harder and longer, pushing themselves to the point of exhaustion.

When our own expectations exceed reality, when demands of others become excessive, or our roles are ill defined, you can be sure that job burnout will probably follow. Burnout is simply another name for fatigue caused by stress, the wear and tear on the body and mind. Job stress quickly overflows into other parts of one's life, affecting motivation, attitude, and self-esteem. But, for better or worse, most of us have to work, either at the office or at home. When the job is satisfying, it can be invigorating and challenging, but when it is not, stress, frustration, and tension lead to job burnout, a common ingredient in fatigue.

Work has become more closely associated than ever with self-image and self-esteem. If we are successful at work, we feel successful as human beings. When we see ourselves as failures in our work, we tend to see ourselves as failures in life. The balance needed to keep things in perspective is lost when our work consumes us. Family, hobbies, friends, recreation, and other social supports are neglected when we let work dominate our lives. Many people are devastated when they are fired or lose their jobs during a recession because they have failed to achieve a balance between their work and personal lives.

The National Institute of Occupational Safety and Health rated occupations based on stress-related diseases and found the most stressful jobs include those of manager, secretary, farmer, machine operator, waitress, inspector, and laborer. Among the least stressful occupations are maid, child-care worker, college professor, personnel worker, craftsman, heavy-equipment operator, and farm laborer. Under any conditions when the person doesn't quite "fit" the job, stress is a common result.

Job satisfaction is one of the most important determinants of our mental health. When it is going well, we feel great. The trouble is that for many of us work is drudgery. The primary cause of burnout is simply too much work. Occupational overload is especially common during economic downturns when companies trim their work force. Overload may be a combination of too much responsibility and too many tasks without enough time to do them. The result is over-stimulation of the mind and body as the worker strains to meet deadlines and get things done.

When the job is complex and demands high intellectual skills, such as those required in medicine or law, the overload can be twofold, both quantitative and qualitative. The mental stress exerted to do the work at the high level of quality required can lead to emotional fatigue, ulcers, and migraines.

Sometimes the problem is not overwork but lack of work or work that fails to challenge the employee. Boredom and frustration arise when the job provides no meaningful stimulation. Monotonous, repetitive tasks, such as work on an assembly line, can cause significant stress if workers view their assigned tasks as dehumanizing and self-destructive.

Expectations set by the employer or the worker himself are another determining factor in job satisfaction. When the employer fails to specify standards and duties, the worker's role and objectives may be ambiguous and unclear, leading to confusion and anxiety. If the worker sets unrealistic standards for himself, he is inviting disappointment and feelings of failure later.

Careers and jobs constantly change. Workers who adapt to new technologies, foreign markets, and other forces are able to grow and develop in their careers. Long-range planning is crucial and proper training, education, and specific goals ease the transitions along the way.

Many changes in a career result in stress, disrupt lives, and present their own unique challenges. Promotions, relocations, transfers, reorganizations, and retirements create stress and difficulties. A worker's attitude and ability to cope will determine if such changes are a problem or accepted as just another part of the career path.

SPECIAL CONCERNS FOR WOMEN

Some women are plagued by stress, because of their role in the work force, their family responsibilities, and their reproductive systems. Mothers who balance full-time jobs with child-care duties are legendary and are sometimes called "supermoms" or "superwomen."

These workers must cope with three demanding and often conflicting roles—mother, wife, and careerist. Additionally, she also must find time to meet her own needs as an individual. Because these women are often of childbearing age, they must deal with the stress of pregnancy and childbirth and their effects on the family and career.

Single working mothers confront the greatest demands of all, since they shoulder the financial burden of the entire family in addition to taking care of the children. Such a life is bound to be fraught with emotional troubles—loneliness, guilt, worry, and stress.

The stress level is also high in two-career marriages, when both partners are committed to professional careers. Strains in the family are bound to surface as transfers, promotions, and other career changes inevitably occur, forcing decisions and compromises, not to mention balancing time and responsibilities.

Even when the woman is not pursuing a professional career, but has a full-time job nonetheless, the stress can be substantial. Many times, women work in busy offices under considerable stress. Overworked, underpaid, and rarely appreciated, these women do not enjoy the prestige or benefits of professions but may experience similar or even greater levels of stress.

The most stressful emotional problem confronting the working mother is the care of her children. A busy career demands time and a mother may feel guilt and anxiety if she believes her children are neglected in the least. Balancing career and child care requires patience, insight, and understanding from all family members, especially the husband, who often must reorder his own working life to spend more time with their children.

Although men are taking on more of the chores at home, including childrearing, the bulk of the responsibility continues to be dumped on the woman. Paid outside help for the domestic chores, when affordable, is one option to alleviate stress for all concerned. In any case, an enlightened attitude on the part of the husband in a two-career marriage can be crucial for the success of the relationship. It is imperative that both partners communicate openly and frequently with each other, discussing career decisions, delegating responsibilities, sharing free time, and compromising when conflicts arise. The relationship should be reviewed regularly to insure balance and fairness to both partners.

Pregnancy creates both physical and psychological stress for women. In the first months of pregnancy, fatigue and depression are common, while the final months may be filled with anxiety about delivery and the health of the baby. Childbirth may be followed by postpartum depression. In other cases, the depression may be the result of problems encountered in delivery, an ill baby, financial difficulties, or trouble with a spouse. About half of all mothers experience a mild depression after childbirth.

Stress is also associated with menstruation, specifically menstrual cramps and premenstrual syndrome (PMS). Both can cause stress but may also be aggravated by stress, so it is sometimes difficult to tell which is causing which.

While menstrual cramps respond to drugs like Motrin® and Ponstel®, which work quite well for most women, PMS has many symptoms and is more difficult for doctors to treat. Among the most common symptoms are anxiety, irritability, fatigue, depression, retention of fluids, and mood swings. Contrary to the popular impression, however, most women do not experience these PMS symptoms to any significant degree.

CONCLUSION

All people experience stress in their lives, though everyone copes slightly differently. As we each make our way through life, we should keep in mind that we are not alone. Others around us, our friends, families, and co-workers, have experienced, or will experience at some time, many of the same stressful events. Talking with them and sharing experiences can help us all cope a little better.

Nothing eases stress more than genuine, intimate communication between fellow human beings. Reaching out and connecting with others is extremely useful during stressful moments.

As we will see in the next chapter there are a number of simple techniques we can learn to reduce stress, both physical and emotional. But an important thing to keep in mind is that escape from stress would mean escape from life itself. Facing the pain and stress in life allows us to experience its fullness. Stress challenges us to be our best. Accept the challenge and let stress revitalize your life.

CHAPTER SEVEN

RELAXATION TECHNIQUES TO BEAT FATIGUE

INTRODUCTION

Deep relaxation relieves fatigue because it reduces stress and its associated problems, such as insomnia, anxiety, and depression. Relaxation allows the body to rebuild its energy and promotes alertness and vitality, particularly if one wants to reduce use of cigarettes, alcohol, or illicit drugs.

We have countless ways of relaxing—fishing, knitting, reading, and so forth. Nevertheless, many people need to learn how to relax, just as they learned how to walk or talk. In the simplest terms, anything that lowers the level of arousal can qualify as relaxation. It is a skill that takes practice to master. The more one practices, the better one will get at it.

As we learned from our discussion of stress-related disorders, chronic tension leads to exhaustion unless it is somehow relieved. Relaxation methods can be very helpful in providing this relief. For the most part, the techniques are simple and inexpensive, rarely cause any harm, and usually lead quickly to renewed vitality.

Various relaxation methods exist, all of which generally induce approximately the same physiological responses. The methods fall within two groups—physiology and imagery. The physiological methods involve concentration on some sort of bodily activity, such as breathing or tensing and relaxing muscles. This group includes such methods as progressive muscle relaxation, self-hypnosis, meditation, or autogenic training, which is a form of autosuggestion. The second type enlists the imagination and visual images to promote relaxation. Visualization of quiet, calm scenes, such as a deserted beach, grassy meadow, or cold mountain stream, create feelings of general relaxation.

A clinical study of patients with fatigue, treated with only relaxation methods, found that 14 out of 17 patients showed a very marked improvement. Of 82 patients suffering from nervous hypertension with fatigability, 76 showed marked or very marked improvement from relaxation techniques. The study was done in the 1930s by one of the pioneers in relaxation therapy, Dr. Edmund Jacobson. He found that relaxation was also effective in treating mild depression, insomnia, and anxiety.[1]

The ultimate goal of any relaxation method is a tranquil mind at peace with itself. This means eliminating any negative emotions that may create turmoil and stress, such as guilt, fear, anger, and depression. True relaxation represents the absence of these negative feelings. By learning to experience life without these stresses, even for 20 minutes a day, a person can find the path to a life free of fatigue.

WHAT IS DEEP RELAXATION?

It seems ironic that a person suffering from fatigue should need to be told to relax. Tired people "relax" a lot, don't they? If they are too tired to do anything but lie in bed or watch television, why would they need to relax?

The fact is that many people who suffer from persistent, unremitting fatigue never relax. They are simply idling their revved-up engines. The stress in their lives has accumulated to such an extent that the more common means of relaxation are no longer effective for them.

People exhausted by stress usually choose inappropriate ways to relax. When they feel tired or stressed, they take drugs, light up a cigarette, pour another cup of coffee, or drink a beer. Others turn to foods, such as chocolate, sodas, or other junk foods. These activities may provide a brief respite from stress, and temporarily calm a person, especially if they are part of a social occasion, but in the long run, such habits simply add to fatigue and lead to alcoholism, obesity, drug addiction, or chronic illness as the person comes to rely on them more and more often. Such ineffective relaxation methods deplete already marginal energy reserves and push people into complete exhaustion.

True relaxation is really quite simple. It is easily recognized by the way the body responds to it. The heart slows down and beats evenly. Blood pressure drops and breathing becomes deeper, slower, and more regular. Oxygen consumption declines and tension eases in the muscles throughout the body. The mind feels quiet and at rest. A feeling of peace and well-being flows over the person.

Many activities may promote these responses. However, individuals often react differently to the same activity, so something that is relaxing for one person may not be for someone else. For example, watching television might relax you but lead to frustration, anger, or fear in someone else, depending on the program being viewed. By trial and error, you can find the appropriate methods that fulfill your individual relaxation needs.

THE PHYSIOLOGY OF RELAXATION

Relaxation is the physiological opposite of stress. While stress excites the central nervous system, relaxation decreases arousal and tension. The mechanism that triggers this relaxed state is complex and not fully understood. A reduction in certain hormones, such as vasopressin, which increases blood pressure, is thought by some researchers to play a role, but the evidence of studies has not been conclusive.

During a relaxed state, the breathing rate declines, resulting in both a decrease in the intake of oxygen and removal of carbon dioxide. The body needs less oxygen because it is not burning off as much energy. A relaxed person, as we know from popular deodorant commercials, does not perspire as much as someone under stress.

This is why some biofeedback machines can monitor the sweat glands in the skin to measure a person's level of stress.

Changes also occur in the blood—both in its biochemical makeup and the way it flows through the body. In particular, relaxation reduces blood pressure, the rate of the heartbeat, and blood lactates, which are normal organic by-products of the metabolism of glucose and glycogen. Excess lactate production, resulting from an increase in the flow of adrenaline, has long been associated with anxiety and stress.

Certain physical sensations are sometimes associated with deep relaxation, such as momentary tingling or numbness in fingers or toes. Relaxation may also prompt certain psychological effects, such as euphoria, dissociation, or a floating sensation. Although people generally find these feelings pleasurable, some may feel uncomfortable, at least until they become accustomed to the new sensations.[2]

SELF-HYPNOSIS

Hypnosis is a state of deep relaxation induced by suggestions, either by oneself or through a trained health professional. It represents a trancelike state of mind between sleep and wakefulness. The level of hypnotic trance may be light, medium, or deep.

Hypnotism has been used since the 1800s as treatment in many areas—stress, pain control, smoking cessation, dieting, sexual problems, hysteria, insomnia, and low self-esteem. Because it can be used to reduce stress or end unhealthy habits, hypnosis can also be effective in the relief of many causes of fatigue.

Successful hypnosis depends on conditioning. Many hypnotists use a combination of relaxation techniques, such as autogenic training, guided imagery, or progressive muscle relaxation in order to get their subjects to relax. Autogenics relies on autosuggestion, usually suggestions that a person feels heavy or warm in his or her arms, then legs, and so forth. Guided imagery evokes vivid, dreamlike descriptions of scenery, such as fields of flowers, cool brooks, or sunny meadows. A third technique, progressive muscle relaxation,

Seven Steps to Relaxation

Martin Shaffer, author of *Life After Stress*, has developed seven general rules for preparing for any type of relaxation:[3]

1. **Get into a comfortable position.** Sit down in your favorite chair, put your feet up, and get your body into a comfortable position. A sofa, bed, and recliner are all good prospects. Put a pillow under your knees for support. Make sure your head is supported.

2. **Loosen collars, jewelry, and belts.** Eliminate anything touching you that might feel uncomfortable. Remove eyeglasses, wallets, watches, bracelets, ties, and anything else that might distract while you try to relax.

3. **Choose a quiet, peaceful setting.** Find a location that is free of noise, lights, smells, and motion. The setting should be cool, quiet, and free of all distractions. Take the telephone off the hook, turn off the lights, pull the shades, and lock the doors.

4. **Adopt an observing attitude.** Don't force the issue. Take a passive, unquestioning attitude to the session. Step back and outside yourself and watch yourself watching yourself. If you simply breathe and observe, relaxation will follow.

5. **Allow enough time.** Different techniques require different amounts of time. Some can be done in five to ten minutes, while others may take a half hour. Through practice, you will learn to relax more quickly and receive the benefits in just a few minutes.

6. **Fit relaxation into your daily schedule.** Pick a time of the day that you usually have free. Some people prefer nights, others mornings. Make sure the time is convenient and fits into your lifestyle. If you practice before going to bed, it should improve your sleep.

7. **Practice relaxation.** Like any other skill, relaxation takes practice. The more you practice, the more proficient you become. With practice, relaxation becomes quicker and deeper.

concentrates on specific muscle groups in succession, first tensing, then relaxing them.

These techniques help relax the mind, making it more susceptible to the hypnotic suggestion. The suggestion itself—to quit smoking, reduce tension, or whatever—distinguishes hypnosis from other relaxation methods, not the state of consciousness it evokes. Furthermore, there is no typical physiological response to hypnosis, as there is with other relaxation methods. These responses apply to breathing rates, heartbeat, blood pressure, and perspiration, all of which decrease in other forms of relaxation but follow the suggested response under hypnosis. If the suggestion is to relax, then the typical response is one of lower arousal, similar to any other relaxed state. On the other hand, if the suggestion is disturbing or exciting, a higher arousal level is experienced.

Hypnosis is also physiologically distinct from sleep, since the subject remains conscious and open to suggestions. Brain wave patterns under hypnosis also differ from those of sleep or meditation. During the deepest periods of sleep, brain waves follow the delta pattern, which is the slowest. The brain waves modulate three or four times as fast during meditation, for example, when they follow the alpha pattern. During hypnosis, the brain waves follow whatever state of mind has been suggested. Thus, there is no brain wave typical of hypnosis.

The suggestions made under hypnosis are designed to implant ideas into the subconscious that will direct the person's conscious behavior after the hypnotic session is over. The most common posthypnotic suggestion is for the person to fall into a deeper level of hypnosis at the next session, which reinforces the hypnotic conditioning.

When you meet with your family physician, ask him his opinion about hypnosis as a relaxation method. He may want to refer you to a trained therapist. You might ask him to listen to a tape of the guided imagery of the script provided in the panel on page 162 to see if he feels it would be useful for you.

If your physician approves, it may be helpful to include a positive posthypnotic suggestion at the end of the imagery text to facilitate conditioning. One example of this type of suggestion might be: "You will be able to return to this stream or meadow whenever you like. Remember how you feel right now. You may think of one or two words, such as leaf and water, whichever is best for you. To experience this calm and easy feeling all you have to do is think of these words."

By repeating the key words "leaf and water" over and over, you may experience relaxation at any time. Some hypnotists use a different approach. Instead of key words, they ask the subject to count to three or concentrate on a special color emphasized in the script.

The best way to learn hypnosis is to attend at least one session with a reputable psychologist who practices hypnosis and ask him to record a tape tailored to your needs. A live session is recommended, because it is common for people to resist the hypnotic trance at first. Besides, people who have never been hypnotized have no idea what hypnosis is like, so they are trying to achieve something that they cannot recognize. Once you have had a session with the psychologist, he may agree that you can continue along on your own by listening to the tape at home.

AUTOGENIC TRAINING

Autogenic training is a form of self-hypnosis that uses suggestions directed by the subject himself to induce deep relaxation. The term autogenic means self-generating or self-regulating. In a sense, all forms of relaxation rely on self-directed messages or images, but autogenic relaxation has come to mean a specific, muscle-relaxing technique.

The autogenic method brings on a general feeling of relaxation by means of a shallow hypnotic trance, in which consciousness is diminished and the subconscious is closer to the surface, as in a light sleep. Through autosuggestion, the individual reaches relaxation by focusing on the heaviness and warmth of first his hands and arms, then feet and legs, abdomen, and forehead, and finally his heartbeat and breathing.

Autogenic training was pioneered in Germany at the turn of the century by Oskar Vogt, a physician. Dr. Vogt developed the idea of having the patient focus on warmth and heaviness in the various parts of the body. His work was continued and developed by Dr. Johannes H. Schultz, an Austrian physician. Their ground-breaking technique is documented in a six-volume work written by Drs. J. H. Schultz and W. Luthe entitled *Autogenic Methods*.[4]

The technique involves the repetition of several direct suggestions like the ones listed below. Each suggestion should be repeated at least five times—the more times the better. First, get comfortable, close your eyes, and then recite the following instructions to yourself. (Before following these or any other relaxation scripts, please consult a physician.)

1. My right leg is warm and heavy.
2. My left leg is warm and heavy.
3. Both legs are warm and heavy.
4. My right arm is heavy and warm.
5. My left arm is heavy and warm.
6. Both arms are heavy and warm.
7. The trunk of my body is warm and heavy.
8. My head and neck are warm and heavy.
9. My entire body is warm and heavy.
10. My forehead is cool.
11. My breathing is easy and calm.
12. My heartbeat is calm and regular.
13. My entire body is warm and heavy.
14. I pause for a few minutes to feel sensations.
15. Reorienting myself, getting reoriented. When I count back from five I will open my eyes and feel relaxed and refreshed.

You might find it easier to write your own script and have someone tape it for you, but first, you will want to have it approved by your physician. The suggestions should be given in a calm, pleasant voice. Synchronize the voice with the exercises. Vary the text to avoid monotony and help concentration. As an example, the text might read something like this:

> Get comfortable. Close your eyes. Focus on your body and get a feeling
> for how your body is doing right now.

Starting with your left leg now. Focus on your left leg. Your left leg is warm and heavy. Left leg is warm and heavy. You feel the leg becoming heavier. Left leg warm and heavy. Left leg heavy and warm. Left leg warm and heavy, heavy and warm.

Let's move to the right leg. The right leg, becoming heavy and warm. Warm and heavy. Heavy and warm, etc., etc.

Continue through the rest of the exercise, moving from one part of the body to the other. Finally, do the breathing (easy and calm) and then the entire body.

As with other methods, autogenic training takes a few days of practice. In time, individuals should be able to reach deeper levels of relaxation more quickly. At first, the response may be light and barely noticeable for some people.

Caution: If you have ulcers or other stomach problems, you should omit the abdominal exercise, because the sensations produce acids and can cause discomfort.

Because distractions will interfere with concentration, the place and time to practice are important. The room should be quiet. Lights should be low, telephones unplugged, and the room temperature should be comfortably cool. A person should try to practice at least twice a day, ideally once in the morning and again in the evening or late afternoon. The essential thing is to work the sessions into your daily routine so that regular practice is maintained.

MEDITATION

Meditation predates modern civilization. Some Eastern religions used meditation more than 2,000 years ago. It still plays a central part in many of the world's religions today.

In the broadest sense, meditation is simply focusing one's thoughts on something.

Clinical forms of meditation have applied ancient concepts to stress management and stripped away cultic and religious rituals. Medical science has discovered that meditation relieves many common complaints, including fatigue, mild depression, insomnia, and hypersomnia, as well as the abuse of drugs, alcohol, and tobacco.

Research has determined that one form of meditation is about as useful as another in terms of relieving stress. Meditation induces a profound rest that is similar to sleep. Both are hypometabolic states, which means that they are characterized by a significant decrease in metabolism. Oxygen consumption, for example, drops dramatically in meditation to a level normally seen only after several hours of sleep.

In some studies, meditation has actually restored more energy than sleep restored, dramatically reducing fatigue and lethargy. Meditators report a surge of energy after a short course of regular sessions. Increased stamina, higher job productivity, and a reduced need for naps or sleep are common. Meditation has psychological benefits as well, providing enhanced mental stability and reduced anxiety.

Transcendental Meditation

There are many different types of meditation, but the best known is Transcendental Meditation or TM. It has been widely studied and practiced in the West since the 1960s, when it was introduced in the United States by Mararishi Mahesh Yogi. He became known in the West when he taught meditation to the Beatles. The form of meditation he taught was adapted from Yoga.

Transcendental means "extending beyond ordinary experience" and refers to the mind's ability, through meditation, to travel beyond the boundaries of normal human experience. Although rooted in the Eastern religions, TM is not a religion or philosophy but a mental process whose purpose is to establish deep relaxation and a keener sense of awareness.

The TM method is easy to learn. Like other forms of meditation, it requires repetition of a word or sound, known as a mantra, for 20 minutes two times a day. The tenets of TM require a trained instructor to give an individual this secret mantra, which is taken from ancient Hindu texts.

Repetition of the mantra prevents the appearance of distracting thoughts. TM practitioners recommend sitting comfortably in a quiet room, then repeating the mantra slowly and silently over and over again. Followers of this approach believe the repetition of the mantra dissolves stress and allows the mind to reach a higher state of consciousness.

TM has been adapted for clinical use in treatment of stress-related disorders. The method, known as the Relaxation Response, was scientifically developed and, in contrast, does not make any claims to raising consciousness and uses no religious texts.

Benson's Relaxation Response

Dr. Herbert Benson, a cardiologist at Harvard Medical School, developed the Relaxation Response in the 1970s after years of research on stress and its physical effects on the body. This method, sometimes called the "respiratory one method" or ROM, is very similar to TM and produces the same physiological response. The difference is that it does not have the spiritual dimension associated with TM and other forms of meditation.

In his book, *The Relaxation Response*, Dr. Benson describes how the technique is used by his group at the Harvard Thorndike Memorial Laboratory:

1. "Sit quietly in a comfortable position.
2. Close your eyes.
3. Deeply relax all your muscles, beginning at your feet and progressing up to your face. Keep them relaxed.
4. Breathe through your nose. Become aware of your breathing. As you breathe out, say the word 'ONE,' silently to yourself. For example, breathe IN . . . OUT, 'ONE'; IN . . . OUT, 'ONE'; etc. Breathe easily and naturally.
5. Continue for 10 to 20 minutes. You may open your eyes to check the time, but do not use an alarm. When you finish, sit quietly for several minutes, at first with your eyes closed and later with your eyes opened. Do not stand up for a few minutes.
6. Do not worry about whether you are successful in achieving a deep level of relaxation. Maintain a passive attitude and permit relaxation to occur at its own pace. When distracting

thoughts occur, try to ignore them by not dwelling upon them and return to repeating 'ONE.' With practice, the response should come with little effort. Practice the technique once or twice daily, but not within two hours after any meal, since the digestive processes seem to interfere with the elicitation of the Relaxation Response."*5

Dr. Benson found that the majority of people felt calm and relaxed after a session. A small percentage of people became ecstatic, while others reported feelings of pleasure, refreshment, and well-being. One common reaction, based on reports from his patients, was a renewal of energy, both physical and mental. Nonetheless, Dr. Benson cautions people to use moderation because some individuals may experience disturbing thoughts.

PROGRESSIVE RELAXATION

Progressive relaxation helps people recognize the difference between having tense muscles and relaxed muscles. By contracting and releasing various muscle groups, people learn to relax all of their muscles.

This method was pioneered by Edmund Jacobson in the early 1920s in his laboratory at Harvard University and has been refined over the years. Dr. Jacobson realized that many people have no idea how to relax because they are unable to identify where the tension resides in their bodies. In some cases, people may not even be conscious of the tension their muscles are storing. Jacobson devised tensing and relaxing exercises to give people a "muscle-sense," which allows them to find the tension in their muscles and gain greater control over it. In effect, this "muscle sense" acts as an internal biofeedback mechanism that alerts the body to undesired tension.

Stressful incidents automatically create tense reactions in our

*Reprinted with permission from pp. 162–163 of *The Relaxation Response*, by Herbert Benson, M.D. (New York: Avon Books, 1976). Copyright 1975, William Morrow & Co.

muscles. These reactions are caused by emotions, such as fear, surprise, excitement, and pain. A prolonged, stressful situation can quickly lead to exhaustion, both physical and emotional. According to Dr. Jacobson, if we can control this automatic, muscle-tensing activity, we can reduce the amount of stress and fatigue in our lives.

Progressive relaxation is best learned from a reputable therapist trained in this technique. The therapist leads the client through an exercise involving 17 muscle groups, giving instructions to tense the muscles and then release them suddenly. The session begins with the right hand (left hand if the client is left handed) and then the right upper arm. The routine continues with the other hand and arm, then forehead, cheeks and nose, lower face, abdomen, neck, chest, both thighs, both calves, and both feet.

The therapist tells the patient to hold each muscle contraction for 6 seconds, release it, pause for 10 seconds, and then make a second contraction, release, and pause for 45 seconds. Then the process starts all over again with the next muscle group.

After several sessions, the exercises can be done with fewer muscle groups. In abbreviated programs, the number of groups is reduced to seven after three sessions and then to four muscle groups after a few weeks. The sessions with four muscle groups can be done in about 10 minutes. Once the person has mastered the technique, the state of relaxation can be induced by simply recalling the sensations without tensing the muscles at all. The goal is to gain enough control to call up this response in daily situations that cause stress.

GUIDED IMAGERY

Images have the power to create intense emotion. The most obvious examples are the images in our dreams, which run the gamut from pleasure to terror. Certain imagery suggested to our imaginations can lead us into deep relaxation.

The body responds to various images with a range of physiological changes involving heartbeat, breathing, and muscle tension. Pleasant images produce quiet, calming responses, whereas unpleasant, fearsome images trigger heightened physiological reactions.

Guided Imagery Text

Guided imagery is a simple and pleasant way to relax. Ask your physician or therapist to record the following passage on a tape. They may want to make some changes. They should talk in a calm, soothing voice and emphasize key sensory words, such as mountain, meadow, sun, warmth, leaf. The speaker should pause from time to time to allow the listener to relax fully.

Just get as comfortable as you can. Then let your eyes close and allow your mind to drift. Just let it float. And if you will, let's go to a mountain. A nice green, tree-covered mountain. Let's just imagine a nice open meadow. A blue sky and a bright sun. A nice warm, bright sun. Feel the warmth of that sun on your forehead, your shoulders, and all over your body. Just see the bright blue sky and the view of the white clouds. Just imagine yourself looking over the meadow and looking at the flowers that are growing, the colors, smelling the fragrance. Imagine yourself walking through this meadow. Feel the warmth that's on your head. Perhaps there's a little breeze. Imagine what the grass feels like under your feet. Just walk through the meadow, listening, looking. Perhaps there are some small animals wandering through the meadow. Perhaps there are rabbits. Perhaps some chipmunks. Perhaps some birds. I don't know what kind. Perhaps some birds that sing. Perhaps some butterflies. Think of all the colors they are. Just a warm sun and slight breeze, a bright blue sky, walking through the meadow. And we come to the edge and there are lots of trees. All kinds of trees. Some pines, some oaks. Perhaps you can feel the breeze through the trees, hear the sounds it makes as it goes through the needles of the pine trees. Hear the soft sound it makes. Notice the kind of rattle it makes when it blows through the leaves of the oaks. Just walk along these trees, perhaps touching the bark of the trees. Feel the roughness. Notice how it gets a little bit cooler as you walk into the shade of the trees. Perhaps you notice some little squirrels jumping in the trees from branch to branch. Perhaps some different kinds of birds are calling. Let's continue the walk on this path. We hear a brook, somewhere in the distance. And then we come upon the brook, nice clear water, perhaps bubbling or gurgling down the stream. Perhaps you put your hand out in the water. Feel the temperature of the water. Then just watch the water, listen to it. Notice there are leaves floating in the stream. And perhaps, just imagine that on each leaf there is a problem or a worry or discomfort. And imagine those leaves drifting off down the stream—going further and further away. Then they disappear around the bend in the stream. And as each leaf disappears so does each problem, discomfort, or worry. We watch the last leaf go around the corner, around the bend, and you turn and you go back towards the meadow. Back into the sun, feeling the warmth of the sun again. Looking out across the meadow, perhaps seeing an eagle fly across the meadow. Relaxed and comfortable. More comfortable, peaceful, looking out across the meadow. Enjoying that moment. And then returning your attention now to this room, this time. You are becoming more and more alert. Open your eyes but hold on to that sensation, relaxation. You are in this room, at this time, waking with your eyes open, you feel relaxed and refreshed, calmer than before.[6]

As an example, imagine yourself on a raft floating down a quiet river. You are lying on your back in the sun watching the white, fluffy clouds. The sun warms your skin. You almost fall asleep as you float along past the quiet, tree-lined riverbank.

Next, imagine yourself stepping into a darkened alley in the middle of a cold, rainy night. You hear a high-pitched screech and a flutter of bats dive erratically over your head. You turn and run away, your heart pounding like a drum.

Your response to these imagined scenes underscores the power of the imagination. We think and feel in reaction to envisioned pictures. These pictures are closely related to arousal and stress. Unfortunately, most of us experience the negative aspects of imagery more often than the positive ones. Disturbing images create stress, while pleasant images promote relaxation.

Recall some of the most vivid memories of your childhood. You probably do not experience these memories as thoughts but as images. You may see the faces of your parents, perhaps, or a house you lived in years ago. These images elicit feelings similar to an actual experience. The more vivid the image, the closer to reality it seems.

Guided imagery or visualization is an exercise in which a professional therapist guides you through a scene with images that will induce deep relaxation. You may use the script on page 162 of this chapter or write one of your own but first make sure to have it approved by your physician or therapist.

Think of the most pleasant experiences in your life, times when you were especially happy and relaxed. Draft a story similar to the mountain scene. Include as many sensory images as possible—use smells, colors, textures, and sounds—to heighten the imagery. You can either tape the story or write it out and have your therapist read it to you.

It may help to relax some before listening to the script. Take a few deep breaths and count backwards from 10 to 0. Imagine climbing down a ladder and taking a step down towards deeper relaxation with each number you count. Once you have reached the bottom of the ladder, turn on the tape recorder or just try to imagine the scenes you have written.

Guided imagery is one of the simplest forms of relaxation. We all daydream about things that make us happy and less tense. Capturing these daydreams and guiding them into a productive framework can lead us into deep restorative relaxation.

BIOFEEDBACK

Biofeedback uses sophisticated equipment to monitor a person's level of tension by measuring body functions, such as breathing, heartbeat, skin temperature, perspiration, or muscle contractions. The machines feed information back to the person from electrodes attached to the skin. The person uses this information to control his or her physiological reactions with relaxation techniques, usually autogenic training.

Besides stress management, biofeedback is used in the treatment of high blood pressure, headaches, sleep disorders, stroke, cardiac arrhythmias, and other illnesses. The patient must use a relaxation technique to control the stress level since the machine is simply a tool that reports data and does not by itself promote relaxation.

The most widely used instrument in the biofeedback laboratory is the electromyography machine or EMG, which monitors electrical impulses given off by the nerves involved in muscle contractions. Electrodes attached to the skin feed data to a variety of devices, such as computers, lights, or sounding instruments, which make the information easily comprehensible to the patient.

Another biofeedback machine measures skin temperature since it is sympathetically related to the blood flow. The amount of blood in the skin varies and is determined by the constriction or dilation of blood vessels. These readings provide indicators on the level of relaxation. Cold hands, for example, are a common symptom of stress. Some inexpensive machines on the market provide feedback on body temperatures by monitoring the fingertips.

A third type of machine measures electrical processes involving the sweat glands and is based on the same principles as the modern lie detector. The term galvanic skin resistance (GSR) has been adopted to describe this sort of electrodermal activity.

With training, the patient learns to control his biological response to stress and is gradually weaned from the machine. The patient first learns to become aware of the stress, then how to control it by responding to the biofeedback data, and finally, he learns how to control the stress without getting feedback from the machine.

Because of the training and equipment required, most people seek treatment from biofeedback therapists. Training usually involves biofeedback sessions of 10 to 20 minutes, followed by a discussion with a professional therapist about stress-related events in the person's life—money problems, marital strife, family stress, or work pressures. In this sense, the biofeedback sessions are similar to psychotherapy. Autogenic training is usually the technique of choice and is taught to help the person relax in response to the biofeedback data.

SPECIAL CONCERNS ABOUT
RELAXATION THERAPY

Relaxation techniques are not appropriate for everyone and people should first consult with their family physicians or reputable psychologists before choosing a method to insure that it is the best one for them. In some cases, the exercises may do little good and may even cause some discomfort, but such incidents are rare and the potential for good far outweighs the risks for most people.[7]

Anyone suffering from severe depression or other mental illness, such as schizophrenia, mania, paranoia, seizure disorders, or mental retardation would not benefit from this sort of treatment because he or she could easily be overwhelmed by negative feelings and disturbing thoughts.

If a person is taking medication for other illnesses, the treating physician should be consulted. Medications prescribed for diabetes mellitus, hypothyroidism, seizures, hypertension, glaucoma, and asthma may need to be reduced.

Some of the negative side effects of relaxation are primarily psychological, although some muscle reaction, such as tics, cramps, or jerks, or an increased heartbeat, may occur in some people. Others may experience feelings of sadness, anger, depression, fear, or other disturbing thoughts. Some people report a fear of losing control.

BENEFITS OF RELAXATION

Some relaxation methods are more effective for certain conditions than others and at times a combination of treatments may be the best solution. Most theorists believe that all techniques prompt pretty much the same response, although there may be subtle differences. A person who is emotionally overwhelmed by meditation may find progressive muscle relaxation or biofeedback more effective. The primary response to any of the relaxation methods is a reduction in stress. Therefore, all methods appear to be useful in reducing fatigue in most people when it is caused by mild depression, anxiety, stress, or insomnia.

You may want to try out a few methods to determine which works best for you. If you are uncomfortable with machines, for example, biofeedback would be less apt to work for you. On the other hand, if you have a strong faith in the spiritual world, then meditation may be an effective choice.

As a general rule, combinations of techniques, especially if tailored to the individual by a credentialed therapist, are more effective than any single method used alone. Much depends on the nature of the person's dominant symptoms and his or her general receptivity to relaxation techniques.

Let us review the effectiveness of these methods on three common disorders: anxiety, depression, and insomnia.

Anxiety

All of the relaxation methods appear to provide some help in reducing anxiety, particularly symptoms such as headaches, insomnia, and phobias. More severe anxiety states, such as anxiety neurosis and panic disorder, are not as responsive to these techniques. A combination of cognitive therapy and relaxation may be effective for these more severe disorders. Autogenic training, hypnosis, and meditation are the methods used most often to reduce these sorts of anxiety-related symptoms.

Depression

Studies have provided mixed reviews on the effectiveness of relaxation techniques on depression.[8] The use of relaxation training to treat depression has not received much attention, but a few studies have shown some improvement in mood. Progressive muscle relaxation has gotten some encouraging reports, but it is still not considered as effective as cognitive-behavioral therapy or antidepressant medication. Meditation and autogenic training have also been shown to relieve depression in some studies. Relaxation therapy is not recommended for severe depression, however, since it may evoke disturbing thoughts and deepen the patient's depression.

Insomnia

Troubled sleep seems to respond to a variety of relaxation methods, including progressive muscle relaxation, meditation, autogenic training, hypnosis, and EMG biofeedback. For insomnia, all of these relaxation techniques are more effective than no treatment at all. Combinations of progressive relaxation and meditation seem to be the most effective.

The primary benefit of any of these methods is the reduction in stress, since stress is a principle cause of fatigue and nervous tension. Deep relaxation will restore energy reserves and help overcome the most debilitating aspects of fatigue.

CONCLUSION

Most of the relaxation methods we have discussed are easy to learn. You will know quickly enough whether or not they are helpful. If you feel calm and refreshed after a session, it is a good indication that stress has been causing your fatigue.

If you are experiencing an inordinate amount of stress in your life, either at work, school, or home, a relaxation technique may help. The first step is to find a health professional to help you find the best method for your individual needs. Ask your family physician to refer you to a psychologist who has been trained in relaxation therapy.

Without proper intervention, the stress will likely increase and it could eventually undermine your emotional and physical health. In this sense, fatigue caused by stress is a warning to slow down and relax. A few minutes is probably all that will be needed. As with anything else, relaxation is a skill that gets better and better with practice.

CHAPTER EIGHT

EXERCISE
THE BEST REMEDY FOR FATIGUE?

The physical fitness boom in the United States over the past two decades has obscured a dismal reality—only about 28 percent of all Americans exercise on a regular basis. Just as many people are completely sedentary and only slightly more are occasionally active.[1]

People who suffer from fatigue usually have no particular medical problem but may be so unfit that the demands of an ordinary day leave them exhausted. Physical fitness is directly related to an ability to function and cope with the stresses of life.

The President's Council on Physical Fitness and Sports has defined physical fitness as: "The ability to carry out daily tasks with vigor and alertness, without undue fatigue and with ample energy to employ leisure-time pursuits and to meet unforeseen emergencies."[2]

As a general rule, fatigue that is alleviated by exercise is most likely caused by emotional distress. If a person feels rejuvenated and relaxed about an hour or so after a workout, emotional stress is more likely the cause of the fatigue. Regular exercise is certainly recommended in such cases.

Despite frequent and widespread publicity about the benefits of exercise for prevention of heart disease, a 1985 national survey found that only 11 percent of Americans exercise long enough, frequently enough, and with enough intensity to gain the recommended level of cardiovascular benefits.

The physical benefits associated with exercise—slower heart rate, good muscle tone, weight control, and so forth—often receive the most attention, but psychological benefits can be just as dramatic. This is especially true for people who suffer from fatigue caused by depression, stress, and anxiety. Hundreds of studies have linked psychological well-being to exercise and physical fitness.

Typically, the people who are tired and depressed are the least likely to exercise, which tends to perpetuate their fatigue. A sedentary life-style and fatigue are synergistic, so each tends to reinforce the other. In theory, one could argue either side of the equation, that fatigue causes inactivity or that inactivity causes fatigue, but as a practical matter, the two usually coexist and feed into each other.

In 1986, research by the National Center for Health Statistics found that inactivity was a consistent predictor of fatigue. Inactive individuals were found to be twice as likely to suffer from fatigue as those who were active.[3] People who exercised vigorously displayed a greater tolerance to fatigue.

Much like the fads in diets and fashion, the popularity of various physical activities fluctuates with the times. The most intensive, aerobic exercises are best for elevation of mood, reduction of fatigue, and improved physical health. "Aerobic" means "with air," so the aerobic exercises require replenishing significant amounts of oxygen over a sustained period of time. These exercises, such as swimming, brisk walking, bicycling, aerobic dancing, or jogging are considered best for building cardiovascular fitness. Most are convenient, inexpensive, require little equipment, and can be done close to home.

Demographic studies tell us something about active people who exercise. We know that men exercise more often than women, for instance, but both sexes exercise less as they grow older. People with more education and higher incomes exercise more during their leisure hours than those with less education and income. The most active Americans live in the west, while those in the northeast and south exercise the least.

Recreational activities and the leisure time to enjoy them have increased substantially in the last few decades, and more people seem to be participating in some form of exercise. But those who need exercise the most are least likely to get it. Those who are depressed or considerably overweight, for example, tend to avoid vigorous physical activity of any kind. The people who join organized exercise programs are usually already active. Surveys of programs at worksites and health facilities indicate that the dropout rates are high—as many as 70 percent quit after six months.

BENEFITS OF EXERCISE

The physical and emotional benefits gained from regular, vigorous exercise are substantial. Growing evidence in the medical literature continues to support the importance of exercise in mental and physical health.

Most of the physical benefits of exercise are objectively evident, easily measured, and generally undisputed. The typical advantages are: reduction in percentage of body fat, increased lung capacity, improved flexibility, greater muscle strength, lower resting heart rate, and lower blood pressure.

The benefits for the mind, however, remain somewhat controversial, although a consensus is emerging that the psychological benefits of exercise are just as significant as the physical. Exercise relaxes muscles, reduces fatigue, promotes sound sleep, and reduces blood lactate, an acid by-product of the metabolism of glucose and glycogen that has been linked to anxiety and panic attacks.[4]

PSYCHOLOGICAL BENEFITS

More than 1,000 studies have been done on the psychological effects of exercise on anxiety, depression, sleep, fatigue, socialization, and work performance.[5] The results have been mixed, which is not really surprising because each study differed in methods and subjects.

A review of four major studies in the United States and Canada found several links between mental health and physical activity. An active life-style correlated to reduced depression and anxiety, improved self-esteem, and more tolerance to stress for both sexes. This correlation was particularly strong for men and women over 40 years old.[6]

In general, people who exercise regularly report feeling more relaxed, less tired, more attractive, more self-confident, and more productive in their work. The sense of discipline, mastery, and commitment to improving health are also commonly suggested as positive feelings that result from regular exercise.

Active people invariably have a better psychological profile than their sedentary counterparts. They have higher self-esteem, better self-image of their bodies, more vitality, and less stress, depression, and anxiety. Whether this healthy personality is the result of exercise, or the exercise is the result of the personality remains a question for some researchers.

Exercise has been shown to be most effective in reducing fatigue caused by depression, anxiety, and stress. All three states of mind are alleviated by vigorous exercise. As fitness improves, the body develops a higher tolerance for emotional distress.

Anxiety and depression are not caused by a lack of physical fitness, but fitness does allow a person to handle the stressful events in life more effectively. Vigorous, regular exercise is certainly a more desirable way to counter stress than alcohol, tobacco, tranquilizers, or illegal drugs. Not only is exercise cheaper, it has an enviable side effect—physical fitness.

Depression

The broadest consensus among the studies seems to be that vigorous exercise, particularly running, reduces depression and the fatigue that accompanies it.

A study at the University of Wisconsin in 1973 found that running was as effective in the treatment of depression as two types of psychotherapy, time-limited and time-unlimited.[7] A variety of factors was suggested to explain the results, including distractions from preoccupations, improved self-image, replacement of negative habits with running, and relief from anxiety and stress.

According to the authors of the Wisconsin study, six of eight patients seemed "essentially well" after running for three weeks. The patients ran three times a week for 30 to 45 minutes of walking and running. The study also suggested that the exercise was as effective as psychotherapy in reducing depression. All the runners suffered from moderate depression, and the researchers noted there is no evidence that exercise alone would be as effective in cases of severe depression. No follow-up was reported and the long-term effectiveness was not addressed by this study.

A similar study at Duke University found that middle-aged men and women showed less fatigue, anxiety, and depression after jogging 45 minutes three times a week for ten weeks. They also experienced renewed vigor, less confusion, and elevated mood.[8]

Psychologists who prescribe jogging and other aerobic exercises for depression report that their most difficult task is obtaining the depressed patient's continuing cooperation. Overcoming the inertia of despondency requires motivation, something undermined by the patient's depression.[9]

Anxiety

Although light exercise does not seem to have much effect on anxiety, vigorous exercise does. The reason is not known, but the results have often been compared to other therapies, such as biofeedback and meditation.

Generally, anxiety increases at the onset of exercise, levels off during the workout, then declines significantly afterwards. The person's anxiety then begins to build once again until the next exercise session. The primary physiological factor may be the decrease in blood lactate that results from exercise. Lactate or lactic acid has been associated with anxiety. Some researchers believe a build-up of blood lactate in anxiety neurotics occurs because of an overproduction of adrenaline.

The reduction in anxiety has held true for both "normal" as well as highly anxious individuals who participate in a vigorous form of exercise. These forms of exercise include brisk walking, jogging, swimming, aerobic dancing, and other aerobic exercises.

Stress

Exercise may be nature's way of ventilating the stresses associated with the stress response we discussed in Chapter Six. Faced with a stressful threat, the body prepares itself by tensing and preparing to flee or fight. Exercise gives us a way to vent this tension and energy in a constructive way, using the stress response to energize the body to run, swim, jump, and so forth.

The tension released in exercise leaves a person more relaxed and counteracts the disease-causing properties of stress. Although light exercise may have little or no effect on anxiety, even very light exercise can reduce muscle tension and alleviate stress with exercise periods as short as 12 minutes.

Vigorous exercise appears to be as effective as other relaxation techniques, such as cognitive-behavioral therapy and meditation. Coincidentally, exercise increases alpha waves, the brain waves associated with meditation and relaxation.

Researchers at the University of Virginia determined that fatigue, tension, and anger decreased significantly for individuals who jogged 30 minutes five days a week for ten weeks. The benefits were only slightly less for those who jogged three times a week. The study, however, found little benefit in less vigorous sports, such as softball or volleyball.[10]

HOW EXERCISE AFFECTS THE MIND

Although the evidence is not conclusive, one can make a convincing case that regular vigorous exercise such as brisk walking, swimming, and jogging reduces depression and anxiety, improves mood, and decreases fatigue while increasing energy and vitality. What is it about exercise that produces all these changes?

Several theories attempt to answer this question, but none of them has been able to explain the answer completely. One of the most popular theories centers on beta endorphin, a morphinelike chemical found naturally in the hypothalamus and limbic systems of the brain.

The beta endorphin, an opiate whose levels rise sharply during vigorous exercise, is produced by the pituitary gland. Some believe its presence may explain the "runner's high" experienced by some joggers. Its chemical structure is similar to opium, but endorphins are 20 times more potent.

When people have high levels of endorphins in their blood, they are unlikely to experience fatigue. Yet the evidence is not as clear that endorphins are responsible for reducing depression. They are, nonetheless, thought to decrease pain, sharpen memory, and exert some control over appetite, sex drive, blood pressure, and respiration.[11]

Because it is not possible to measure the concentration of endorphins in brain tissue, it is not known if they can cross the blood brain barrier into the brain. This leaves unanswered the question of whether or not their levels rise and fall inside the brain as they do in the bloodstream where they can be measured accurately.

Another popular theory about exercise and mood concentrates on a physiological explanation related to stress. The benefits of personal fitness, such as improved heart rate and reduced muscle tension, allow the body to tolerate stress more easily. This, in turn, reduces the stress-related emotions of anger, anxiety, and depression. Some question this theory because elevation of mood is relatively immediate after exercise, whereas fitness generally takes two months or more of training.

Several researchers are studying the alpha waves emitted by the brain during exercise. These brain waves appear after about 20 minutes of jogging and linger for a while after exercise ends. The more intense the exercise, the higher the alpha wave activity. Alpha waves are normally associated with a relaxed but alert state. People in this state of mind are calm, at ease, and describe a sense of floating and peace.

An alternate theory focuses on the effects of exercise on the neurotransmitters in the brain. Some studies suggest that exercise may alter the levels of norepinephrine, dopamine, and serotonin. All of these neurotransmitters, which act as communication links between nerve cells, have been associated with depression, although there is no conclusive evidence that they cause the disorder. As we discussed in Chapter Five on depression, the tricyclic antidepressant drugs also alter the levels of these hormones.

It is important to note that although there is no definitive explanation for the psychological benefits of exercise, there is overwhelming statistical evidence that exercise elevates mood, increases vigor, reduces fatigue, and improves self-esteem. The research has virtually settled this issue, even though an undisputed scientific explanation for this phenomenon has yet to emerge.

EXERCISE AND THE BODY

Most people probably exercise to keep their bodies in shape, not necessarily to feel better. Their primary motive is not conditioning but weight control. It is well known that exercise reduces body mass, if not weight, replacing flabby fat with tight, trim muscle.

This is because vigorous exercise burns off fat, reducing the size of the body while conditioning the muscles, heart, and lungs. The net gain is both psychological and physical, reducing self-consciousness, guilt and anxiety about one's body while fending off stress and illness, particularly heart disease.

Besides reducing body fat, exercise increases cardiovascular efficiency, lowers blood pressure, relaxes muscles, diminishes the effects of stress, and improves lung function and circulation. The lean, efficient body produced by exercise can perform more work with less effort. The added endurance creates a higher threshold to fatigue.

In some ways, the effects of physical exercise actually resemble those encountered in the stress response that we discussed in Chapter Six. Heart and respiration rates increase, while muscles tense and hormones rush into the bloodstream. However, the difference is striking: Physical exercise strengthens the body, while mental stress wears it down.

The physical changes that take place in the body from regular, vigorous exercise—sometimes called the "training effect"—are:

1. Increase in heart rate, stroke volume, and total output—these three factors account for the improvements in cardiac fitness. People who are physically fit have a slower resting heart rate, which means the heart needs to beat fewer times to accom-

plish its tasks. On average, the resting rate drops about one beat per minute for every couple of weeks of aerobic exercise. Stroke volume, which is the amount of blood pumped per beat, also increases as the heart gets stronger with exercise. Cardiac output is the product of these two factors or the stroke volume times the heart rate, which equals the output of blood pumped per minute. These factors all combine to make a more efficient heart.

2. A stronger heart means an increase of blood flow to all of the muscles, improved circulation to the brain, and a greater ability to tolerate stress without fatigue.

3. The improved efficiency of the muscles helps increase the amount of oxygen these fibers can extract from the blood. This added power, combined with cardiac output, contributes to higher oxygen uptake for people who exercise. Exercise increases the number of capillaries in muscle fiber, which also facilitates easier blood flow.

4. Ventilation, or the rate of respiration, is lower for trained individuals than for their sedentary counterparts. The physically fit individual actually breathes less but receives the same amount of oxygen because of his higher oxygen intake.

5. Training increases high-density lipoprotein (HDL) cholesterol, sometimes called the "good cholesterol," and decreases the triglycerides, which have been identified as a risk factor in heart disease. During exercise, fatty acids in the blood are burned off that would otherwise be converted to triglycerides and low-density lipoprotein (LDL) cholesterol.

These factors work together to allow the fit individual to accomplish tasks with less effort than the sedentary person. Less effort means that more energy is conserved to apply to other things.

WEIGHT CONTROL WITH EXERCISE

Although most people exercise to lose or maintain their weight, any weight-loss program should include a diet to reduce calories.

Exercise alone has not been found to be effective in shedding excess weight.

About 34 million Americans—roughly one in four adults—are more than 20 percent overweight, which is the medical definition of obesity. A person is considered mildly obese if he is 20 to 40 percent over his ideal weight, moderately obese if 41 to 100 percent over. Anything greater is classified as severe obesity. (See Table Seven, Chapter Nine for recommended weights.)

As we learned in the previous chapter, losing excess weight can reduce fatigue. Obesity damages self-esteem and causes guilt, depression, and anxiety, especially for women and adolescents. All of these factors contribute to fatigue. Additionally, just carrying the excess weight around depletes energy and promotes a sedentary lifestyle.

Exercise is crucial to any weight control program. The average sedentary person burns an average of 300 to 800 calories in normal physical activity, such as walking or climbing stairs. Exercise specialists recommend that a person expend 200 to 400 additional calories in some form of planned exercise. This is the equivalent of jogging two to four miles a day.

To lose one pound, a person must burn off 3,500 calories. This is the equivalent of jogging 35 miles! As you can see, a person would need to run hundreds of miles to lose any significant amount of weight.

If this is the case, why recommend exercise to reduce weight at all? There are several reasons. By exercising and dieting at the same time, a person attacks the problem from two ends—reducing the number of calories taken in and burning off others. The exercise also has psychological benefits that are positive for weight reduction. It improves self-esteem and self-confidence, and alleviates depression and anxiety, which sometimes cause people to eat too much. Furthermore, exercise strengthens muscle and reduces fat.

While helping to reduce excess weight, exercise also combats diseases that have long been associated with obesity. Vigorous, aerobic exercise helps prevent heart disease, diabetes, high blood pressure, and excessive cholesterol levels.

Anyone who is overweight and out of shape must take special care to avoid injury. Intense forms of exercise should be approached carefully and slowly. The risk of injury to muscles and joints is higher for the overweight person because excess weight puts more demand and pressure on the musculoskeletal system.

BEFORE YOU START

A careful evaluation by a physician is necessary before starting any vigorous exercise program. All too often this suggestion is ignored by the enthusiastic exerciser who is eager to get started despite the hidden dangers.

For some people the potential trouble is obvious if they have suffered from heart disease, respiratory disorders, or diabetes. The complexity of the effects of training on the human body deserves respect. The danger of injury, even among trained athletes, is ever present.

Healthy individuals of any age can benefit from regular vigorous exercise, as long as they follow a sensible plan. The most essential advice is to go slowly. Introduce exercise into your life-style gradually to allow your body to adapt to the new stresses on muscles and joints.

There are many fitness tests to measure a person's level of conditioning. With the proper test, your physician can offer the most appropriate exercise guidelines. The physician may ask for a treadmill test to measure the stress on your heart and lungs, especially if you are more than 30 years old. Some doctors use a simple step test. These tests measure the heart rate after stepping up and down from a 12-inch-high step for several minutes.

Once you have gotten a clean bill of health from your doctor, you are ready to start your program. In your enthusiasm to begin, don't forget to limit your exercise for the first few weeks.

THE BEST TYPES OF EXERCISE

Aerobic exercises are clearly the best for both physical and mental health. Weight-lifting may build muscles, but it does little for cardiovascular conditioning. The best exercises work the large muscle groups—legs, arms, and abdomen.

The guiding factor in choosing any exercise program is enjoyment. If it isn't fun, it is unlikely to hold your interest very long. Fitting exercise into a busy schedule requires discipline and a certain amount of sacrifice. The drop-out rate from exercise programs is high. Most people give up running programs after six weeks unless they really enjoy it.

Another critical factor in a successful program is convenience. If you need to drive an hour to an indoor swimming pool, then swimming may not be the one to choose. Often, the climate and geography will dictate your choice. For some, a variety of exercises may be the best idea, in order to maintain interest. Others may want to concentrate on only one type of exercise so they can observe their progress.

The type of aerobic exercise does not seem to matter, as long as it meets certain criteria. The preferred aerobic exercises are vigorous, continuous, and rhythmic and use the major muscle groups.

According to Paul M. Ribisl, an exercise authority at Wake Forest University, the ideal exercises are:[12]

Aerobic dancing	Kayaking
Badminton	Racquetball
Basketball	Rope skipping
Bicycling	Soccer
Canoeing	Squash
Cross-country skiing	Swimming
Fencing	Tennis
Handball	Walking/jogging/running

All of these activities meet the criteria for vigorous, aerobic exercise and all of them provide a good workout. Other activities are useful as supplements, such as downhill skiing, hiking, nature walking, skindiving, backpacking, golfing, and gardening. These are good things to add to your repertory, but they are not vigorous enough to provide the intensity needed to gain maximum benefits.

It is sometimes best to choose one vigorous aerobic exercise to do at least three times a week. Other days can be used for one of the other sports. If the activity is a team sport, like basketball, then it may be more difficult to do regularly since you must find other teammates and a facility.

This brings us back to convenience. If at all possible, choose an exercise that allows you to walk out the front door, exercise for a half hour or more, and then return to the front door. Walking, running, or bicycling generally fit the bill. Such convenience precludes the hassles of driving, parking, finding teammates, and changing clothes in locker rooms three or four times a week. Depending on your geographical location, you might alternate bicycling during warm months and cross-country skiing in winter. Of course, walking and jogging can be done year round just about anywhere in most kinds of weather.

Here are some of the advantages and disadvantages of five of the most popular aerobic exercises:

1. **Running/Jogging**. One of the best aerobic exercises, running costs little and can be done anywhere, anytime, though preferably in weather that is neither too hot nor too cold. Although the popularity of running has declined in recent years, marathons and 10K races are still common around the country, and these events offer the long-distance runner an occasional contest. Injuries, some serious, may occur, especially to the knees, feet, and ankles, which take a pounding on the concrete or pavement. It is crucial to pay attention to proper training and warm-up exercises. Physical conditioning is assured with running just 10 to 15 miles a week, so the time commitment is not great.
2. **Walking**. The main advantage of this exercise is safety for all ages and levels of fitness. Many of the same advantages of running are true for walking, too, and injuries are rare. Just about anyone with normal health can participate. It takes more time to gain the same training effect as jogging, but conditioning can be increased by adding weight to a backpack or walking up hills. Some people have taken to using hand weights to work upper muscle groups. Walking is one of the fastest growing forms of exercise and the most commonly prescribed by physicians.
3. **Swimming**. This exercise is one of the best of all exercises because it involves both lower and upper muscle groups, so it offers a good workout without the danger of injury associ-

ated with running. The main disadvantage is access to a place to swim. Health spas with pools are more common these days, but membership fees can be high. In any case, swimming is a great adjunct to other exercise programs.

4. **Bicycling.** Except for the hazards of the road, bicycling offers less chance of injury than running since much of the weight is off the feet. Bicycling is something the whole family can do together and can be very enjoyable. Be careful in traffic and wear a helmet to guard against head injury. New technologies have revolutionized the bicycle, adding lightweight materials, sophisticated gears, and special features for various terrains. Bicycles can be expensive, some selling for more than a thousand dollars, but some bicycle shops accept trade-ins and have many refitted bicycles for sale at secondhand prices.

5. **Cross-country skiing.** Perhaps the best aerobic exercise, cross-country skiing works both upper and lower muscle groups. The sport burns off plenty of calories while getting people out into natural scenery, which in itself can be very relaxing and refreshing. One can progress at a pace of one's own choosing, and the chance of injury is fairly low, certainly less than downhill skiing. Of course, equipment for this sport is expensive and it can be done by most people only during the winter months, and only then if there is sufficient snow. For those with the proper climate, however, this is an excellent exercise, combining enjoyment with conditioning.

WHY DO PEOPLE EXERCISE?

All of the knowledge we have about exercise is useless if we don't put it to good use. Two things seem to motivate people to exercise: They want to look and feel better. A good exercise program is aimed at meeting both of these goals.

The exercise should also be geared to the individual's own interests and schedule. Although convenience is crucial for long-term success, so is social support and positive feedback on progress. Once people start feeling more energetic and less tired, lose some excess weight, and receive compliments about their looks, they will have plenty of motivation to continue their exercise program.

The most common explanation for quitting an exercise program is lack of time. But this is a poor excuse. Most people, no matter how busy, should be able to find 15 to 20 minutes three days a week to exercise. Before starting your own program, review the time management techniques in Chapter Twelve to schedule time for exercise.

It is not necessary to spend a great deal of money to become physically fit. Joining a health spa can be expensive and studies indicate that modern, fancy facilities do not significantly improve compliance. The truth is that exercise is not expensive. Chances are that you already have a pair of sneakers, a sweatsuit, a bicycle, or a bathing suit. Take advantage of the equipment you already have. If

---

Make Exercise Convenient and Fun

1. Pick a sport or exercise you enjoy. If it isn't fun, it won't last long.
2. Fit the exercise into your schedule at least three times a week. If exercise disrupts your routine, you may find it too troublesome to continue.
3. Alternate the forms of exercise to avoid boredom or disruptions caused by climactic changes. For example, you might swim twice a week and jog once a week.
4. Seek support from others. Invite someone to join you in your exercise. Many close friendships have been forged in this way and it offers you encouragement.
5. Start out slow to avoid injury and overtraining, both of which could ruin your plans before you get your program underway.
6. Set some goals, for both the long term and short term. If you smoke, use exercise as a reason to quit. If you are overweight, make a commitment to lose a set number of pounds by exercising and dieting.
7. Keep expenses down to the bare minimum to insure that exercise won't be jeopardized should your household budget shrink.

you spend a lot of money, then quit for some reason, you will just feel more guilty.

The other major reason people quit is because of injury or overtraining. Caught up in the initial burst of enthusiasm, these exercisers overdo it. The price of overtraining is high. Besides injury to muscles or joints, overtraining may cause fatigue, tension, irritability, insomnia, weight loss, poor appetite, and an increased resting heart rate. When exercise stops being fun and starts hurting, people stop exercising.

HOW MUCH IS ENOUGH?

The amount of exercise needed to gain psychological and physical benefits depends on three factors: intensity, duration, and frequency. One must train hard enough, long enough, and often enough to become physically fit.

Most exercise specialists recommend at least 15 minutes of continuous, vigorous exercise three times a week to derive the cardiovascular benefits. The same is true for psychological gains, but the level of intensity can be lower.

The American College of Sports Medicine (ACSM) recommends that the minimum three sessions a week be no more than two days apart. An average of fewer than two sessions a week will result in few, if any, benefits, according to the ACSM.

Intensity of exercise is measured by the training heart rate, which can be computed using a formula developed by Dr. M. Karvonen, a Scandinavian physician.[13] The formula includes a rate from 50 to 85 percent that corresponds to minimal, optimal, and maximal intensity. Also part of the formula are the maximum heart rate (MHR) (see the panel on page 185) and the resting heart rate (RHR).

Training Heart Rate = [(MHR − RHR) × 50 to 85%] + RHR

Your resting heart rate can be measured by either counting your pulse (at the neck or on the wrist) for 10 seconds and then multiplying by 6 or counting your pulse for a full minute. It is best to check the rate in a sitting position the first thing in the morning after waking up.

Let's figure out the training heart rate for a 35-year-old woman with a maximum heart rate of 188 beats per minute. She has a resting heart rate of 70 beats per minute and plans to exercise at the minimal percentage of 50 percent. Using the formula, the training heart rate would be [(188 − 70) × 50%] + 70 = 129 beats per minute.

At the beginning of any exercise program, it is always best to warm up slowly to avoid injury. If you find yourself straining at the minimum target heart rate, slow down and build back up gradually. Stop every five minutes or so to take your pulse and determine your heart rate to make sure it is within the target range. It is a good idea to exercise on alternate days at first to give your body time to adjust between sessions.

Depending on the initial level of conditioning, a person should try to maintain the training heart rate for at least 12 to 15 minutes. Most gains from exercise are greatest in the first 15 minutes and then taper off.

WALKING—THE NATURAL EXERCISE

Walking is one of the fastest growing forms of exercise and is the most prescribed by physicians. It offers moderate, safe, and longer

Maximum Heart Rates by Various Ages	
Age	Maximum
25	200
30	194
35	188
40	182
45	176
50	171
55	165
60	159
65	153

duration exercise as well as the psychological benefits found in running without the risks of injury. In fact, the only disadvantage to walking is that it takes more time.

Walking at a brisk pace fits the bill for convenience, low cost, safety, and equipment. One can leave the front door, walk around the neighborhood, and return to the front door. There is no need to purchase expensive memberships in health spas or drive to a gymnasium to work out.

Walking at a 4-mph pace burns off 420 calories an hour, about the equivalent of jogging for 30 minutes at 7 mph. One can gain the same benefit in terms of weight control as running by simply doubling the time commitment. You can also increase the number of calories burned by carrying weights, either in your hands or in a backpack.

To gain the maximum health benefits of walking, your pace should be steady and rhythmic, as close to the target heart rate as possible. Taking your pulse regularly during the walk will quickly familiarize you with the appropriate pace. A good brisk pace is about 3.5 mph.

Most people find it easier to maintain a walking program than other exercise activities, probably because it is convenient and safe. The primary problem is generally fitting the program into an already busy schedule.

Find at least three hours a week in which you can walk. Pay special attention to any sedentary activities in your schedule. By eliminating television viewing for three or four hours a week, your benefits will be twofold—replacing sedentary behavior with physical activity. At the same time, be careful not to reduce other physical activities since this will offset the plusses you gain through walking.

CONCLUSION

The next time you arrive home tired and worn out from the tasks of the day, take a few minutes to change clothes, put on your sneakers, and leave the house for a brisk walk around the neighborhood. Keep the pace sprightly, rhythmic and steady. Make a point of noticing the details in the scenes around you.

About an hour or so after your walk, make a quick check of your mood. Chances are that the fatigue has faded away. Maybe you weren't so tired after all.

We all need this sort of boost at one time or another. Exercise, when properly prescribed, is a wonderful and simple antidote to fatigue. Whatever your exercise program, pay attention to the feedback from your emotions as well as your body. Your feelings have a lot to do with fatigue and exercise has a great deal to do with your feelings.

CHAPTER NINE

LOSING WEIGHT TO BEAT FATIGUE

INTRODUCTION

Obesity is a common cause of fatigue, but fatigue may also contribute to obesity. The two often coexist and reinforce each other. Tired, overweight people eat poorly and rarely exercise, compounding their weight problems. Why are they tired? Three reasons are commonly suggested:

1. An obese person must carry around a heavy load. A 210-pound man whose ideal weight is 140 lifts or carries one half of his desirable weight every time he stands up or takes a step.
2. Obese people lead sedentary lives, and are almost always physically unfit. They walk less, climb fewer stairs, and exert themselves less than people of normal weight.
3. The obese also suffer emotionally, both in their personal relationships and in the workplace. In the past, it was thought that depression and anxiety caused overeating, but at least some authorities now believe obesity is actually the cause of these negative emotions.

The evidence on the emotional consequences of obesity is mixed, however, partly because of relatively sparse research on the subject.

A person who is tired, bored, and chronically exhausted may seek solace in food. On the other hand, a person who is already overweight may feel depressed, lonely, and anxious because of the weight. Changing behavior and the person's emotional relationship to food is necessary to end these tendencies.

Modern life-styles have a propensity for making people over-weight. Despite the cultural forces of fashion, youthfulness, and health concerns, an epidemic of obesity afflicts almost every segment of the population of the United States. About 34 million Americans— roughly one in four adults—are more than 20 percent overweight, which is the medical definition of obesity. A person is considered mildly obese if he is 20 to 40 percent over his recommended weight and moderately obese if 41 to 100 percent over. Anything greater is classified as severe obesity. A person is overweight when his body weight exceeds his ideal weight by 10 percent (see Table Seven for recommended weights).

Most research has focused on the physical consequences of obesity, although we know that the psychological impact can be just as devastating. The diseases linked to obesity include cardiovascular illness, diabetes, arthritis, gallbladder disease, hypertension, and gout. The psychiatric problems are not as easy to identify, but depression, anxiety, and low self-esteem are commonly associated with obesity, particularly among women.

If fatigue causes obesity and obesity causes fatigue, what can be done to end this vicious cycle? Should one concentrate on curing the obesity or the fatigue? The answer is to concentrate on both. The chicken-or-the-egg question has scientific interest, but in practical terms the conditions support each other. A person must confront them both.

Fatigue caused by obesity is more common among women than among men according to the first National Health and Nutrition Examination Survey (NHNES) of American adults. The women who were described as heavy had one and a half times the risk for fatigue as those women described as light. Variance between heavy and light men was not statistically significant.[1]

No explanation was provided for the disparity between the sexes, but other research has shown that women suffer more from

Table Seven.   *Height-Weight Tables*

Men				Women			
Height (ins.)	Frame			Height (ins.)	Frame		
	Small	Medium	Large		Small	Medium	Large
62	128–134	131–141	138–150	58	102–111	109–111	118–131
63	130–136	133–143	140–153	59	103–113	111–123	120–134
64	132–138	135–145	142–156	60	104–115	113–126	122–137
65	134–140	137–148	144–160	61	106–118	115–129	125–140
66	136–142	139–151	146–164	62	108–121	118–132	128–143
67	138–145	142–154	149–168	63	111–124	121–135	131–147
68	140–148	145–157	152–172	64	114–127	124–138	134–151
69	142–151	148–160	155–176	65	117–130	127–141	137–155
70	144–154	151–163	158–180	66	120–133	130–144	140–159
71	146–157	154–166	161–184	67	123–136	133–147	143–163
72	149–160	157–170	164–188	68	126–139	136–150	146–167
73	152–164	160–174	168–192	69	129–142	139–153	149–170
74	155–168	164–178	172–197	70	132–145	142–156	152–173
75	158–172	167–182	176–202	71	135–148	145–159	155–176
76	162–176	171–187	181–207	72	138–151	148–162	158–179

the social and psychological stigma attached to obesity. Two other groups that suffer more emotionally are adolescent girls and severely obese men.

The NHNES found no correlation between fatigue and nutrition for either men or women. The diets of fatigued and nonfatigued subjects showed little difference in protein, carbohydrate, fat, phosphorus, iron, the B vitamins, and vitamins A and C. In fact, the only difference was in calcium, which was higher among the nonfatigued men.[2]

This indicates that excess calories, not nutrition, generally distinguishes those who are tired from those who are not. Reducing excess weight, rather than improving the nutrients in the diet, therefore, seems more effective in combatting fatigue.

As anyone who has tried to lose weight knows, it is not an easy thing to do. Only about 5 percent of those who lose weight maintain the loss for two years, despite a multibillion dollar industry that has arisen to help people lose weight. A torrent of commercial programs, diet books, exercise videos, patent remedies, liquid diets, food powders, and diet pills has flooded the market.

Adding to the general confusion of the issue, the medical research on the subject is frequently inconclusive, contradictory or ambiguous. Theories abound but solid and useful evidence is hard to find.

The need for an individualized, rational strategy to attack obesity in a methodical and effective way is essential. This chapter is designed to provide a framework for such a program. Faced with the array of choices, conflicting claims and testimonials, consumers are understandably confused. All programs look easy on paper but real change is hard.

The rewards can be substantial, however, for the person who suffers from fatigue due to obesity. The prize is a renewed vitality that will enrich one's life.

WEIGHT CONTROL—A COMPLEX PROBLEM

The bodily mechanisms that control weight are unknown, but several theories attempt to explain this complex process. Whatever the weight regulators may be, they can be overridden by genetic variables, high calorie diets, sedentary life-styles, and certain psychological conditions.

Some researchers have compared the process of weight control to the body's temperature. The temperature may rise or decline, but the body always seeks to return to "normal." Unlike body temperature, however, the normal range for weight varies from one individual to another.

Obesity is probably the result of many factors, which vary among individuals. At times, one theory of the cause of obesity emerges to show more promise than others, but none seems to have all the answers.

Any successful weight-loss program should include three elements: diet, exercise, and a change in eating habits. One without the other two will probably result in failure. To maintain any loss, modifying eating behavior is the most important of the three and this means a lifetime commitment.

ENERGY BALANCE

The energy balance refers to an equation in which energy input equals output. The body takes in energy as food and burns it off during physical activity and metabolic processes, such as the production of body heat. Some researchers believe obesity results from a disruption in this delicate balance.

Stated in simple arithmetical terms the equation is:

Change in Body Fat Stores = Energy Intake − Energy Expenditure

As this indicates, if intake exceeds expenditure, then body weight increases. Weight decreases if expenditure exceeds intake.

This equation focuses on the crux of the problem but it is not especially practical. It is almost impossible to count every calorie consumed or to know how many calories are burned off for every specific activity. Calorie counts for foods are based on weight, so it would be necessary to weigh all food before eating it for a caloric estimate. Ingredients vary in food products anyway, so even these estimates would not necessarily be reliable.

Most of a person's calories are expended in metabolic processes, such as digestion, breathing, and production of body heat. Except in cases of unusually heavy exercise, this metabolic process, called the resting metabolic rate (RMR), accounts for 65 to 75 percent of the energy expended daily. This RMR varies depending on sex, age, ambient temperature, genetic factors, height, weight, and body composition. Pregnancy, growth, and lactation increase the RMR. Assuming normal levels of physical activity, the average male expends about 3,000 calories a day, while the average woman expends about 2,200 calories.

Two common factors seem to lead to higher stores of body fat. First, a person's caloric intake may increase slowly over decades while physical activity declines, resulting in obesity. Second, certain psychological conditions, such as depression, fatigue, boredom, or stress, may develop and contribute to overeating.

FAT CELLS

The percentage of fat a person carries is determined by the size and number of his fat cells. The number of fat cells in the body can double and their size can expand by as much as 70 percent. Young adults of normal weight have between 28 and 38 billion fat cells, but some obese adults may have as many as 88 billion.[3]

New fat cells are formed once the existing cells reach their maximum size. Most fat cells are added during the first year of life, but new ones can form at any age.

A special type of body fat, commonly referred to as brown fat, comprises about one percent of all body weight. This fatty tissue is deposited at various sites in the body—near the kidneys, around the heart, and between the shoulder blades. These cells burn off excess energy as heat at a much higher rate than the ordinary "white" fat cells do.

There are different opinions about whether or not a person can reduce the number of white fat cells. Some nutritionists believe the number can be reduced if a person loses weight and maintains the lower weight for seven to nine years. Others disagree, saying the number is set for life and cannot be reduced.[4]

Heredity and eating habits both play a role in determining the number of these cells. Everybody is born with a certain number, based on inherited characteristics. If one overeats, new cells will be formed to store varying amounts of fat.

According to one theory of fat cells, the body fights to maintain the cells at a certain size. If the size is reduced, the cells trigger a physiological mechanism involving the hypothalamus—the lower part of the brain responsible for autonomic functions. This reaction causes a person to either eat more or reduce physical activity to restore fat cells to their former size.

Some studies have shown that it is more difficult for people with a higher number of fat cells to lose weight. At least, these people lose weight more slowly and with greater effort than those with fewer fat cells. A variety of other factors hinders weight loss, such as the level of obesity, the duration of the condition, any harmful eating habits, and emotional problems associated with food and eating.

SET POINT THEORY

The set point theory suggests that obesity is caused by a biologically predetermined number of fat cells. It is closely associated with ideas discussed earlier about the fat cell. The set point proposes that the total number of fat cells is "set" early in life by eating habits and heredity.

This theory, popular in the 1980s, would explain why some people find it so difficult to lose weight and why they regain the weight they lose later on. The theory takes an especially pessimistic view of the problem, since it believes efforts to lose weight are opposed by strong biological forces.

Adherents point to a vague physiological mechanism that they believe regulates weight much like the body maintains its temperature. According to this theory, weight is controlled within a narrow range by some sort of interaction among hormones, enzymes, and fat cells.

The set point theory has not been proven, so it remains theoretical. If nothing else, the idea that each individual has a different body-weight set point has helped deflect claims that obesity is a purely psychological problem.

Two treatments have been suggested to reduce the set point—exercise and drug therapy. The treatments attempt to stabilize weight at a lower set point, where energy intake equals output. Exercise helps facilitate this objective by increasing the number of calories expended. As a tool in weight loss, however, exercise is more effective if it is part of an overall weight-reducing program.

A second treatment involves use of an appetite suppressant, fenfluramine, which is thought to lower the set point by altering the body's metabolism. Fenfluramine and amphetamine are both members of the phenylethylamine class of chemicals and both have been prescribed for weight control. A physician would likely recommend fenfluramine only in the first few weeks of a diet, however, since its appetite-reducing benefits are temporary. For this reason, fenfluramine is not considered effective for continuous use in diet control, although it can be helpful for people while developing new eating habits. Side effects of this medicine include depression, mental confusion, and skin rashes. These effects generally go away as the body adjusts to the drug.

GENETICS

The idea that genetics predestines a person to obesity is not a new one, but it has enjoyed a resurgence of scientific interest over the past few years because of studies done with identical twins. One of the most influential of these studies in 1990 at the University of Pennsylvania found that identical twins reared apart had virtually the same weight as adults. The researchers compared 673 pairs of twins by body-mass index, which is weight adjusted for height. The twins had virtually the same body-mass whether they were raised together or apart. The study concluded that childhood environment and experiences had little influence on obesity, whereas heredity accounted for as much as 70 percent of the differences in body–mass in adult life.[5]

Studies of adopted children have come to similar conclusions, finding that children resemble the weights of their natural parents, not their adoptive parents. Inheritance plays such a crucial role that if one parent is obese, a child has a 40 percent chance of becoming obese. This chance doubles if both parents are obese. On the other hand, the chance dwindles to only 7 percent if neither parent is obese.[6]

Genetics is not necessarily destiny, however, and social and environmental influences can be a strong determinant in weight control, especially over several generations. This is particularly evident in studies of obesity in lower and higher social classes. Almost twice as many adult American women in the low socioeconomic group are overweight compared to women in the upper class.

The same trend is seen among children in lower social classes. Scientists believe the children of the poor are at higher risk for obesity because their parents do not have the skills to manage their own weight or teach the children how to manage theirs. This situation could continue for generations.[7]

Another study in 1990 indicated a strong link between obesity and genetics of 12 pairs of identical twins in Quebec. Each twin was fed an extra 1,000 calories each day over four months and maintained similar levels of physical activity. All gained the same amount of weight as their twin, but the gain varied among pairs of twins by as much as 20 pounds. This indicates that some people can eat all they want and not gain much weight, while others will gain quite a bit. Researchers attribute this difference to the fact that some people burn off more calories than others in converting food to energy.[8]

If genetics is such a powerful determinant in obesity, you might wonder why anyone should even try losing weight. How can anyone buck such seemingly overwhelming odds? The genetic studies provide some crucial information and guidance for those who wish to lose weight.

People who can't lose weight on a low-calorie diet are probably genetically prone to obesity because their bodies are very efficient in storing fat. These people have two options: burn more calories by exercising or reduce the proportion of fat in their diets.

A combination of both is probably the best approach. Exercise has many other benefits for health and improves mood. Reducing fat intake is critical, however, because the body converts about 90 percent of dietary fat calories into body fat. In contrast, the body burns off about 25 percent of the calories from carbohydrates and protein in the process of converting them to fat.

The genetic research provides a reasonable, nonjudgmental explanation for a weight problem. The adherents of the genetic school believe that people should not blame themselves for lack of willpower or some other emotional weakness. It may be more difficult for them to lose weight, but they should be able to reach a desirable weight with the proper weight-reducing program.

HORMONES

It has long been suspected that hormones play a role in obesity, but definitive evidence has never been found to link the two. The recent genetic research has again revived interest in a hormonal cause of obesity.

At the turn of the century, there was a widespread belief that some undiscovered hormone was responsible for obesity. This theory was discredited because of a lack of evidence and the hormone theory fell into disrepute. The present theory suspects that some hormonal imbalance plays a minor role, at least in cases of severe obesity.

Hormones are secreted by the glands of the endocrine system, such as the thyroid, pituitary, pancreas, adrenal, and others. The hormones are carried through the bloodstream and help stimulate metabolic functions throughout the body. Hormones affect appetite as well as the rate at which calories are burned off.

Insulin, which is secreted by the pancreas, is one of the hormones that may contribute to overeating. The sight and smell of food triggers a small increase of insulin in people of normal weight but a more significant release for obese individuals. This is not caused by obesity, however, since even after they have reduced their weight to normal levels, previously obese individuals show the same exaggerated response to insulin.[9]

The thyroid gland, which is located at the base of the neck, has also received special attention. Obese subjects have been given injections of thyroid hormone because it accelerates loss of lean and fatty tissue by increasing the body's metabolism. Because of the dangers of hyperthyroidism from an excess of this hormone, physicians do not recommend its routine use. Hyperthyroidism causes nervousness, insomnia, irritability, and rapid heartbeat.

Imbalances in hormonal systems are almost always the result of obesity, not the cause of it. With the loss of weight, the systems generally return to normal. This is the case, for example, when the pancreas is impaired by obesity and secretes an excess of insulin, causing diabetes. With the loss of weight, the diabetes can be cured or significantly reversed.

PSYCHOLOGICAL INFLUENCES

Some people overeat for emotional reasons, although this is not true for all obese people. For many, however, eating serves to ease negative feelings like anger, boredom, fatigue, loneliness, anxiety, rejection, or stress. When life becomes too overwhelming, they turn to food for solace.

Some psychologists believe that overeating represents a craving for love and affection that originates with feelings associated with the need for a nurturing, attentive mother. Another theory suggests that some individuals cling emotionally to their obesity as a means of avoiding deeper, more troubling psychological problems.

It is important to note that the negative emotions that afflict the obese are not necessarily any more serious than they are for people of normal weight. The problem is that their emotions are entangled with overeating and result in obesity. When these people are tired, lonely, or depressed, they turn to food for emotional support.

Emotional problems involving eating habits must be sorted out first if any weight control program is to succeed. If the problems are transitory, such as loneliness caused by a temporary separation, social support from friends or relatives may help a person reassert control. At other times professional counseling may be advised.

Different moods trigger overeating in different individuals. Identifying the relationship between the specific mood and the eating behavior is an essential first step. This is doubly important if the person eats when he feels tired or depressed, since this encourages inertia and a sedentary life-style, which makes weight control all the more difficult.

Other psychosocial factors, such as marital adjustment, social interaction, self-esteem, and body image all contribute to the dynamics of overeating. Life events, such as the breakup of a romantic relationship, the loss of a job, or the death of a loved one, may cause overeating among some people.

The obese are caught up in a relentless cycle of overeating, obesity, and emotional distress that leads to more eating, obesity, and distress and so on. When observing this cyclical process, it may become impossible to separate the emotions causing the obesity from those being caused by it.

PSYCHOLOGICAL CONSEQUENCES OF OBESITY

Information on the emotional consequences of obesity is scarce compared with the extensive studies done on its physical complications. Although the psychological evidence is ambiguous at times, a consensus is emerging to challenge the long-held belief that the obese have serious emotional problems.

The moods that encourage overeating in some people should not be confused with serious psychological disturbances, such as severe depression or anxiety. Various studies using psychological tests have found only a small difference in terms of emotional disorders between the obese and people of normal weight. In some studies, the obese actually score better. The findings for obese children follow the same trend as for obese adults.[10]

These studies should not be taken to mean that the obese do not have any psychological problems. Many standard psychological tests are not appropriate measures of the specific problems faced by the obese, such as their lack of confidence in maintaining their weight and a sense of isolation from others. Many obese individuals are obsessed with their weight and view their bodies as grotesque, even deformed. This image seriously erodes confidence and self-esteem, creating the frustration that perpetuates overeating.[11]

This disparaging self-image is reinforced by a society that seems obsessed with slimness. A strong prejudice exists against fat people, even within the health professions that treat them. In our culture, fat means ugly. The social and psychological consequences, even for those who may be only slightly overweight, can be emotionally disturbing, even devastating.

It is not easy to overemphasize the American culture's contempt for the obese. The stereotype is depressingly familiar—lazy, sick, stupid, ugly, weak willed, dirty, smelly, ignorant, and self-indulgent. This is not a prescription for psychosocial stability. Indeed, these stereotypes undermine social interaction and emotional growth.

This social attitude follows the obese into the work place, where they pay a financial penalty as well. Not only are the obese less likely to be hired, but they are also more likely to earn less than other, slimmer employees.

The social stigma of obesity is most evident for women. Physical attractiveness is a strong predictor for a woman marrying into a higher socioeconomic class, for instance. One study found that only 12 percent of those women moving up into a higher class were obese, while 22 percent of those dropping to a lower class were obese.[12]

DIETS

Americans seem to be obsessed with diets. At any given time, nearly half of all American women and more than a quarter of the men are trying to lose weight one way or another. Health spas, diet programs, low-calorie foods, diet pills and powders have developed into a multibillion dollar industry.

Given such a large, widespread effort to control the weight of Americans, the net results are abysmally low. Nothing seems to be more difficult for people to do. Even quitting smoking and alcohol are said to be easier habits to break. After all, a person never needs to smoke another cigarette or drink another highball, but everyone has to keep eating.

The success of any diet depends on the dieter. The best diet in the world will fail if the dieter is unprepared emotionally or socially for change. Any diet should begin with a physical examination by a physician. Most doctors have a variety of dietary plans from which patients may choose. The doctor can set a target calorie intake and suggest a proper exercise program.

The diet should be approached with realistic expectations. You should accept that it is you, not the doctor or diet counselor, who is responsible for your own weight loss. Prepare yourself. Pick a time when you are emotionally stable, sufficiently motivated, and then educate yourself about the problem.

An array of fad diets flood the market every year, sowing

confusion among consumers. These diets offer simplistic solutions to complex problems. Advertisements promise they are "easy" and "guarantee success." When the diet fails, the consumer is left poorer and more frustrated than ever.

Fad diets don't work. There are no "secrets" about weight loss. Nothing is easy about losing weight and any diet that pretends otherwise is simply not credible. Many diets are based on misinformation and nutritional fallacies, rarely address behavioral problems, and sometimes even neglect to mention exercise. Worst of all, they may be nutritionally inadequate and even dangerous.

Fad diets come and go like the seasons of the year. Consumers apparently don't stop to realize that if any of them were truly effective, there would be no need for new ones.

Some of these diets emphasize one type of food, such as rice, grapefruit, bananas, or watermelon. Some concentrate on either carbohydrates or proteins, often excluding one entirely in favor of the other. Any low carbohydrate or low protein diet should be approached with caution, because both can lead to chemical imbalances.

Other diets target vegetables or fruits. Diet powders are also subject to fads, but the attrition rate is high for such products. If you can't live the rest of your life on the food recommended in the diet, it will most likely fail in the long run.

For this reason, low-calorie balanced diets are best. These are safe and nutritionally sound. The weight lost is primarily fat, rather than lean body tissue. The diets contain normal table foods from all of the major food groups. A good diet will educate the dieter in good eating habits, so that a desirable weight can be maintained for a lifetime.

Generally speaking, a weight-loss plan should follow these general guidelines:

1. Make sure it contains all the necessary nutrients, especially if it is a low-calorie diet of 2,000 calories or less. A vitamin and mineral supplement provides some insurance.
2. Reduce or eliminate alcohol consumption altogether, since alcohol is high in calories and provides no nutrients.
3. Review the junk foods you eat and replace them with other foods, such as raw vegetables, fruits, or juices. Stop between-

meal snacks of sweet or fatty foods, such as cookies, potato chips, candy, and soft drinks.

4. Reduce the calories in a diet by lowering its fat content because fats are high in calories and more easily converted to body fat. Instead, eat more complex carbohydrates found principally in starches, such as cereals, potatoes, tapioca, peas, and beans. Also, substitute foods high in fiber, found in whole grains, fruits, oatmeal, root vegetables, and beans.

5. Introduce an exercise program into your daily routine. Exercise combined with a diet attacks body fat from both directions, burning off more calories while taking in less.

6. Plan to consume more calories on one day, less on others. Eat more frequently but more carefully. Although many low-calorie diets recommend a certain number of calories, it is easier to stay on a diet if you add variety and alternate the number of calories from day to day.

Chronic dieting can be worse than not dieting at all, especially if a person loses the weight quickly, then regains it. This cycle is called the "yo-yo syndrome" because weight goes up and down. The problem is that rapid weight loss reduces lean body mass as well as fat, so when the weight is regained as fat, the body ends up with a higher percentage of fat. This not only makes future weight loss more difficult but threatens to make the person even fatter.

Given the complexity and pitfalls of weight loss, it is advisable to write down a strategy before adopting any diet. Record the foods you eat regularly, when you eat them, how much, and why. Add up the calories in these foods and determine your daily energy intake. How much do you need to cut back to lose two pounds a week? How much exercise do you need?

DIET PILLS

Many people who want to lose weight are searching for a magic pill. A variety of over-the-counter and prescription drugs is available on the market. Some of these drugs have the potential for abuse, especially amphetamines.

Behavioral Weight Control Techniques[a]

I. **Stimulus Control**
  A. Shopping:
   1. Shop for food after eating.
   2. Shop from a list.
   3. Avoid ready-to-eat foods.
   4. Don't carry more cash than needed for shopping list.
  B. Plans:
   1. Plan to limit food intake.
   2. Substitute exercise for snacking.
   3. Eat meals and snacks at scheduled times.
   4. Don't accept food offered by others.
  C. Activities:
   1. Store food out of sight.
   2. Eat all food in the same place.
   3. Remove food from inappropriate storage areas in the house.
   4. Keep serving dishes off the table.
   5. Use smaller dishes and utensils.
   6. Avoid being the food server.
   7. Leave the table immediately after eating.
   8. Don't save leftovers.
  D. Holidays and Parties:
   1. Drink fewer alcoholic beverages.
   2. Plan eating habits before parties.
   3. Eat a low-calorie snack before parties.
   4. Practice polite ways to decline food.
   5. Don't get discouraged by an occasional setback.

II. **Eating Behavior**
  A. Put the fork down between mouthfuls.
  B. Chew thoroughly before swallowing.
  C. Prepare foods one portion at a time.
  D. Leave some food on the plate.
  E. Pause in the middle of the meal.
  F. Do nothing else while eating, such as reading, watching television, etc.

III. **Reward**
   A. Solicit help from family and friends.
   B. Have family and friends provide this help in the form of praise and material rewards.
   C. Utilize self-monitoring records as basis for rewards.
   D. Plan specific rewards for specific behaviors (behavioral contracts).

IV. **Self-Monitoring**
   A. Keep diet diary that includes:
      1. Time and place of eating.
      2. Type and amount of food.
      3. Who is present and how you feel.

V. **Nutrition Education**
   A. Use diet diary to identify problem areas.
   B. Make small changes that you can continue.
   C. Learn nutritional values of foods.
   D. Decrease fat intake; increase complex carbohydrates.

VI. **Physical Activity**
   A. Routine Activity:
      1. Increase routine activity.
      2. Increase use of stairs.
      3. Keep a record of the distance walked every day.
   B. Exercise:
      1. Begin a very mild exercise program.
      2. Keep a record of daily exercise.
      3. Increase the exercise very gradually.

VII. **Cognitive Restructuring**
   A. Avoid setting unreasonable goals.
   B. Think about progress, not shortcomings.
   C. Avoid imperatives like "always" and "never."
   D. Counter negative thoughts with rational restatements.
   E. Set weight goals.

[a]From reference 13. Copyright 1985 American Society of Clinical Nutrition.

None of the drugs is particularly effective unless used in conjunction with an overall weight-loss program. Even then, results have been disappointing. Drug treatment for obesity is typically not recommended because the weight loss is short lived.

The most popular and widely marketed diet pills are the anorectic drugs, which suppress your appetite. One class of these drugs is commonly known as "speed," since it stimulates the central nervous system and may cause nervous agitation. This type of anorectic includes amphetamine, dextroamphetamine, methamphetamine, and other derivatives. All have the potential for addiction and abuse.

For the fatigued patient, the amphetamines have some undesirable side effects, such as insomnia, agitation, and panic states. Several other adverse effects may occur, including palpitations, rapid heartbeat, confusion, dry mouth, and unpleasant tastes.

Other types of anorectic or appetite suppressants include fenfluramine, mazindol, phentermine, and diethylpropion. Chronic use of these drugs is restricted because of side effects. For example, fenfluramine is a depressant and can induce sedation and mental depression. These also have the potential for abuse.

The effectiveness of the anorectic drugs has been found to be about the same, so most physicians prescribe the nonamphetamines. A review by the Federal Drug Administration (FDA) of clinical studies of the anorectic drugs found weight loss was negligible and "clinically trivial" when compared to diet alone.[14]

Many people eat without any hunger sensations, so suppression of the appetite isn't always as effective as one might think. Furthermore, the pills may give people the false idea that they can lose weight without changing their eating habits. Unless behavior changes, weight gain will result once the person stops taking the drug.

EXERCISING AND DIETING

As mentioned earlier, exercise can have a profound effect on expenditure of calories. Vigorous exercise, such as running, swimming, or bicycling, can increase a person's resting metabolic rate by six to eight times. Even when the number of calories expended in daily exercise is small, the impact on weight can be significant over weeks and months.

People abandon exercise programs as readily as diets, so integrating the exercise into a daily routine is essential. Prospects of success are best if the exercise is inexpensive, convenient, and enjoyable. Alternating the form of exercise—walking one day, bicycling the next—helps fend off boredom.

Once the weight has been lost, exercise helps maintain the loss. Individuals who expend 200 to 400 extra calories in daily physical activity have a good chance of keeping the weight off. This can sometimes be done with changes in the daily routine, such as parking farther away from work or climbing stairs instead of using an elevator.

Few dieticians believe a weight-loss plan can be effective without some exercise. Joined with a reducing diet and behavioral changes in eating, exercise provides greater flexibility to any weight-loss program. The diet can be less restrictive, for instance, allowing a person to eat more calories.

As we learned in Chapter Eight, exercise is an antidote to fatigue, depression, anxiety, and stress. If a person's obesity is linked to one of these negative emotions, then exercise plays a twofold role—removing the emotional cue as well as burning off excess calories.

Statistics show that the heavier people get, the less they exercise. Obese men and women walk about half as much as people of normal weight. They also spend more time in bed and less time on their feet.

Exercise increases the lean body mass, thus the body's proportion of metabolically active tissue. This raises the body's metabolic rate, which consumes more calories. Aerobic exercise also burns free fatty acids in the bloodstream before they can be converted to body fat.

Despite its advantages, exercise should not be viewed as a cure-all for obesity. Some critics even suggest that exercise plays only a marginal role in weight reduction. It is generally accepted that an average person must expend 3,500 calories to lose one pound. This would require a lot of exercise. For example, a 200-pound man would have to walk 35 miles to lose a single pound.

This strict formula is somewhat simplistic, however, since it neglects two crucial points. First, exercise increases the RMR for several hours after exercise ceases, burning up additional calories. Second, certain levels of exercise suppress the appetite and reduce caloric intake.

Exercise increases the metabolic rate—the rate at which the body uses energy for life functions—by 7.5 to 28 percent for four to six hours after exercise.[15] Such a postexercise metabolism burns 40 to 50 calories in addition to the calories expended during the activity.

In general, 15 extra calories are burned off for each 100 calories expended during exercise. This may seem like a small amount, but the daily loss of those extra 40 to 50 calories means a loss of four to five pounds over a year.

Additionally, certain levels of exercise suppress the appetite, reducing caloric intake. This occurs when the activity falls within a mild to moderate range. Appetite is stimulated, however, if the activity falls within a lower rate or if it is brief but strenuous.

Any person considering an exercise program should first consult a physician. Exercise poses special concerns for people who are severely overweight. Any weight-bearing exercise could cause this special group problems with feet, legs, and lower back. Heat and humidity also present special dangers, particularly dehydration and heat stroke.

Despite the potential problems, the overweight individual has much to benefit from a regular exercise program that is properly planned. The physician can best assist in selecting the proper exercise and determining the rate of increase in intensity. Any program should begin at a reasonable level and build slowly.

Exercise is most effective if it replaces sedentary activities, such as watching television. This brings us to the third element in weight loss—behavioral changes.

CHANGING BEHAVIOR FOR WEIGHT CONTROL

Behavior modification is an essential part of any weight-control program. Its principles focus on the whole person's life-style to change adverse behaviors that contribute to obesity and replace them with positive ones.

Fatigue is usually only one of several factors in someone's life-style that triggers overeating. Exhausted by the hectic pace of living, many people turn to food for reassurance or for a pick-me-up. Over time, this behavior leads to obesity, more fatigue, and more over-eating.

Behavioral treatment concentrates on these cues that stimulate overeating. Food behavior is a product of many life experiences and attitudes that are deeply rooted in personality. Changing them requires a broad approach.

The techniques used in behavior modification aim at control of all actions related to food—shopping, storage, meal preparation, kitchen cleanup, holiday meals, eating styles, and nutritional knowl-edge. The treatment includes exercise components, social support, and methods to change negative attitudes about weight control.

Behavioral approaches incorporate both diet and exercise, inte-grating them into a program designed to alter the person's emotional relationship with food. Early behavioral programs emphasized con-trol of things that stimulated appetite as well as ways to monitor eating behavior. More recent techniques incorporate positive rein-forcement and cognitive restructuring.

Stimulus Control

This refers to control of cues or triggers so that a positive outcome is more probable. The dieter does certain things to influence a positive result. Techniques might include shopping with a list, not shopping when hungry, not eating while doing other activities, eating from smaller plates, storing food out of sight, pausing during a meal, putting down a fork between bites, and drinking sips of water after swallowing.

Self-Monitoring

The dieter is urged to keep a careful watch on himself or herself and write down everything he or she eats. This information can be used to compute calories. Time and place of eating are sometimes noted along with meal partners and the feelings associated with the meal. This practice helps the dieter and counselor identify problems.

Positive Reinforcement

This aspect offers social support and provides encouragement for change. A person might buy himself or herself small gifts after reaching certain goals, for example. Family members and friends should be enlisted to provide praise and recognition of success. Other social supports, such as group meetings, are part of many commercial programs.

Cognitive Restructuring

Cognitive restructuring in this case means changing the way people think about food and obesity. Setting realistic goals, avoiding unreasonable expectations, and challenging negative thinking are recommended. This technique has much in common with cognitive psychotherapy discussed in the chapter on depression.

The emphasis of the behavioral approach is on changing eating habits. The diet itself is modest, perhaps 1,500 to 2,000 calories, depending on sex, age, and body frame. The usual advice is to eat regular meals and smaller portions rather than specific types of foods. This allows the dieter to eat with the family and requires no special foods or preparation.

The idea of changing habits for both eating and physical activity is integral to the behavioral approach. As we stated earlier, exercise burns off fatty tissue, rather than lean muscle, and expends extra calories. It also improves mood, so exercise is especially helpful for "emotional eaters." But the attrition rate for exercise is high. Only about half of those who start an exercise program continue for six months or more.

Maintenance of weight loss also gets special attention in the behavioral treatment of obesity. Exercise may help maintain weight. Not only does exercise burn off extra calories, but some research indicates it may reset a person's normal weight. Whether or not this is true, individuals who continue exercise after weight loss have more success at maintaining their new weight over the long term.

Other factors identified as important for weight maintenance are: continued self-monitoring, social support from spouse, absence of stressful life events, and setting a specific weight limit at which control strategies would be reinstated.

Behavioral approaches take into consideration that, at some point, a person is going to regain some weight. A strategy should be developed to deal with the relapse early on rather than later, after the behavior has gotten out of control. If viewed as a single episode rather than a complete failure, corrective action can be taken and the dieter can return to the earlier weight-control strategies.

CONCLUSION

Tired people eat on the run. Fast foods, TV dinners, and snacks become tempting conveniences. Exhausted at the end of the day, the last thing these people want to do is exercise. The result is more excess calories to store as body fat.

Imagine carrying around the equivalent of a soldier's field pack all day. No wonder obesity breeds inactivity. Climbing stairs becomes a dreaded challenge and even bending over to tie your shoes is an effort. Physical fitness is a wistful, distant hope. Demoralized and unhappy, the obese become vulnerable to depression, anxiety, and poor self-esteem.

To change this course requires motivation, knowledge, and support. By far the most effective treatment has been a combination of a reducing diet, exercise, and behavior modification.

This approach can parallel an individualized program to reduce fatigue. Both require basic changes in life-style. As changes occur, new sources of vitality can be tapped. Regular exercise, a balanced diet, and enhanced self-esteem not only reduce weight but fatigue as well.

Obesity is usually not the only factor causing fatigue, but for some people it may be the most important. Losing weight for these individuals should be the first order of business.

CHAPTER TEN

VITAMINS AND MINERALS
A PILL FOR FATIGUE?

INTRODUCTION

Few topics have been subject to as much quackery, myth, misinformation, falsehoods, and abuse as that of vitamin and mineral supplements. The claims for these vital nutrients range from cures for cancer and the common cold to enhanced sexual prowess and even prevention or reversal of the aging process. There seems to be a vitamin or mineral for everything that ails us, whether it's baldness, sunburn, obesity, or varicose veins. Invariably, fatigue can be found on this list of ailments, which continues to grow infinitely.

Americans who must cope with the pace of modern life look longingly at these claims, tempted by the simplicity of the solution— just take a pill and forget it. Unfortunately, unless a person has a vitamin or mineral deficiency, supplements are not likely to help much, if at all. One of the most persistent myths is that vitamins give a person "pep" and "energy." This is not true for healthy people. Vitamins have no calories to charge the body with energy. They provide no extra vitality unless the person has a specific deficiency.

A person with a vitamin or mineral deficiency may suffer chronic fatigue along with a host of other symptoms, but the deficiency may be only one of several factors contributing to the tiredness. Eliminating the deficiency by itself will not necessarily cure the fatigue. An underlying cause—smoking, alcoholism, stress, poor diet, or malabsorption—may need to be corrected as well.

Vitamin requirements are influenced by many of the things that cause fatigue, such as coffee, drugs, cigarettes, alcohol, oral contraceptives, and emotional problems. All of these increase the body's requirements for certain vitamins or minerals. Any combination of these other factors and a vitamin or mineral deficiency can cause severe fatigue.

A vitamin supplement, however, should not be approached as a panacea. Many health care professionals, particularly nutritionists, dismiss most claims for supplements as unscientific, inexact, or even downright dangerous. They warn of the hazards associated with taking large doses of vitamins and minerals, while urging consumers to eat balanced meals for all of their nutrients.

In politics, honorable men may disagree, but medical issues are supposed to be black and white, right or wrong. At least that is the public's perception. The truth is that medical experts are just as likely to disagree as politicians. This certainly seems to be the case with recommendations on supplements.

Vitamins and minerals are essential for good health. Nobody disputes this central precept of good nutrition. The great debate centers on the proper dose and the best way for people to obtain it. Determining the correct dose for individuals is not as easy as it might appear, the ubiquity of the United States recommended daily allowances (RDAs) notwithstanding.

In terms of dosage, one school adopts the philosophy that if something is good, then a lot of it must be better, and even more must be even better. This sort of logic has given rise to a $2 billion food supplement industry in the United States. This megavitamin school often recommends ten times or more the RDA dosage.

Another school espouses a different well-established principle of pharmacology. This idea, promoted more than four centuries ago by Paracelsus, the Swiss-born alchemist and physician, simply states, "All substances are poisons; there is none which is not a poison. The right dose differentiates a poison and a remedy."

The consumer is left to wonder if vitamin and mineral supplements are cure-alls or poisons. The conflicting information given by respected physicians and nutritionists has left people frustrated and confused. Guidelines from the government in the form of RDAs have only intensified the debate, even while providing a convenient standard over which to argue.

For proper health, it is important to strike a balance between two extremes—a deficiency on the one hand and toxicity on the other. Both conditions can cause fatigue and a number of other health problems.

Iron, or the lack of it, is a good illustration of the dilemma faced by consumers. Iron is commonly associated with fatigue because an iron deficiency can lead to anemia. Iron supplements are widely advertised as invigorating and healthful. The public is largely unaware, however, that 2,000 cases of iron poisoning are reported in the United States each year. Given the wide availability of iron supplements, this should not be surprising. Megadoses of iron supplements can cause diarrhea, constipation, drowsiness, and vomiting.

In search of answers for their fatigue, people should not expect to find miracles in a bottle of vitamins if they are otherwise healthy. Any healthy person who eats a varied diet composed of the basic food groups should never need a vitamin supplement.

That said, there are millions of others who may need additional vitamins and minerals, either because of illness, pregnancy, or a lifestyle that includes coffee, alcohol, cigarettes, or other things that increase the requirement for certain vitamins.

Deficiencies in a number of vitamins and minerals will cause fatigue and weakness. National studies have found that millions of Americans do not obtain the RDA for one or more vitamins or minerals. The effects of a minor and prolonged deficiency are not well understood and are the subject of conflicting evidence.

If you suspect that you have a deficiency, the simplest thing to do is to ask your doctor for a blood test to determine the levels of vitamins and minerals in your system. Then your doctor can recommend the appropriate dose of vitamin or mineral supplements if they are needed.

Serious vitamin deficiency diseases are rare today in the United States. Rickets, beriberi, scurvy, and pellagra, for example, have been virtually wiped out in the United States, but in other parts of the world, vitamin deficiencies continue to claim many lives each year, most of them children.

Between 40 and 50 percent of all Americans use vitamin supplements on a regular basis. Doctors are rarely consulted, so the practice is a form of self-medication. Vitamin supplements generally have all the RDA for each vitamin or mineral, although some contain much more.

In terms of quantity, the healthy body needs only tiny amounts of vitamins or minerals. The amount is so small that we use the microgram (μg) as the unit of measurement. The μg has replaced International Units (IU) as the form of measurement for most vitamins. The IU is a measure of a material needed to create a certain biological effect that has been agreed upon internationally, so the quantity varies from one vitamin to another. It continues to be used sometimes for vitamins A, D, and E, although these vitamins are increasingly represented in μg. A μg is one millionth of a gram. An ounce has 28.4 grams or 28.4 million micrograms. The adult RDA for vitamin D is 10 μg, so an ounce would supply the recommended daily allowance for 2.84 million adults.

For a proper, healthful diet, it is helpful to understand the different types of vitamins and minerals, why each is important, in which foods and in what quantities they can be found, and the dangers of deficiency and toxicity. Armed with this information, a consumer should be able to plan meals that contain all the necessary nutrients.

TYPES OF VITAMINS

Vitamins are not foods. They are chemicals found in foods that act as catalysts and allow the body to utilize food, turning it into energy. Vitamins fall into two categories—oil- or fat-soluble and water-soluble.

The four fat-soluble vitamins are A, D, E, and K. These dissolve in fats and are absorbed in the intestine along with fats and lipids in foods. They are stored in the body longer than their water-soluble cousins. The liver, for example, stores enough vitamin A for a year.

Water-soluble vitamins are excreted from the body in urine and waste. They are more fragile than fat-soluble vitamins and are damaged or destroyed by cooking. The water-soluble vitamins are ascorbic acid (vitamin C) and the B complex, which includes thiamine (B_1), riboflavin (B_2), niacin, pyridoxine (B_6), cobalamin (B_{12}), biotin, pantothenic acid, and folic acid.

Fat-Soluble Vitamins

More danger is associated with megadoses of the fat-soluble than water-soluble vitamins, particularly A and D, which are more readily stored than E and K. The two vitamins, A and E, along with C, are the most likely to be taken in excessive doses, apparently because of the popular myths surrounding these particular vitamins.

Vitamin A

Fatigue may be caused by too much or too little vitamin A. Deficiency can cause a general debility and a loss of resistance to infection.

Vitamin A deficiency is rare in the United States, because manufacturers use it as an additive in milk and butter. Vitamin A is derived from two sources: carotene, a pigment in vegetables and fruits, which the body converts into vitamin A, and retinol, which is vitamin A that has been converted and stored by animals in such foods as liver, eggs, and milk. Unlike retinol, carotene is virtually nontoxic.

The RDA for vitamin A is 4,000 IU for women and 5,000 IU for men and pregnant women. The IU for vitamin A is equal to 0.30 μg of retinol or 0.60 μg of β-carotene. An egg contains about 260 IU, a tablespoon of margarine has 470 IU, a cup of orange juice has 270 IU, and an apple has 120 IU. A cup of tomato juice provides 1,940 IU and a whole carrot has about 7,500 IU.

One of the paradoxes of vitamin A is that toxicity and deficiency frequently share the same symptoms, including fatigue. Other signs of deficiency are dry eyes, rough skin, nightblindness, hair loss, and faulty tooth and bone development.

Toxic side effects include fatigue, headache, anemia, weakness, dizziness, vomiting, liver damage, sleepiness, and sluggishness.

Other signs of overdose include nausea, fever, sweating, and peeling of the skin. Signs of toxicity usually appear only with sustained daily intake, including food and supplements, exceeding 50,000 IU in adults and 20,000 IU in infants and young children. Single doses of one million IU in adults have resulted in only transient side effects.[1]

While oral contraceptives deplete the body of some vitamins, they increase the amount of vitamin A in the blood. Even so, present research indicates that women taking the pill can safely use multi-vitamins with the usual dose of 5,000 IU without suffering harmful effects.

Smokers metabolize vitamin A at a faster rate than nonsmokers, putting them at greater risk of deficiency. A Norwegian study found that smokers with lower vitamin A levels were three times more likely to contract cancer than other smokers with adequate levels of the vitamin. This is one reason that the American Cancer Society recommends a diet high in vitamin A, particularly for those people at risk for lung cancer. Researchers have found that vitamin A makes laboratory animals more resistant to cancers of the skin, bladder, and breast. Unfortunately, no similar evidence exists for humans.

Alcohol abuse can also cause deficiencies in vitamin A, since the liver must synthesize large amounts of the alcohol, impairing its ability to process retinol, a form of the vitamin.

Vitamin D

Like vitamin A, the symptoms of deficiency and toxicity for vitamin D are frequently similar. Both may cause fatigue. However, there is greater danger from too much vitamin D than from too little, though too little can harm the body.

Vitamin D aids in the absorption of calcium and phosphorus in forming bone and teeth. Natural sources of vitamin D are canned fish, liver, butter, and egg yolk, as well as a host of fortified foods, such as milk, cereals, and cocoa. Vitamin D is often called the "sunshine vitamin," because it is synthesized in the skin from the ultraviolet rays of the sun.

The RDA for adults and children is 400 IU. Without fortified foods, people eating a proper diet would only receive about 100 to 150

IU daily. An egg yolk contains 35 IU, a cup of fortified milk has 100 IU, four ounces of liver has 34 IU, and one ounce of dry fortified cereals has 40 IU.

A deficiency is most frequently seen in children and the elderly. Besides fatigue, other symptoms are insomnia, stress, and nervousness. A severe deficiency will cause rickets, which is a deformation of the skeletal structure, marked by bowed legs and a deformed spine.

Toxic doses are potentially lethal. The toxic amount is highly individualized and has been variably reported as between 50,000 to 300,000 IU daily. Early signs of toxicity include fatigue, weakness, dry mouth, headache, vague muscle pains, and a metallic taste in the mouth. Other symptoms include hypertension, weight loss, vomiting, anorexia, and the formation of kidney stones.

Vitamin E

Fatigue is more apt to be caused by toxicity to vitamin E than by a deficiency, although the published research on the vitamin has presented conflicting evidence.

Vitamin E acts as an antioxidant that prevents oxygen from destroying other chemicals in the body, including vitamin A. Many other functions have been ascribed to vitamin E as well, but these have not received wide acceptance. Vitamin E has been the subject of many exulted, but as yet unsubstantiated, claims about sexual potency, baldness, longevity, and heart disease, among others.

The RDA for vitamin E is 10 mg for men and 8 mg for women. Vitamin E is commonly found in polyunsaturated oils and margarine, including products derived from corn, safflower, or soybeans. Other sources include egg yolk, beans, wheat germ, leafy vegetables, and whole grains. A tablespoon of corn oil contains 11.3 mg of the vitamin, slightly less than soybean oil. A quarter cup of roasted almonds contains 8.3 mg, roasted pecans 5.8 mg, and sunflower seeds 12.3 mg.

Vitamin E is so common in our diet that deficiency is unlikely. Some studies have indicated that the vitamin may help combat premenstrual syndrome and it has been used therapeutically for menopause symptoms. Other research has found improvement in the depression of elderly women who have taken vitamin E supplements.

Some anecdotal evidence indicates that megadoses of vitamin E may cause fatigue. At least two small studies have found that fatigue and weakness occurred in some people with daily doses as low as 800 IU. Other reports have linked similar doses to depression, withdrawal, mood swings, and tiredness.

On the other hand, some research has found no link between fatigue and vitamin E supplements. In some cases, experts counsel that megadoses of vitamin E may even alleviate fatigue and depression. This is a minority view, however, and is not widely accepted in the medical community.

Vitamin E may be helpful to smokers, because it can assist in blocking the formation of nitrosamines, some of which are powerful carcinogens that develop from the compounds in tobacco smoke.

The Food and Nutrition Board of the National Academy of Sciences opposes the use of supplements of vitamin E for healthy individuals but has found little harm in doses of 400 to 1,000 IU daily for most people. There is no established toxic level for vitamin E, but therapeutic doses recommended by nutritionists do not exceed 150 mg a day.

Water-Soluble Vitamins

The water-soluble vitamins dissolve in water and are not stored in the body for more than a few days, so frequent or daily replenishment is important. The only exception is B_{12}, found in meats, which is stored in the liver for several years.

Water-soluble vitamins are more vulnerable to heat and cooking, which may destroy them, so special care must be taken in preparation of foods containing these nutrients. For example, vegetables that are steamed will retain more of these vitamins, than those that are boiled.

Because excess doses of the water-soluble vitamins are easily passed through the urine, the risks of toxicity are much less, although overdoses can have serious health consequences in specific cases. These vitamins also obscure certain laboratory tests, particularly in the case of vitamin C, which masks tests for sugar in urine specimens.

Vitamin C

Vitamin C is a critically important vitamin and severe deficiencies will, among other things, cause tiredness, weakness, depression, and a loss of appetite.

The most famous of the water-soluble vitamins, vitamin C or ascorbic acid is also the most popular among consumers, who continue to buy supplements of the vitamin in record amounts. Unlike other vitamins, vitamin C is virtually nontoxic.

Vitamin C helps heal wounds, reduces vulnerability to infections, facilitates absorption of iron, helps form teeth and bones, produces collagen, and performs other vital functions.

The adult RDA for vitamin C is 60 mg. It is found in many fruits and vegetables, including cantaloupe, watermelon, citrus fruits, cucumbers, strawberries, peas, beans, lettuce, and radishes. An orange contains about 80 mg; a grapefruit has 76 mg; a baked potato has 20 mg; and a banana has 12 mg.

Vitamin C has been described as an antidote to fatigue because it helps the body absorb iron. Several studies have documented this over the years. One sample study found that 80 percent of those suffering from scurvy were also anemic, indicating that anemia might involve a combination of deficiencies in iron and vitamin C. In any case, the vitamin's contributions to fighting iron deficiency anemia are well established.

Vitamin C is the subject of various health claims. One of the most famous has been made by Dr. Linus Pauling, a two-time Nobel laureate, in his book *Vitamin C and the Common Cold*, in which he recommends 1 to 5 grams a day to reduce the incidence and severity of cold symptoms. Unfortunately, other studies by equally qualified scientists have never been able to corroborate this research claim.

Other hopes for vitamin C have also gone unfulfilled. Research has never verified various claims that vitamin C enhances athletic performance, improves memory, alertness, or concentration, despite suggestions to the contrary.

The classic symptom of deficiency is scurvy, which develops within 60 to 90 days of total elimination of vitamin C. Fatigue and lassitude are symptoms of this disease, a fact that has led some researchers to theorize that even minor deficiencies of vitamin C may cause fatigue by causing a "miniscurvy." The body maintains a pool of 1,500 mg of vitamin C and the scurvy develops when the level drops below 350 mg.

People who smoke are more vulnerable to deficiency, since their bodies use more vitamin C. Smoking one cigarette breaks down about 25 mg of the vitamin, which may explain why smokers have been found to have 30 to 50 percent less vitamin C in their blood than nonsmokers. Some researchers consider heavy smokers to be in a chronic state of subclinical scurvy, which means the scurvy is not advanced enough to be detected by the usual clinical tests.

Large doses of vitamin C are lost during periods of stress and trauma, so special care should be taken to safeguard deficiency at such times. The adrenal gland releases large quantities of vitamin C during stress along with stress hormones norepinephrine and epinephrine, which were formerly known as noradrenaline and adrenaline, respectively. It is not clear what vitamin C has to do with the stress reaction, but it is known that stress increases demand for the vitamin. Trauma also increases demand, particularly with infections, burns, and major surgical operations. Chronic use of aspirins, barbiturates, and oral contraceptives as well as cigarette smoking also deplete body stores of vitamin C.

Dr. Pauling, a tireless advocate of megadoses of vitamin C, recommends a minimum of 240 mg a day for stress. After major surgery, daily intake of vitamin C may be 1,000 mg or more a day.

Since vitamin C is virtually nontoxic, dangers of overdose are minimal compared to those of the fat-soluble vitamins. But megadoses have caused diarrhea in some people, as well as nausea and abdominal cramps, and may interfere with vitamin B_{12} absorption, creating a deficiency. Some evidence exists that megadoses may also cause the formation of kidney stones. Furthermore, a dependency develops if megadoses of vitamin C are taken over prolonged periods, making adjustment to smaller doses difficult later.

The debate over the benefits of vitamin C is likely to continue for a long time. One thing is clear, more research needs to be done to uncover the possible benefits of this most interesting vitamin.

The B-Complex

The B-Complex refers to a group of water-soluble vitamins that performs a host of vital metabolic functions in the human body. They work together with the various enzyme systems that break down carbohydrates, proteins, and fats. The B vitamins are closely involved in the mechanisms that release energy, carbon dioxide, and water as the by-products of our metabolism.

Rarely will a person suffer a deficiency of only one of the B vitamins. When one is low, others are generally low as well.

Thiamine

Sometimes called the morale vitamin, a deficiency of thiamine (vitamin B_1) will cause fatigue, depression, insomnia, irritability, loss of interest in work, and a loss of stamina. All these symptoms may present themselves within 10 days of a deficiency.

As is true of other B vitamins, thiamine is a coenzyme that is central to the metabolism of carbohydrates, fats, and proteins. Its coenzyme action produces energy from glucose. Thiamine is, therefore, crucial in providing the energy necessary for the normal functions of the brain, nerves, muscles, and heart. A deficiency impairs the central nervous system, reducing alertness and reflex reactions, which results in general fatigue and apathy.

The RDA is 1.5 mg for men and 1 mg for women. Thiamine can be stored in the body for about 10 days and is available from a wide range of foods, including nuts, wheat germ, potatoes, liver, beef, peanuts, brown rice, molasses, and fish. A slice of wheat bread contains .09 mg, equivalent to a half cup of brown rice. Three ounces of turkey have .04 mg compared with .78 mg for the same amount of pork. A cup of orange juice has .22 mg.

As with vitamin C, thiamine is virtually nontoxic. Doses as high as 500 mg a day have been taken by adults for up to a month with no symptoms of toxicity. Allergic reactions to thiamine are also rare.

The chief symptom of severe deficiency of B_1 is beriberi, a disease that affects the nerves, heart, and intestines. Beriberi is rare in the United States, although some of its early symptoms involving the gastrointestinal system are reported each year. Among these symptoms are anorexia, indigestion, constipation, and a lower secretion of hydrochloric acid because glands and muscles do not receive sufficient glucose to provide the energy they need to perform their work. In later stages, the nervous and cardiovascular systems are also impaired because of this lack of energy, eventually causing paralysis and cardiac failure.

Drinking alcoholic beverages increases the need for vitamin B_1 and niacin (B_3), because alcohol destroys some of these two B vitamins and impedes the body's ability to absorb them. Vitamins A and D are also affected because of the impaired functioning of the liver caused by alcohol abuse.

Alcohol is burned as a carbohydrate, but unlike other carbohydrates, it contains no B_1 to replace the B_1 used to metabolize it. This makes alcoholics more susceptible to Wernicke-Korsakoff Syndrome, sometimes called cerebral beriberi, which is a neurological disorder caused by a B_1 deficiency. Symptoms of the syndrome include disorientation, apathy, and jerky, rhythmical movements of the eyes. If a person is a heavy drinker, the need for some sort of vitamin supplement might be advised by his or her physician, since such a person often eats poorly anyway, compounding the risk of a deficiency of this important vitamin.

Others who are vulnerable to B_1 deficiency are the elderly, junk food eaters, drug addicts, and the chronically ill, primarily because of their diets. Athletes are also susceptible because intensive physical exercise increases the requirement for B_1 because of the increase in the body's use of glucose for energy.

Tannic acid or tannin, a substance used in tanning animal skins, destroys thiamine in the body. The acid is a natural component of tea. A quart of tea will eliminate up to twice the RDA of thiamine. The same amount of coffee taken within a three-hour period has been shown to eliminate more than half of the body's stores of thiamine. Decaffeinated coffee has the same effect, since it is not the caffeine, but the chloregenic acid, a crystalline acid found in the coffee bean and other plants, that causes the problem. Heavy coffee drinkers should be extra vigilant for B-vitamin deficiency and take supplements, if advised by their physician.

Thiamine is very significant to the brain and central nervous system. Both systems are dependent on the assistance of thiamine to metabolize glucose for energy, so they are seriously affected by deficiencies of thiamine.

Several studies have found mild deficiencies among many Americans, particularly the elderly. A deficiency is generally determined by a biochemical test. These tests have found thiamine deficiency in 10 to 35 percent of the American elderly tested. It is thought that the thiamine deficiency may contribute to mental confusion among the elderly.

Riboflavin

Deficiency of riboflavin or vitamin B_2 has been associated with fatigue and depression for years. Several studies at mental hospitals have actually found lower levels of riboflavin in patients suffering from depression.

Riboflavin is vital for the metabolism of protein, so any condition requiring more protein increases the requirement for this vitamin. It is essential for healthy eyes and for the transport of hydrogen in the body.

Vitamin B_2 is found in a wide range of foods, including spinach, nuts, peas, beans, milk, whole wheat, eggs, cheese, liver, leafy vegetables, and dried fruits. The adult RDA for riboflavin is 1.7 mg. A cup of cottage cheese has .60 mg; an orange or half a cup of orange juice has .10 mg; a slice of enriched bread has .05 mg; and a cup of milk or yogurt has .40 mg.

Some of this vitamin will be lost in cooking, particularly when vegetables are boiled rather than steamed. Riboflavin in wheat is lost when processed for flour and must be restored by a supplement. Fortifying bread with B_2 is a widespread practice in the American food industry and a policy that has proved very effective in reducing B_2 deficiencies. This vitamin breaks down when exposed to sunlight, which is why supplements are stored in dark brown bottles.

Riboflavin is so abundant in foods that severe deficiencies are rare, although studies have consistently shown that many Americans have mild deficiencies. A mild deficiency may appear first with symptoms involving the eyes. Eyestrain, sensitivity to light, and itching around the eyes are frequent symptoms. More serious deficiencies include anemia, cracks in the lips, sores around the mouth, and scaly skin.

Orthomolecular psychiatry has linked vitamin B_2 deficiencies with depression and fatigue. A British study of a psychiatric unit at a general hospital found that about 25 percent of the patients admitted had B_2 deficiencies. Many of these patients suffered from depression. In controlled studies of patients treated with a riboflavin-deficient diet, lethargy and depression were among the first symptoms to show themselves. It took about two weeks for all psychiatric symptoms to disappear once a normal diet was resumed.

The use of oral contraceptives increases the need for B_2 and other B vitamins because estrogen drugs must be detoxified by the liver, a process that requires B vitamins. Several reports have linked B_2-deficiency to the Pill. One study found that half of the women on the Pill were deficient in B_2—a percentage that was even higher among those who had taken the Pill for three years or more.

Toxicity from B_2 is considered unlikely because excess amounts are excreted through the urine, giving it a bright yellow color. Furthermore, the capacity of the gastrointestinal tract to absorb the vitamin is limited.

Niacin, Nicotinic Acid

Fatigue is one of the early signs of a deficiency of niacin or vitamin B_3. Other symptoms include insomnia, stress, agitation, headache, and depression. Supplements usually resolve these symptoms quickly.

Niacin has a primary role in cellular respiration and the ability of cells to use nutrients. It releases energy to the body by enabling the oxidation of glucose.

Niacin is one of the most stable vitamins. It is abundant in lean meats, peas, beans, fish, liver, milk, poultry, cheese, peanuts, and leafy green vegetables. The RDA is 29 mg for adults. A prepared cup of frozen peas and a baked potato both contain 2.7 mg. A cup of broccoli has 1.2 mg and a cup of asparagus has 2.0 mg. Three ounces of tuna have 10.1 mg, compared to about 20 mg for the same amount of hamburger.

The body also gets niacin from foods and by converting tryptophan, an amino acid commonly found in milk, bananas, turkey, and natural cheese. Roughly 60 mg of tryptophan in the diet converts to 1 mg of niacin.

Niacin is widely used by physicians to treat heart disease and mental illness. In the form of nicotinic acid, supplements of niacin reduce triglycerides, sometimes called neutral fats, as well as cholesterol levels in the blood, thereby reducing the risk of heart disease.

Severe deficiency of niacin causes pellagra, a disease characterized by depression, psychosis, dementia, diarrhea, and skin disorders. Pellagra, Italian for "rough skin," spread in epidemic proportions in the southern United States during the 1930s, when the average diet was heavy in corn and fatback, a type of pork. A national effort to fortify corn and flour with the vitamin virtually eliminated this disease.

Schizophrenia has some of the same symptoms as pellagra, which has prompted some orthomolecular psychiatrists to prescribe niacin in large doses to treat schizophrenia. The association between pellagra and schizophrenia, if any, has not yet been identified.

Alcoholics, drug addicts, and individuals eating poor diets are the most susceptible to niacin deficiencies. People under extraordinary stress, such as patients recovering from surgery or extensive burns, are also at risk.

Women who are pregnant or breast-feeding are at increased risk for deficiencies in one or more vitamins, including niacin, riboflavin, folic acid, and pyridoxine. The additional demands for growth of fetal tissue and losses of vitamins through milk are enough to insure that the mother will be low in one vitamin and, likely, low in others. As a result, most physicians recommend multivitamin supplements during pregnancy and lactation.

Large doses of niacin should not be taken without medical supervision, because megadoses may cause an irregular heartbeat as well as flushing, itching, hair loss, peptic ulcer, nausea, and a burning sensation in the hands and face.

Vitamin B$_6$

Deficiency of vitamin B$_6$ has long been associated with fatigue, but it can also be a symptom of toxicity. Other symptoms of deficiency include depression, weight loss, dizziness, nausea, and sometimes severe nerve disorders.

Vitamin B$_6$ is the common name for three vitamins—pyridoxine, pyridoxal, and pyridoxamine. The three work together to enhance the formation of niacin from tryptophan. Vitamin B$_6$ is essential for the proper functioning of the nervous system and the cells of the brain.

B$_6$ is found in liver, potatoes, red meats, corn, green leafy vegetables, bananas, eggs, milk, poultry, and whole grain cereals. The RDA is 2 mg for adults. A small banana has .50 mg; a medium potato has .20 mg; a half cup of tomato juice .20 mg; a cup of milk .10 mg; and an egg has .05 mg.

For people suffering from chronic fatigue, supplements may help if they are deficient in B$_6$. A British study in 1957 found improvement in people suffering from chronic fatigue after they were given 20 mg of pyridoxine a day for a week.

Depression has been found in patients with low levels of B$_6$. Research at the Virginia Polytechnic Institute found that levels were 48 percent lower in depressed patients, although the study group was a small one. Vitamin B$_6$ may also ease depression in women taking oral contraceptives, which deplete this vitamin. Women with a history of depression or premenstrual depression that becomes worse after taking the Pill, are especially likely to benefit from B$_6$ supplements. Several studies have found that the vitamin improves mood and relieves headaches for those experiencing PMS.

Megadoses of the vitamin—10 times or more the recommended daily allowance—may cause serious side effects, including fatigue, headaches, bloatedness, and sensory neuropathy, a disease accompanied by numbness and tingling in the limbs. Modest doses—80 to 200 mg a day—have not presented any adverse side effects. A seven-year study of 600 women, which concluded in 1985, found these doses to be safe and effective for treating premenstrual syndrome.

Fatigue caused by iron-deficiency anemia may also respond to B$_6$ supplements. A deficiency of B$_6$ may indirectly cause this form of anemia because the vitamin is necessary to produce hemoglobin. The usual symptoms are fatigue, shortness of breath, and muscle weakness.

Given its serious toxic effects in high doses, consumers should be careful about taking supplements of B$_6$. As with any drug, reactions vary depending on the individual.

Folic Acid

Marginal deficiencies of folic acid cause irritability, fatigue, and a sleep disorder known as restless leg syndrome in which the sleeper is awakened by violent spasms in the legs. If a deficiency worsens, anemia occurs with related symptoms of exhaustion and depression.

Folic acid is essential for normal metabolism of food into energy. It is also important for the maturation of red blood cells, synthesis of DNA, and promotion of cell growth. As one of the least stable vitamins, it can be easily destroyed in cooking, so nutritionists recommend raw vegetables as the best source.

Folic acid is best found in green leafy vegetables, or broccoli, asparagus, dry beans, fish, beef, soybeans, peanuts, liver, and whole wheat. The adult RDA is 0.4 mg. A medium orange or half a cup of orange juice has 70 μg; a half cup of cooked broccoli has 50 μg; an egg has 25 μg; and half a cup of peanuts has 70 μg.

This vitamin is not considered toxic, even at high doses, but some people have reported irritability, sleeping problems, nervousness, and excitability caused by doses hundreds of times the RDA.

Folic acid plays a vital role in the formation of heme, which carries iron in the red blood cells. A severe deficiency of folic acid will cause either megalocytic or megaloblastic anemia. Symptoms of this type of anemia include diarrhea, depression, fatigue, drowsiness, pallor, and a slow pulse.

A number of studies have found lower folic acid levels in the blood of psychiatric patients. One study of mental patients found that folic acid supplements shortened hospital stays for patients with depression and schizophrenia.

Alcohol interferes with the absorption of folic acid and may contribute to a deficiency. Oral contraceptives, aspirin, barbiturates, and anticonvulsant medicines also may interfere with absorption.

Cobalamin

Pernicious anemia, accompanied by severe fatigue, is the result of a deficiency of cobalamin (B_{12}), since this vitamin is essential for proper formation of red blood cells. Pernicious anemia is usually not caused by an inadequate diet but is the result of a lack of intrinsic factor—a gastric secretion required to absorb B_{12}. Symptoms of this anemia include fatigue, general weakness, diarrhea, depression, drowsiness, irritability, and pallor.

Vitamin B_{12}, or cobalamin, is unique among the B-complex vitamins because it is extremely rare in plants, but is commonly found in meats or animal products. It works with folic acid in the synthesis of DNA and facilitates the growth of cells.

B_{12} is necessary for the normal development of red blood cells and the functioning of cells in bone marrow, the nervous system, and intestines. The body can store an adequate supply of B_{12} in the liver for up to five years, so severe deficiencies are rare.

Abundant sources of B_{12} include liver, eggs, tuna fish, shellfish, meats, poultry, milk, cheese, and fish. The RDA is 3 μg. An egg contains 1 μg; a cup of milk has 1 μg; and 3 ounces of beef or lamb have 2 μg.

Other than allergic reactions, no toxic side effects from megadoses of this vitamin have been identified. Injections of B_{12} as high as 10,000 times the RDA have not produced adverse effects.

Most deficiencies of B_{12} have been linked to a lack of intrinsic factor, a substance secreted by the stomach that allows the body to absorb the vitamin. The elderly are more susceptible to this condition, because the body's ability to secrete intrinsic factor diminishes with age. A study in Denmark several years ago found that one in three patients admitted to a geriatric center had low levels of B_{12}, a situation that can be remedied easily by vitamin supplements or adjustments in a diet to increase intake of animal products.

Besides problems associated with intrinsic factor, certain substances interfere with absorption of B_{12}, particularly alcohol, oral contraceptives, and certain compounds in tobacco smoke.

Orthomolecular psychiatrists have found that some psychological disorders occur years before the appearance of pernicious anemia as the supply of B_{12} is slowly depleted. Dementia, paranoia, hallucinations, appetite loss, diarrhea, and depression are among the psychological symptoms observed among mental patients with low B_{12} levels, even though there was no evidence of pernicious anemia.

Smokers may suffer from B_{12} deficiencies because they excrete more of the vitamin than nonsmokers. This tendency is a possible cause of tobacco amblyopia, a disease that causes dimming of vision. B_{12} also helps detoxify cyanide found in tobacco smoke and may help the body repair damage to the lungs caused by smoking.

Reports in the mid-1970s that megadoses of vitamin C destroy B_{12} have since been contradicted and discredited by subsequent research.

Injections of B_{12} have been used for years in treatment of fatigue and depression, but this course is hardly recommended unless a severe deficiency is evident. Any lift from B_{12} injections is short lived.

MINERALS

Minerals are found all around us in rocks, soil, plants, animals, and in our own bodies. These minerals or elements are chemically simple compared to vitamins but perform roles just as vital to proper health.

Minerals regulate many bodily functions, activate processes, transport other chemicals, and control many different cell functions. Some minerals, such as calcium, are found in our bodies in relatively large amounts, while others are present in mere traces.

Calcium

Fatigue can result from too little or too much calcium, a mineral most often associated with strong bones and teeth. It is the main structural mineral in the body, comprising almost 2 percent of the total body weight, and is vital for proper growth and development.

Calcium, a whitish compound, is abundant in milk, cheese, and other dairy products but is also present in some vegetables, such as turnip, collard, kale, and broccoli. The RDA for adults is 800 mg but this increases to 1,200 mg a day for women during pregnancy and lactation.

A cup of skim milk contains 296 mg; an ounce of American cheese has 198 mg; a cup of cooked broccoli has 136 mg; two large eggs have 54 mg; and an ounce of sardines has 125 mg.

Calcium from vegetables is not as easily absorbed by the intestine and is, therefore, less effective in providing the minimum daily requirement. Sugar enhances the absorption of calcium and is a good dietary companion to this mineral.

Orthomolecular psychiatrists have linked calcium deficiency to anxiety, general weakness, fatigue, depression, and psychosis. The brain is also sensitive to excessive levels of calcium and too much can cause depression, fatigue, delusions, kidney stones, and hallucinations.

Marginal calcium deficiency is fairly common, although severe deficiencies are rare. National surveys have found that many adult women obtain 30 to 50 percent less than the recommended daily allowance. Deficiencies are most common among alcoholics, people on high protein diets, and pregnant or postmenopausal women. Besides fatigue, other symptoms of deficiency include tetany, insomnia, bone pain, heart palpitations, and muscle cramps.

About $200 million in calcium supplements are sold in the United States each year. Additionally, many food producers have fortified their products with calcium, including flour, soft drinks, orange juice, and cold cereals.

Research has found some evidence to suggest that osteoporosis and hypertension respond to calcium supplements. Osteoporosis, which results in porous and brittle bones, affects mostly women. Hypertension or high blood pressure is a leading cause of heart disease and affects some 60 million Americans. Calcium supplements, however, should be monitored carefully. The ground dolomite that is a popular substitute for calcium has been found to contain lead, arsenic, mercury, and aluminum.

There has been growing evidence that the recommended daily

requirement of calcium for middle-aged and older adults is not sufficient, because the efficiency of absorption varies widely among individuals.

Iron

The mineral most commonly associated with fatigue is iron. Even a marginal iron deficiency can cause fatigue, decreased alertness, and muscle weakness.

Despite the wide availability of supplements, iron deficiency anemia is the most common mineral deficiency in the United States. As much as 20 percent of the population is estimated to be iron deficient.

Deficiency is much more common among women. Men store about 500 to 1,000 mg, but women store less than 500 mg. When anemia occurs, a normal diet will not supply enough iron and therapeutic supplements of ferrous sulfate or another form of iron are necessary.

The best source of iron is liver, but other meats, oatmeal, fish, shellfish, egg yolk, nuts, legumes, dates, beans, molasses, and green leafy vegetables are also good sources. Cooking in an iron pot can add iron to foods. The RDA is 10 mg for men and 18 mg for women under the age of 50. Beef liver contains 2.5 mg per ounce; hamburger has 1 mg per ounce; a cup of raw spinach contains 1.7 mg; and half a cup of cooked lima beans contains 2.9 mg.

In addition to exhaustion, symptoms of an iron deficiency include irritability, dizziness, sore tongue, itching, hair loss, diarrhea, constipation, heartburn, and loss of appetite.

Often the deficiency is caused by problems in absorption. Iron in meat is more readily absorbed than is the type found in vegetables. Excessive amounts of copper, zinc, or manganese will interfere with iron absorption, too. Vitamin C facilitates absorption and will reduce stomach upset from iron supplements.

In iron deficiency anemia, the body does not create enough red blood cells and body tissues are deprived of oxygen, which is carried from the lungs by hemoglobin in the blood. The body loses stamina and tires easily. An anemic person also experiences irritability, ringing in the ears, and loss of sex drive.

Marginal deficiencies may not show up in blood tests, but may cause many of the same symptoms. Depression, fatigue, insomnia, and loss of concentration are common complaints. Iron deficiency reduces immunity to infection, leaving the body open to attack from bacteria, viruses, and disease.

Deficiencies are most common among menstruating and pregnant women, although any condition that causes a loss of blood—hemorrhoids, ulcers, hernia, nosebleeds—can cause iron deficiencies. Poor diet is a likely cause among young people and the elderly. Junk foods, poor food selection, and crash diets are also common causes. Once deficiency sets in, fatigue, loss of appetite, and apathy compound the problem of a poor diet and aggravate and perpetuate the iron deficiency.

Too much iron may lead to dangerous toxicity. Megadoses of iron supplements may cause diarrhea, drowsiness, and vomiting. Iron toxicity, otherwise known as hemosiderosis, is common among chronic alcoholics who drink inexpensive wines, which contain iron.

About 6 percent of child poisonings in the United States are related to iron, most commonly from iron-enriched multivitamins. As few as six of these pills can cause death in a child. This problem is more widespread than most people realize. Nonetheless, iron deficiency anemia remains one of the most common nutritional disorders among children in the United States. It is most prevalent in low-birthweight infants, babies up to two years of age, and children in low-income families. The recommended daily allowance for children from 6 months to age 10 is 10 mg, the same as the RDA for adult males.

Potassium

Fatigue may be caused by too little or too much potassium, since it is a common symptom of both deficiency and toxicity. Both conditions cause muscle weakness.

Potassium acts with sodium to maintain the balance of body fluids and facilitate exchange of fluids between cells. It is needed to convert glucose in the blood to glycogen, which can be stored in the tissues for later use.

There is no established RDA for potassium, but the Food and Nutrition Board recommends from 1,875 to 5,625 mg a day as safe and adequate. Potassium is found in bananas, lettuce, broccoli, potatoes, peanuts, fruit, wheat germ, nuts, and orange juice. One potato contains up to 800 mg; half a cup of raisins, 553 mg; a medium banana has 440 mg; and a cup of milk has 350 mg.

Since there is an abundance of potassium in common foods, deficiency is usually the result of diuretics, laxatives, fasting, vomiting, or diarrhea. Besides fatigue, common symptoms of deficiency are depression, muscle weakness, loss of concentration, disorientation, irritability, and cardiac irregularities.

The most common factor increasing the requirement for potassium is exercise and physical work, since potassium is lost through sweat. Runners may lose half their total potassium levels after a long distance race. If the potassium level is not restored, chronic fatigue will result.

Persons with eating disorders, particularly anorexia and bulimia, create severe deficits of potassium in their bodies, a condition known as hypokalemia. This condition is brought on by vomiting, abuse of laxatives and diuretics and may lead to sudden death.

Toxicity from too much potassium may cause fatigue, anxiety, confusion, low blood pressure, and a loss of feelings in the limbs. Toxicity may result from daily doses of 25 grams or more of potassium chloride.

Magnesium

Supplements of magnesium and potassium have been used by some doctors to treat "housewife syndrome," a form of fatigue that afflicts homemakers and is often accompanied by headaches, insomnia, and vague pains. The depletion of magnesium among these women is apparently linked to stress, which leaches the magnesium from red blood cells.

Some magnesium is found in all body cells, but the mineral is especially important in controlling heart function and formation of bones and teeth. It is also vital for the production of energy.

The RDA is 400 mg for men and 300 mg for women. Magnesium

is found in whole grain products, nuts, green vegetables, seafood, and beans. A quarter cup of wheat germ contains 97 mg; a banana has 58 mg; a potato 51 mg; a cup of oatmeal, 50 mg; and a tablespoon of peanut butter has 28 mg.

Increased intakes of magnesium show no improvement for otherwise healthy individuals, but high doses may cause increased excretion of phosphorus and lead to a phosphorus deficiency, resulting in bone loss, weakness, anorexia, and malaise.

A deficiency in magnesium results in a wide range of symptoms, including fatigue, depression, agitation, anxiety, muscle weakness, dizziness, nausea, apathy, psychotic behavior, tremors, and seizures.

Large numbers of Americans are thought to suffer marginal deficiencies. Men appear to be more susceptible than women, since women metabolize the mineral more readily. The body absorbs magnesium slowly and only about 10 percent is absorbed from foods eaten. Severe deficiencies of magnesium are rare. Diabetics, alcoholics, the elderly, pregnant women, athletes, and patients with kidney ailments are the most likely to suffer serious deficiencies.

Megadoses of magnesium can lead to dangerous toxicity, a condition known as hypermagnesemia. Although rare, it can and does occur among people who abuse magnesium-based laxatives or stomach antacids, but those containing relatively low amounts of magnesium are regarded as safe. Toxicity may also cause fatigue, drowsiness, nervousness, diarrhea, vomiting, low blood pressure, coma, and even death.

Zinc

Fatigue and depression are common symptoms of zinc deficiency. Although zinc is relatively nontoxic, it may cause chronic fatigue when taken in high doses.

Zinc is necessary to human growth and reproduction, and is vital to the proper functioning of more than 70 enzymes in the body. It is found in a variety of foods but is most commonly available in meats and fish.

The normal American diet contains slightly less than the RDA, which is 15 mg. Four ounces of beef have 7 mg; four ounces of beef liver have 5.8 mg; a quarter cup of cashews, 1.5 mg; an ounce of cheese 1.1 mg; and four ounces of fish have 1.1 mg.

Fatigue and listlessness are early signs of a deficiency and these symptoms are accompanied by weight loss, reduced appetite, and rough or scaly skin. Other symptoms include reduced sense of taste and smell, depression, hair loss, and reduced resistance to infection.

Certain life-styles contribute to deficiency. Strenuous exercise excretes zinc in perspiration. Institutional meals, particularly in schools, are often short of zinc. Vegetarians are susceptible because the zinc in plants is more difficult for the body to absorb. Abuse of alcoholic beverages depletes stores of zinc.

It takes three to twenty-four weeks for any symptoms of deficiency to appear, but supplements will relieve symptoms in a matter of a few days. Pregnancy and lactation increases the need for additional zinc.

Sodium

Found most abundantly in salt and salty foods, too much or too little sodium will cause fatigue.

Commonly linked to hypertension, sodium is critical for the maintenance of the equilibrium of the cells and bodily fluids. It plays an important role in tissue formation, nerve transmission, and contraction of the muscles.

The maximum intake is usually recommended to be between 6 and 8 grams a day. The minimum is quite low and patients on severely restricted low sodium diets have experienced no problems. The safe and adequate level recommended by the Food and Nutrition Board is 1,100 to 3,300 mg a day for adults.

A large dill pickle alone has 1.4 grams; 3 slices of bologna have 1.1 grams; a hot dog has .63 grams; and 4 ounces of corned beef have 1.0 gram.

Sodium is so common in our foods, particularly processed foods, that deficiencies are usually the result of diarrhea, prolonged vomiting, excessive sweating, or the abuse of diuretics.

Deficiency will lead to fatigue, dehydration, depression, weakness, restlessness, muscle twitchings, nausea, vomiting, headache, and loss of appetite. Heavy exercise causes depletion of sodium through sweat and loss of fluids. Dieters intent on losing water weight may inadvertently cause a deficiency in sodium, especially when using "water pills" or other diuretics.

Too much sodium is more of a problem than too little is. Since sodium makes the body retain more water, a person may feel bloated and tired if his diet is high in sodium. Additionally, sodium and salt have long been associated with hypertension or high blood pressure, although many other factors contribute to this condition.

TO SUPPLEMENT OR NOT? A GOOD QUESTION

If you are uncertain whether or not to take vitamin and mineral supplements, you should make a careful review of your diet to determine first if you are getting all the proper nutrients. Once an approximate tabulation is in hand, the question will usually answer itself.

In choosing from available supplements, those with 100 percent of the RDA are probably the safest, since these levels have been established by extensive research to be safe and adequate for most people.

As we have seen, fatigue is not only a symptom of deficiency, it is also a side effect of toxicity for many vitamins or minerals. Taking megadoses of vitamins, therefore, may cause fatigue rather than cure it.

Millions of Americans take vitamins with no adverse consequences. Except for a few vitamins, excess amounts are passed out in the urine and pose little problem of building up to toxic levels.

A person's life-style often indicates a need for supplements. If you smoke or drink alcohol, take drugs, drink a lot of coffee or tea, eat poorly or take oral contraceptives, suffer from depression or unusual stress, you may be more vulnerable to vitamin deficiencies and should check with a physician to determine if a supplement is necessary.

If approached with common sense, supplements can be health-

Vitamins and Health

1. To date, no scientific data support a conclusion that healthy people eating a well-balanced diet need vitamin supplements.
2. Natural vitamins are no better and no worse than synthetic vitamins. Both perform the same function, and the body cannot tell the difference.
3. Large doses of vitamins will not overcome the effects of a poor diet.
4. Vitamins alone will not sustain life. They have no calories and are effective only when working with other nutrients.
5. Vitamin supplements can play an important therapeutic role for alcoholics or women who are pregnant or breast-feeding.
6. Contrary to popular belief, no optimum ratios or combinations of vitamins have been established by scientific research.
7. Vitamins do not provide "pep" or feelings of well-being in healthy people, despite anecdotal evidence to the contrary.
8. Many things destroy the effectiveness of vitamins in food, such as sunlight, water and heat.
9. Vitamin supplements may cause problems for people with special medical conditions, such as allergies, diabetes, gout, and various forms of anemia.
10. Supplemental doses of vitamins may interfere with medical tests for diabetes and other conditions.
11. Vitamin deficiencies may result even with proper diet if the body has difficulty absorbing the nutrients in the food.
12. Many symptoms, including fatigue, are present in cases of toxicity as well as deficiency.
13. The only time megadoses of vitamins are helpful is when the body has a severe deficiency.
14. A vitamin by itself is useless. All vitamins are catalysts, so they require other things to work with, such as protein, fat, and carbohydrates.
15. Women may need supplements during pregnancy and lactation or if they take oral contraceptives. Coffee, tea, alcohol, smoking, and exercise all increase the body's need for certain vitamins.

ful additives to our diets, but people should not view them as a cure-all. The fact is that few of us will ever experience a severe vitamin deficiency.

A person who suspects that a vitamin deficiency may be causing his or her fatigue should visit a doctor. A few simple blood tests should indicate if there is reason for concern.

CHAPTER ELEVEN

CHRONIC FATIGUE SYNDROME

A BRIEF HISTORY

Chronic fatigue syndrome (CFS), formerly known as chronic Epstein–Barr virus (EBV) syndrome or the "yuppie flu," is characterized by an extreme weakness and debilitating fatigue, sometimes lasting for months or even years. Patients become so weak that normal routines are impossible.

The syndrome, which usually strikes people in their 30s, can mean a tragic interruption in careers and family life. The fatigue is so prolonged and persistent that a life can be ruined, marriages destroyed, and financial savings wiped out.

Nobody knows for sure how many people suffer from CFS. Although thousands of inquiries are made about CFS to national health officials, authentic cases of the syndrome are considered fairly rare. In many suspected cases, other disorders are usually identified as the culprit.

The mass media has dubbed it the "yuppie flu" because of its tendency to strike educated, upwardly mobile young people. The affliction is called a syndrome rather than a disease because it manifests a cluster of possibly related symptoms that occur together and is not an illness with a single set of definite symptoms.

No reliable diagnostic test exists for CFS, so the syndrome is easily misdiagnosed as something else and physicians tend to dismiss its symptoms as psychoneurotic. Frustrated patients may con-

241

sequently revert to unauthorized, useless treatments at costs of thousands of dollars in search of relief. But progress is being made, at least on this front, and in recent years, CFS has gained acceptance as a legitimate medical condition. This acceptance has led to an intensified research effort in hopes of clarifying the CFS mystery.

The role of the EBV as a cause of the syndrome is a matter of contention and new evidence tends to diminish its role. An emerging consensus believes the syndrome may have several causes.

The condition was poorly defined until 1988, when the Division of Viral Diseases of the Centers for Disease Control coordinated a study that changed the name from chronic Epstein–Barr syndrome to chronic fatigue syndrome and established specific criteria for its diagnosis.

The onset of the syndrome typically occurs in people in late adolescence or early adulthood. The condition has been found twice as often in women as in men, but the reason for the disparity is not understood.

The complex of symptoms that comprise the syndrome has been recognized by physicians since the 1940s and has been known by a variety of names, including chronic mononucleosis, myalgic encephalopathy, postviral syndrome, atypical poliomyelitis, Icelandic disease, and epidemic neuromyasthenia. Medical practitioners now classify these conditions as chronic fatigue syndrome.

DIAGNOSIS

Since no reliable laboratory tests exist to detect chronic fatigue syndrome, physicians must rely on signs and symptoms to lead them to a diagnosis. A diagnosis is made by essentially ruling out any other possible illness, including cancer, psychiatric disease, autoimmune disease, drug abuse, alcoholism, and a host of other potential ailments.

For much of the 1980s, diagnosis was most often based on blood tests for EBV antibodies, but the correlation between the virus and chronic fatigue is presently suspect and medical authorities consider blood tests inconclusive for diagnosis. After examining 134 patients who suffered from an outbreak of mononucleosislike illnesses in Lake Tahoe, Nevada, in 1984, physicians concluded that tests for EBV antibodies could not distinguish the ill from healthy subjects.[1]

The Centers for Disease Control (CDC) has established a set of criteria for CFS, which has become the standard since its publication in the Annals of Internal Medicine in 1988.[2] The group found that the syndrome consists of a combination of physical and emotional symptoms.

The CDC definition is rather formal and restrictive, designed for use by medical research teams rather than practitioners. The definition, however, provides a guidepost for physicians treating patients who complain of chronic fatigue, even though their symptoms may fall short of the literal definition. Under the case definition, a patient must meet certain criteria. First of all, the person must suffer from two major symptoms:

1. There must be a persistent or relapsing fatigue that does not respond to rest and is severe enough to reduce a person's normal activity by 50 percent. The person must have no previous history of the symptom and it must persist for at least six months.
2. Other diseases and conditions must be eliminated by thorough physical examination, laboratory tests, and a medical history. This evaluation would include psychiatric disease, infection, side effects to medication, and a wide variety of heart, pulmonary, blood, neuromuscular, and other diseases.

Additionally, the patient must experience 8 of 11 minor symptoms that persist or recur over six months: mild fever, sore throat, painful lymph nodes, general muscle weakness, muscle discomfort, prolonged fatigue, pain in joints without swelling, sleep disturbance, depression, and an onset of symptoms within a few hours or days. Accompanying this complex of symptoms may be a number of psychological complaints, such as confusion, irritability, depression, inability to concentrate, and trouble thinking.

Among physical symptoms cited by the physicians were: low-grade fever, inflammation of the pharynx (throat), and tender lymph nodes. If a CFS patient has only 6 rather than 8 of the 11 minor symptoms, then he or she must have 2 of the 3 physical symptoms to meet the case definition.

A person might not meet each and every one of the above criteria and still have CFS, since the definition was meant more for researchers than medical practitioners. The latter can be expected to encounter exceptions to the rule in their offices. Still, the CDC criteria remain the standard guideline for diagnosis of CFS.

MORE ABOUT THE SYMPTOMS

Fatigue

The fatigue that lies at the heart of CFS is a constellation of various symptoms—malaise, depression, weakness, and lethargy. It is unlike normal fatigue and can incapacitate a person for months. Normal activity must be drastically reduced. Jobs may be abandoned, housework neglected, and family duties postponed.

The fatigue that accompanies this syndrome is the worst of the symptoms. In one in four cases, the patient is so tired he is virtually bedridden at some point during the illness. Most patients who continue their normal routines complain of feeling exhausted and are unable to do anything else.

The fatigue drains the person emotionally and spiritually as well as physically. Rest, rest, and more rest seems the best antidote to even greater discomfort.

Patients sometimes do not have the strength to carry a bag of groceries or climb stairs. Common routines of the day, such as making a bed or driving to the store, become torturous exercises that leave the person virtually prostrate with exhaustion. The fatigue can become so acute, it is almost painful.

Sleep is disturbed, making matters worse. Patients often complain of waking after a night's sleep as tired as when they went to bed. Sleeping pills are ineffective and the person often needs to sleep during the day or whenever sleep is possible.

Virtually all those who suffer from CFS complain of this debilitating fatigue, though it can be more severe for some than for others. Physical activity seems to aggravate the condition in some cases but relieve it slightly in others. Fatigue is inconstant for some, rising and falling in unpredictable waves.

Fatigue seems to be the most persistent symptom and one of the last to disappear before recovery. After a 3–4 month follow-up, all the patients in a Seattle study still complained of fatigue, while only 40 to 60 percent complained of other symptoms.

Sore Throat

A sore throat is a common symptom of CFS. Aspirin and gargles with hot water and salt or sugar can help, but this brings only temporary relief. The most common complaint is pharyngitis, the inflammation of the pharynx.

In most cases, the sore throat is gone after a few weeks, although it can linger for much longer. The soreness may come and go, providing something of a barometer of the patient's fatigue and strength.

Fever

A mild fever or chills are present in almost every case of CFS. Besides the sore throat, the fever is about the only physical condition that can be easily measured by the patient. The fever usually occurs at the outset of the syndrome, in the first few hours or days.

The oral temperature should be between 99.5 and 101.5 degrees Fahrenheit. A temperature greater than 101.5 degrees is less likely to be related to the syndrome. The fever generally disappears after 10 days.

Tender Lymph Nodes

Another physical symptom of CFS is known as lymphadenopathy, the abnormal enlargement of the lymph nodes. The condition usually disappears after four to five weeks. If the enlargement is particularly severe, a physician might prescribe medication to reduce swelling.

The lymph nodes in the neck become tender and painful. The nodes most frequently affected are in the front or back of the neck or under the armpit. If the nodes become greater than two centimeters in diameter, another cause is more likely.

Headaches

Headaches are usually generalized and different in severity and pattern than those the patient has ever had before. The headache may be worse after exercise or other physical activity. Aspirin and other over-the-counter pain relievers are the best hope to reduce the pain, although these may prove inadequate.

Depression

A majority of CFS patients suffer from depression. Whether or not the depression precedes CFS becomes the chicken-or-the-egg type of question, but the frequent presence of depression in the syndrome is well documented. A 1987 Boston study found 78 percent of the patients examined for CFS complained of depression.[4]

Depression may worsen as personal and family problems mount because of inaction. This is especially true for patients who must give up their jobs and face inevitable financial hardship. Support from friends and family members becomes especially critical during these trying times because the emotional side effects of CFS are quite disturbing. The inactivity caused by fatigue can make a person feel helpless, damaging self-esteem. The duration of the illness prompts dark moods as the patient loses hope in recovery. As the depression deepens, so does the fatigue, and one feeds the other in a vicious cycle.

The role of depression in CFS is a controversial matter and not a settled scientific issue. Some research indicates depression predates the onset of CFS and may itself be responsible for the CFS symptoms in many cases. Depression is often accompanied by other psychological symptoms, such as forgetfulness, confusion, irritability, and difficulty thinking. All of these types of problems are part of the CFS profile.

Sleep Disorders

It seems ironic that people who complain of fatigue should have trouble sleeping, but many CFS patients not only report trouble getting to sleep, but also have problems staying awake during the daytime.

Their sleep is disturbed by the physical and psychological symptoms of CFS. Sleep cycles may change. Patients tend to sleep more frequently during the day and complain of insomnia at night. The 1987 Boston study found 72 percent of its subjects suffered from some sort of sleep disorder. The Seattle study found that CFS patients actually sleep longer than most other people, up to 12 hours a night. Additionally, nearly half of the patients in the study slept some time during the day.[5]

Muscle and Joint Pain

General aches and pains throughout the muscle and skeletal structure are not uncommon. The muscle discomfort is generalized and not specific to any particular part of the body. The joint pain is present without swelling or redness. Aspirin and other widely available analgesics are recommended for symptomatic relief.

Although there remains no cure for CFS, there are steps a patient can take to help alleviate the symptoms. Most of the physical symptoms will respond to medication or therapy. The fatigue, unfortunately, is more stubborn and less likely to respond to treatment. A number of false starts can be expected as the patient experiments with what seems to work best—rest, exercise, psychotherapy and/or medication.

CAUSES OF CFS: A VARIETY OF THEORIES

The cause or causes of CFS are unknown. Until the last few years, EBV was thought to cause the condition, but medical researchers now believe the virus is not the sole cause, even though it may play a role. Current research is concentrating on three major areas—viruses, immune system dysfunction, and neuropsychological problems.

Viruses are Leading Suspects

A broad spectrum of viruses is under intense study for links to CFS. Some of the most recent work is being done with retroviruses, particularly the group of human T-cell leukemia viruses (HTLV), which are frequently designated by roman numerals to indicate their order of discovery. The HTLV-III retrovirus is commonly known as HIV or the AIDS virus. A retrovirus contains RNA that provides a template for the formation of DNA, which is then incorporated into the genetic structure of the diseased cells.

In Great Britain, doctors are studying the Coxsackie viruses, one of which causes herpangina, a childhood disease characterized by fever and sore throat.

EBV continues to receive serious study. This virus was an early suspect because it causes mononucleosis, a disease with similar symptoms that sometimes has preceded CFS. One theory holds that CFS may be a form of recurring mononucleosis.

EBV was discovered in 1964 by a team of physicians at the Middlesex Hospital in London. The doctors, M. Anthony Epstein, B.G. Achong, and Y. M. Barr discovered the virus while studying Burkitt's lymphoma cells under an electron microscope. The virus is a member of the herpes family of viruses. This viral group includes the herpes viruses (cold sores and genital herpes), varicella-zoster virus (chicken pox), the cytomegalovirus (mononucleosis-type flu), and HHV6 (Epstein–Barr-type illnesses).

The EBV antibodies have been found in some people suffering from chronic fatigue syndrome but not in others. Indeed, some healthy people have higher levels of EBV antibodies than those suffering from the syndrome.

About 90 percent of all adults in the United States have EBV antibodies present in their blood by age 30, so a positive blood test for EBV is not conclusive of anything. Infection by the virus in most people results in the flu or mononucleosis. After the infection passes, the virus enters a dormant state.

One theory is that EBV may interact with another virus or act as an agent to cause CFS. The key to this interaction, if it does occur, is not known, but it would explain the repeated findings of the virus in patients suffering from chronic fatigue.

Researchers at the Wistar Institute in Philadelphia have identified a link between CFS and a retrovirus similar to human T-cell leukemia virus II (HTLV-II), which causes hairy cell leukemia, a rare form of blood cancer. The virus was isolated in patients suffering from CFS. The suspected virus is believed to be a different strain of the HTLV-II virus. More study will be needed to confirm these preliminary findings.

Other research has linked a variety of other viruses to CFS patients. For example, the study of a cluster of CFS patients in Lake Tahoe in 1985, found relatively high levels of antibodies to cytomegalovirus (CMV), herpes simplex virus 1 (cold sores) and herpes simplex 2 (genital herpes), and measles.[6] The role of these viruses in CFS, by themselves or in combination, remains ambiguous.

One theory suggests that dormant viruses, such as the EBV, CMV, or herpes-type, lie dormant until some other virus invades the body and impairs the immune system. This reduces or eliminates the natural killers of the dormant virus, allowing it to flourish and cause the CFS symptoms.

Immune System Breakdowns

The immune system protects the body against infection by creating antibodies and chemicals to fend off bacteria, fungi, viruses, and other foreign invaders. The system rivals the nervous system in complexity. If the network breaks down or malfunctions, the body is vulnerable to disease.

If the cause of CFS is a defect in the immune system, it would explain the variety of viruses found in CFS sufferers. The viruses would, therefore, play a role in the syndrome, but the leading cause would be the failure of the immune system to fight them. This possibility has led immunologists to search for a link between immune system dysfunction and CFS.

When people become "run down" and weak, they become more susceptible to colds and flus. This is because the immune system has been weakened and is unable to fight off the infection. Two places in the body—the throat and vagina—are particularly vulnerable because they are ports of entry for many types of invading organisms. People who are tired and under stress are prone to recurrent infections in these areas. As we saw in Chapter Six, stress has wide ranging effects on the body and contributes to a variety of diseases.

Three types of white blood cells are created to help fend off infections: B and T cells and macrophages. The B and T cells are produced in bone marrow and provide the front line of attack against bacteria and viruses. The T cell is differentiated in the thymus, a gland located in the chest near the heart. T cells attack the viruses directly, while the B cells produce antibodies to fight specific viruses. Macrophages are the largest of the white blood cells and envelop the virus as well as the toxins associated with the infection.

Additionally, lymph nodes produce about 20 to 30 percent of the lymphocytes in the blood and assist the immune system in cooperation with the B and T cells.

In order to fend off infection, the immune system must function efficiently. If one part of the process breaks down, the whole system may fail, paving the way for chronic or recurrent infections.

One theory of CFS is that something goes wrong with the fighting machine, resulting in the array of symptoms associated with CFS. The fight against infection drains the body of energy as the immune system floods the bloodstream with antibodies and toxins created to kill the invaders. If the immune system is accelerated to fight off an infection but cannot relax or return to normal afterwards, the body faces a prolonged bout with fatigue and accompanying symptoms such as fever, muscle aches, and depression.

Depression

Several studies have found a history of depression in people suffering from CFS. The depression often predates the syndrome, indicating that it may be responsible for CFS symptoms or predispose certain people to the syndrome. Additionally, there is growing evidence that depression undermines the body's immune system, making it more vulnerable to disease. Additionally, depression tends to prolong convalescence from viral infections.

A study in 1988 at the University of Connecticut Health Center diagnosed psychiatric disorders and ruled out CFS in virtually all of the 135 patients who complained of chronic fatigue. Based on psychological testing, the study found that 91 of the 135 patients (67 percent) had "clinically active psychiatric disorders."[7] Of those 91 patients, 67 were diagnosed with major depression. Only 6 of the 135 met the CFS criteria and further study determined that three of the six also suffered from other psychological disorders.

The symptoms of depression parallel the psychological and physical symptoms usually associated with CFS. For example, a British study in 1981 found that more than three fourths of those suffering from depression complained of impaired concentration, fatigue, agitation, daytime drowsiness, and headaches. About half of the patients reported excessive perspiration, dizziness, dry mouth, rapid breathing, and blurred vision. Less frequent symptoms are constipation, flushing, slurred speech, chest pain, excessive salivation, weight gain, impotency, or reduced or excessive libido.[8]

The difficult question, once again, is whether CFS causes depression or depression causes CFS. Whatever the case, the two are inextricably linked, since depression is such a dominant feature of the syndrome. But because depression is experienced by many people, it is one of the first things that must be ruled out before a diagnosis of CFS is finally made. Compared to CFS, depression is relatively easy to treat in most cases.

It is important to note, however, that an authentic case of CFS is expected to be accompanied by depression, whether or not the patient has a history of depression. If the patient's chronic fatigue is caused by depression, it is unlikely that he or she would meet a strict application of the CFS criteria, since the physical symptoms would not be present.

MAGNESIUM DEFICIENCY

Two preliminary studies by British scientists in 1991 indicated that CFS patients suffer from lower magnesium concentrations in their blood and can improve significantly once the deficiency is remedied.

In the first study, scientists found that 20 patients suffering from

CFS symptoms had slightly lower magnesium levels in red blood cells compared with 20 healthy subjects matched for age, sex, and social class. The study was done because malabsorption of magnesium, a rare disorder, is commonly associated with fatigue and generalized weakness.

A second study seems to confirm the link between magnesium deficiency and CFS. Of 32 patients diagnosed as suffering from CFS, 15 were chosen by the scientists for weekly injections of magnesium sulfate for six weeks. Of these 15, a dozen reported they experienced higher energy levels, improvements in mood, and less pain. Only 3 of 17 of the other patients, who received injections of water, showed any improvement.[9]

The scientists noted that the findings are preliminary, since the number of patients involved is relatively small. The studies do not resolve the question of whether the magnesium deficiency is a cause or a symptom of chronic fatigue syndrome. Furthermore, it is not known if such treatment would benefit vast numbers of CFS patients, since it is unknown if magnesium levels are low in the majority of CFS patients.

TREATMENT

No effective treatment for chronic fatigue syndrome exists. In truth, there is no cure. Treatment of the symptoms—sore throats, fever, depression, malaise—is the best a patient can expect.

Because the duration of symptoms is indefinite, those afflicted with the syndrome require support and reassurance. The fatigue may persist for a few weeks, several months, or longer. Sometimes the fatigue comes and goes intermittently. In any case, the syndrome is not fatal and the vast majority of people recover spontaneously.

A study of 26 patients diagnosed with chronic fatigue by researchers at the University of Washington Medical School found that most patients improved gradually over time. After one year, 4 of the 21 still in follow-up had returned to normal pre-illness activities, 8 had improved significantly, while the others still experienced some fatigue. The improvement occurred without treatment with drugs.[10]

The University of Washington study was conducted from 1985 through 1987 before the formal criteria were established by the Centers for Disease Control. More than half the patients in the study had experienced at least one episode of major depression prior to the onset of fatigue, furthering the theory that psychiatric disorder may play a primary role in such cases.

A variety of drugs are being tried to determine their effectiveness in treating CFS symptoms. The drugs fall into two main categories—antiviral and antinflammatory. Antiviral agents, such as acyclovir, do not kill the viruses but act to inhibit their reproduction and growth. Antinflammatory medicines, particularly cortisone, relieve pain and swelling in joints suffered by some CFS patients. Additionally, antidepressants to reduce depression and malaise and antihistamines for flu-like symptoms are often recommended.

COPING WITH CFS

Coping with chronic fatigue is stressful, discouraging, and frustrating. The sufferer is overwhelmed with anger, helplessness, depression, guilt, and self-pity. Financial hardship aggravates the emotional distress for those who can no longer work.

Some diets claim to bolster the immune system or provide the body with more energy. No evidence suggests, however, that diets can cure CFS or alleviate chronic fatigue. At best, a balanced diet will insure that the depressed, disheartened patient will not become obese or emaciated.

Expensive and useless treatments can make matters worse by raising false hopes, so patients must be selective in choosing the proper therapy. Bee venom, megadoses of vitamins, herbal teas, acupuncture, chiropractic, and unconventional therapies cannot be expected to help, although all have been tried by CFS sufferers.

On the other hand, many of the traditional techniques recommended for combatting fatigue may alleviate some symptoms. Relaxation techniques, good sleep habits, sound diet, psychological counseling, and a positive attitude do not cure this syndrome but should help sufferers cope with the distressing symptoms.

Patients must find ways to cope with the incapacitating aspects of CFS. One of the most significant factors is reassurance from health professionals, family, and friends. In the past few years, physicians have recognized the nature of CFS and are no longer apt to dismiss the symptoms lightly as "all in your head." This is a major step in the right direction. As in any other chronic disease, the support of loved ones and friends is crucial to a patient's well-being.

The emotional consequences of CFS are just as serious as, if not more serious than, the physical effects. Guilt, depression, loneliness, and lowered self-esteem can cause long-term emotional harm. The strain on marriages can be almost unbearable. Sympathy and understanding will help relieve stress for the patient and supporters.

Financial troubles and health insurance problems frequently add to an already deteriorating situation, especially when the patient must give up a job. Because the syndrome tends to strike ambitious, upwardly mobile young people, the traditional social services offered by the government pose an unattractive, ego-crushing alternative to most CFS patients. But governmental programs such as social security, welfare, food stamps, and unemployment compensation may offer financial and medical support when other assistance is not available.

If there is good news in the CFS story, it is that symptoms almost always go away after time. The syndrome is not fatal. Patients do get better and return to full and normal lives. In the absence of an effective treatment, faith and persistence, combined with a will to get better, seem to be the best medicine.

CHAPTER TWELVE

THE YEAST THEORY
EPIDEMIC DISEASE OR MEDICAL FAD?

In the 1980s, some physicians linked yeast infections, specifically candidiasis, to a controversial and growing list of symptoms, the most prominent of which is chronic fatigue.

The concept of generalized candidiasis is not completely accepted by the American medical establishment. The debate is not about whether candidiasis exists or not, but whether it is spreading in epidemic proportions and causing the long list of ills attributed to it. At times, the candidiasis theory invokes elements of faith and seems closer to religion than science. Predictably, the argument between the believers and nonbelievers has led to public confusion.

Candidiasis (sometimes spelled candidosis) has been recognized as a disease since Hippocrates described cases in the 4th century. The yeast organism candida albicans was first identified as a cause of illness in 1839. Candida infections, commonly known as thrush, most frequently occur in moist parts of the body, especially the mouth and vagina.

According to the theory, chronic generalized candidiasis infection displays a myriad of symptoms—vaginitis, depression, fatigue, menstrual cramps, diarrhea, headaches, intestinal gas, muscle aches, constipation, and recurrent infections. Other reported symptoms include anxiety, asthma, bronchitis, colitis, impotence, insomnia, loss of memory, swelling, and gain or loss of weight.

Sorting through the published reports about candida yeast infections does not clarify the controversy. First of all, diagnosis is complicated because no reliable laboratory test exists to detect the condition known as chronic candidiasis. Doctors sometimes initiate treatment with antifungal drugs to confirm their tentative diagnosis: if the patient gets better, they conclude the yeast infection was the cause. Although the treatment itself may be harmless, the danger is that some other serious illness causing the symptoms may go untreated.

Case histories and patient testimonials about candidiasis have indicated dramatic results from treatment and an alleviation of a wide variety of symptoms. Unfortunately, traditional scientific methods—double-blind studies, for example—have so far not been used to corroborate these claims. Without such methods, the results can be discounted and perhaps dismissed as some sort of placebo effect—a medical phenomenon that occurs when people seem to get better even though the treatment is known to be ineffective, such as the prescription of a sugar pill.

Physicians at the Mayo Clinic have called reports of an epidemic of candida albicans infections "premature" and said the condition has "all the trappings of a cultural phenomenon." Pointing out that reliable research is necessary to confirm or refute the theory, the Mayo Clinic warned that "the public faces the risk of unscrupulous promoters who take advantage of widespread anxiety by selling useless treatments."[1]

Proponents of the candidiasis theory, who are certified, experienced medical practitioners themselves, bristle at such criticism and refute it by references to their successful cases. They are confident that their views will eventually be proved.

The American Academy of Allergy and Immunology (AAAI) has reviewed the scientific evidence and found the concept of chronic generalized candidiasis to be "speculative and unproven."[2] The AAAI pointed out that the broad-based candidiasis treatment programs commonly prescribed would alleviate symptoms of many illnesses, since the symptoms of generalized candidiasis are essentially universal.

Despite the controversy, more and more physicians are becoming interested in the condition and future research will no doubt resolve many of these questions. Given the conflicting views, however, individuals should enter any treatment program with their eyes open.

In many instances, family practitioners are not "candidiasis-conscious physicians," as doctors who treat candidiasis are called by theory adherents. Given the nature of the controversy, it is probably a good idea to keep your personal physician advised should you decide to try a candidiasis treatment with another doctor.

WHAT IS CANDIDIASIS?

The candida albicans is a fungus that lives normally in many of us as a parasitic yeast, much like thousands of bacteria and other microorganisms in our bodies. When the body's natural immune system is knocked out of balance for whatever reason, the yeast can grow out of control and cause serious infection, even death in rare cases.

There are more than a hundred types of candida yeasts, but only a half dozen are commonly identified in humans. Two of them, candida albicans and candida tropicalis, account for 80 percent of yeast illnesses. As the yeast grow, they are believed to release toxins that cause the illness and further weaken the immune system.

In most people, the yeast causes no problems and there are no symptoms. When infections develop, they are generally found in the mouth, vagina, intestine, or on the surface of the skin. Treatment is relatively simple: administration of antifungal medication to kill the yeast.

The controversy has grown in the past decade, however, as some physicians have come forward with a theory of chronic candidiasis and claimed that the condition is epidemic in modern society. These physicians estimate that one-third of the population of the Western civilized world has the condition.[3]

Such statements come at a time when the number of cases of yeast infection is growing, mostly due to the increased use of antibiotics and birth control pills. Antibiotics kill the bacteria that control the yeast, and birth control pills tend to promote its growth. Irradiation and chemotherapy, alcoholism and drug addiction all impair immunity and provide other opportunities for overgrowth of the candida yeast. Some evidence indicates that iron deficiency and diets high in yeast and carbohydrates may predispose people to the infection as well.

The initial candida infection experienced by a person is usually not severe and can be fought successfully by a healthy immune system. In some cases, however, recurrent infections slowly take their toll and the body loses its power to fight it. As the yeast replicates itself, an overgrowth of the yeast colonizes in the tissues and begins to release harmful toxic chemicals into the bloodstream. These chemicals attack the immune system and weaken defenses, allowing the yeast to grow even stronger.

Candidiasis, formerly known as moniliasis, has gone by many names, but all refer to the same condition. The terms include the candida yeast syndrome, candidiasis hypersensitivity syndrome, polysystemic chronic candidiasis, disseminated candidiasis, and generalized chronic candidiasis.

Medical researchers classify candidiasis infection into three categories:

1. **Superficial Candidiasis.** This is the most common type and is found in the lining surfaces of the skin in the upper and lower respiratory tracts, vagina, gastrointestinal tract, mouth, or external skin. The disease is commonly known as oral thrush when it infects the mouth.
2. **Locally Invasive Candidiasis.** This category is more severe and is characterized by localized lesions, usually ulcers in the intestinal, respiratory, or genitourinary tract.
3. **Systemic Candidiasis.** The most serious, also called deep candidiasis, is the most rare. It can be fatal because it causes lesions and abscesses on the heart, lungs, liver, spleen, kidneys, brain, or other organ. Postsurgery patients or others suffering from cancer or blood diseases are the most susceptible to this form of the disease.

Invasive and systemic candidiasis are both rare and occur almost entirely among those patients suffering from serious illness or undergoing cancer treatments. Superficial candidiasis does not necessarily or frequently lead to these more serious conditions either, since the immune system must be very weak to allow such deterioration.

DIAGNOSIS

A variety of laboratory tests have been developed in the attempt to diagnose candidiasis, but as of yet, none of them presents a clear-cut answer. Lab tests combined with a detailed patient history should point to candidiasis as a suspect, but often a trial of treatment may be necessary to confirm a diagnosis.

Dr. C. Orian Truss, a Birmingham, Alabama allergist, is considered the pioneering physician and the leading advocate of the theory of widespread candidiasis, which he first introduced to the public in his book *The Missing Diagnosis* in the early 1980s. Dr. Truss said that traditional internists have failed to diagnose candidiasis because:

1. The primary presenting symptoms—depression and anxiety, fatigue and weakness, memory loss and concentration problems—are all easily misdiagnosed as being caused by psychosomatic illness.
2. No definitive laboratory test exists to tell when the candida overgrowth has begun or if it is responsible for the trouble.[4]

The medical laboratory has several means of identifying the candida albicans organism, but has not been able to pinpoint chronic infection reliably. Laboratory diagnosis has focused on two areas: blood tests to measure antibodies and yeast by-products in the blood and tests to identify the yeast in bodily fluids, such as urine, sputum, pus, vaginal secretions, and spinal fluid. Blood tests are negative in as many as 60 percent of authentic infections. Tests on smears are not conclusive because the yeast is a normal inhabitant of the body and would be expected to be present. A series of blood tests taken to monitor changes in levels of antibodies can help clarify whether or not a laboratory finding is truly positive or negative.

Without a clear-cut answer from the laboratory, physicians rely on the history and physical examination of the patient to make their diagnosis. Dr. William G. Crook, author of *The Yeast Connection* and president of the International Foundation, Inc., of Jackson, Tennessee, has compiled a list of ten questions to help identify yeast infections.[5]

1. Have you taken broad-spectrum antibiotic drugs for a prolonged period, such as tetracycline, sulfas, and synthetic penicillins?
2. Have you experienced premenstrual tension or problems, vaginal yeast infections, abdominal pain, cramps, prostatitis, or loss of sexual interest or feeling?
3. Are you bothered by exposure to tobacco smoke or the odors of perfume or other chemicals?
4. Do you crave sugar, bread, or alcohol?
5. Are you troubled by stomach upset and digestive disorders?
6. Are you experiencing fatigue, depression, loss of concentration and memory?
7. Do you have chronic skin rashes, psoriasis, or hives?
8. Have you ever taken birth control pills?
9. Are you bothered by poor coordination, headaches, or pains in muscles and joints?
10. Do you feel bad all over, but the cause has not been found?

Dr. Crook believes 3–4 yes answers mean yeast is *possibly* the problem; 5–7 yes answers mean the cause is *probably* yeast infection, and for 8–10 yes answers, the symptoms are *almost certainly* yeast related.

It is impossible to say how many physicians subscribe to the yeast theory, or use Dr. Crook's questionnaire for diagnostic purposes. The Huxley Institute for Biosocial Research in Boca Raton, Florida, which assists patients in finding medical help for this disorder, lists about 150 physicians nationwide who treat patients for candidiasis.

SYMPTOMS

As we have seen, numerous symptoms have been attributed to candidiasis. The type of symptoms depend largely on the individual, the extent of the infection, its location in the body, and the patient's sex. These variables make it difficult to assess specific symptoms common to all candidiasis victims. Fatigue and depression are prominent in virtually all cases, however, and explain why many patients are referred to psychiatric treatment once physical illness has been ruled out by a physician.

Victims of candidiasis report severe insomnia and a sudden, drastic drop in their energy. Depression and exhaustion drain their resources as the body attempts to fend off the yeast infection. Dr. Truss and other physicians believe the depression and fatigue are caused by the yeast's effects on the brain.

The fatigue is accompanied by anxiety, loss of concentration, and memory lapses. The yeast may also interfere with hormone functions, particularly in women, and cause premenstrual tension.

As Dr. Truss points out in his book, *The Missing Diagnosis*, candidiasis patients suffering from depression should not abandon psychiatric treatment in adopting the candidiasis remedy. "Don't be too positive that this is it; it MAY NOT be," warned Dr. Truss. "This is not the answer to all depression."[6]

Other symptoms associated with the emotions include agitation, irritability, impotence, rapid mood swings, and drowsiness.

Candida affects women far more frequently than men, most commonly as a vaginal yeast infection. Although the precise cause of vaginal candidiasis is unknown, its symptoms are usually itching, pain, and a heavy, white curd-like discharge.

Gastrointestinal infections cause a number of other symptoms, such as diarrhea, gas, sour stomach, belching, bloating, stomach distension, constipation, colitis, abdominal cramps, and heartburn.

Candidiasis patients report a recent aversion to many chemicals, particularly those affecting the sense of smell. Perfumes, tobacco smoke, exhaust fumes, hair sprays, furniture polishes, and deodorants become intolerable.

Other generalized symptoms include those normally associated with allergies, such as runny nose, sneezing, cough, post-nasal drainage, frequent sore throat, sinus infection, and bronchitis. Headaches, psoriasis, hives, swelling, weight changes, and dizziness have also been associated with candidiasis.

With such a wide array of symptoms, it is easy to understand why candidiasis is frequently misdiagnosed. The symptoms are basically universal and would apply to just about any sick person at one time or another.

This has prompted some medical authorities, particularly those at the American Academy of Allergies and Immunology, to raise questions about whether or not all of these symptoms are caused by candidiasis. In fact, the AAAI has noted that there is no published proof linking the syndrome to the candida albicans yeast.

The fact is that some people with these symptoms do not have a yeast problem. The question for a healthy person is whether or not one can acquire candidiasis if the immune system is healthy. The answer is maybe, but there is presently no evidence to support an affirmative answer.

TREATMENT

At this point, there is no long-term cure for candidiasis, nor a reliable way to prevent it. Treatment of symptoms is often effective, however, and relief should be evident within a few weeks.

Treatment programs almost always combine prescription drugs, usually Nystatin, with a low-carbohydrate diet to slow the growth of the yeast. Other factors that may have contributed to the onset of the infection, such as antibiotics, birth-control pills, or chemotherapy are also discontinued whenever possible.

Carol Jessop, an internist in El Cerrito, California, treated 900 patients suffering from chronic fatigue with a sugar free diet and Ketoconazole, an antifungal drug. She found that 529 of the patients returned to their previous health and the condition of 232 others improved.[7]

The medical establishment has no quarrel with the treatment of candidiasis, because mainstream physicians have been treating it for decades. The controversy surrounds treatment of "generalized" candidiasis, a reference to the theory that the ailment afflicts millions of people in Western societies.

The American Medical Association has noted the lack of supporting evidence for generalized candidiasis infection. The association suggests that the ailment is a convenient "catch-all" for people who are sure they suffer a disease, although physicians have not been able to identify it.

In light of the controversy, the obvious question is: Does treatment do any harm? The answer is no and yes. Treatment itself appears harmless, but the neglect of other curable diseases may cause serious problems. For example, severe depression or organic disease might go unrecognized, leading to an exacerbation of the illness. In addition, the antifungal agents prescribed may lead to drug-resistant strains of yeasts. Cynics also argue that treatments are expensive and raise false hope.

Modern medicine is ably equipped to treat the condition when it occurs. Prescription drugs are effective in killing the yeast, but the infection frequently returns within three or four weeks. Prolonged treatment with drugs in low doses has proved somewhat effective in preventing recurrences.

A variety of means have been developed to administer the drugs in different ways, depending on the area of infection. Enemas, douches, and nasal sprays are sometimes used. Women suffering from vaginal infections also use vaginal suppositories and creams.

Nystatin, which is one of the most widely prescribed drugs for yeast infections, is available in a number of forms, including tablets, powder, and cream. In small doses, the drug has few adverse effects, except in those who may be allergic to it. In higher doses, however, it can produce several side effects, particularly vomiting and diarrhea.

Less commonly prescribed is ketoconazole, which can cause damage to the liver under certain circumstances. It is not recommended for those suffering from liver disease, alcoholism, or some stomach disorders.

In severe cases of candidiasis infection, physicians prescribe amphotericin B, another antifungal medication. This is sometimes administered through intravenous or spinal injections, although it also is marketed in a variety of forms. Its most common side effects are fever and chills, headache, indigestion, nausea, irregular heartbeat, cramps, and tiredness.

Other antifungal medicines have been used successfully, so if a patient has allergic reactions to one, another type is usually available to combat the yeast infection.

Some physicians, especially those who practice holistic medicine, a branch of medicine that concentrates on natural treatments, prescribe non-drug therapies that include garlic, coffee enemas, caprylic acid (a natural fatty acid), herbal teas, megavitamins, and yogurt. All of these programs aim to kill the yeast, while rebuilding the body's immune system to fend off recurrent infections. The medical efficacy of such treatments remains to be proven.

Of special interest is the current effort to develop a vaccine for candidiasis, especially for women suffering repeated bouts of vulvovaginal candidiasis. An oral vaccine prepared from ribosomes of candida albicans is being tested by D. A. Levy, a French immunologist, who has reported positive results from preliminary studies.

According to Dr. Levy, the vaccine could be effective for three-fourths of women who have at least one previous infection. A larger study is underway and should provide more information on the effectiveness of this vaccine.

DIETARY GUIDELINES

Yeasts thrive in a sugar-rich environment, so advocates of the candidiasis theory recommend a special diet low in yeast, sugar, and carbohydrates. Cookbooks for candida patients have been published with a variety of menus and recipes.

People should realize that they might need to maintain this type of diet for months or years. The aim is to deprive the yeast of an amiable host by reducing its food. Additionally, molds and yeasts are eliminated from the diet.

Gail Burton, author of *The Candida Control Cookbook*, recommends that dieters should keep their carbohydrate intake to between 60 and 100 grams a day, less than a quarter of a pound. She notes, however, that dieters should rely on health care professionals to set their individual levels.

Here are some dietary guidelines based on the theory advanced by Dr. Crook, Dr. Truss, and others:

1. Sugar should be kept to a minimum in any form, such as cane, beet, or corn sugars. That goes for foods rich in natural

sugar, such as juices and fruits. Fresh squeezed juice is best, since it has less sugar.

2. Alcoholic beverages, which contain brewer's yeast, are also a problem. Beer is especially troublesome. Wine, hard liquor, cider, and root beer are other fermented drinks that should be avoided, too.

3. Baked goods that have baker's yeast as a component must be avoided, so this includes virtually all commercial breads, pastries, and cakes. Substitute such things as muffins, biscuits, pancakes, and breads prepared with buckwheat, corn meal, soy flour, and rice flour.

4. Avoid smoked, cured, or processed meats, since they usually contain sugar and yeast. These meats include ham, bacon, sausage, and hot dogs.

5. Cereals that contain malt, such as oatmeal, should be passed up in favor of oat bran and rice brands.

6. Also avoid any table dressings or sauces that contain vinegar, such as mustard, mayonnaise, salad dressings, and pickled items.

7. Hard cheeses, since they contain molds, are a problem, and cottage cheese should be substituted.

8. Vegetables can be eaten with no problem, although fresh and frozen varieties are recommended. The total carbohydrate count for these vegetables should be included in the daily total.

A FINAL WORD

What is the consumer to do when faced with the medical debate that splits opinion on chronic, generalized candidiasis? How is anyone supposed to know if this debilitating syndrome is the cause of their fatigue when doctors themselves can't agree?

These are questions that may have no easy answers. At present, scientific logic seems to favor those who are skeptical about the extent and symptoms of this disease, but there are many issues left unresolved. How is one to explain, for example, the success reported by doctors and their patients who have been treated for candidiasis?

One thing seems clear, the conditions that promote the growth of yeasts—antibiotics, birth control pills, sugar-rich diets—are all mainstays of modern life in Western societies. It seems likely that if yeast infections are not widespread, at least the conditions in our time are more favorable for their growth.

Although conclusive scientific evidence has not been found to support the theory, there is a wealth of anecdotal information from patients who have found antiyeast therapy to be helpful. Nevertheless, people should approach candidiasis treatment with a healthy skepticism and not rely on it entirely to solve their problems. A combination of therapies, developed in consultation with the family physician, is most likely to provide the best result.

CHAPTER THIRTEEN

TIME MANAGEMENT
SAVING TIME SAVES ENERGY

INTRODUCTION

The key to time management is control. If we take control of our time, we take control of our lives. Managing our lives means taking *action*. For this reason, time management techniques are very useful in plotting a strategy to overcome fatigue.

Time is unique, elusive, and fleeting. Once it is gone, it is gone forever. But, on the other hand, time is the great equalizer. We all have the same amount—24 hours a day.

Time management can help two kinds of people who feel tired: those doing too much and those doing too little. Busy people can use time management to weed out the clutter in their lives to make time for relaxation and enjoyment. Inactive, disorganized, or bored people can use time management to schedule stimulating activities to revitalize their lives.

Poor planning and fatigue go together like matching bookends. One complements the other. Accomplishing something without a plan takes more time and energy. When our disorganized day ends, we find ourselves exhausted even though important tasks may be left unfinished, or worse, never attempted. Our failure results in stress, frustration, guilt, and finally, fatigue.

On some days, we may feel too tired to do anything and just

decide to stay in bed or watch television all day. But this only makes us feel all the more useless, bored, and tired. Instead, we should plan activities to rouse motivation, initiate action, and defeat the paralysis that causes fatigue. Action is an essential element of will power, builds self-esteem and can be exhilarating. After all, we are doing something!

Action and motivation provide the stimulation we need to stop wasting our life's most valuable resource—time. By scheduling activities efficiently, we'll have stimulating things planned to do and more time to do them.

Time management is usually considered a means of *saving* time and energy, but it is also a way to *spend* time and energy. Deciding on the best ways to spend these scarce resources will help eliminate fatigue.

Time management won't solve all problems, but it gives us a crucial weapon to fight the things that deplete our energy unnecessarily. Better organization will help all of us do more in less time with less effort.

TIME MANAGEMENT CONCEPTS

The two major principles of time management are planning and analysis. If you take stock of your time, analyze it, and then schedule it better, you are on the way to mastering the basics of time management.

Our lives are composed of different "types" of time—work time, leisure time, overtime, and so forth. Some of our time is controllable and some is not. That is, either we control it, or someone or something else controls it.

Nobody has complete control over his or her time. Working, sleeping, eating, and other daily routines consume most of our 24-hour allotment. If we have 10 percent or more left over we might consider ourselves lucky.

A variety of theories relate to time management, a subject that has been codified into something of a science for system analysts and business managers. But the elements of time management are very simple, as illustrated by a story that has become legend among consultants.

Ivy Lee's Lesson

R. Alec Mackenzie told the following story in his book *The Time Trap* to illustrate one of the principles of time management. He quoted from an account in Donald V. Schoeller's "How to Find an Extra Golden Hour Each Day."

Charles Schwab, who was then president of Bethlehem Steel, met with Ivy Lee, a time management consultant. Schwab made an unusual offer. "Show me a way to get more things done with my time, and I'll pay you any fee within reason," he said.

Lee scribbled something down on a sheet of paper and handed it to the chief executive. Mr. Lee said, "Write down the most important tasks you have to do tomorrow and number them in order of importance. When you arrive in the morning, begin at once on No. 1 and stay on it till it's completed. Recheck your priorities; then begin with No. 2. If any task takes all day, never mind. Stick with it as long as it's the most important one. If you don't finish them all, you probably couldn't do so with any other method, and without some system you'd probably not even decide which one was most important. Make this a habit every working day. When it works for you, give it to your men. Try it as long as you like. Then send me a check for what you think it's worth."

A few weeks later Schwab sent Lee a check for $25,000 and a note saying the advice was the most profitable lesson he had ever learned. Later, when someone asked him if that weren't a lot to pay for such a simple idea, Schwab replied, "What ideas aren't basically simple?"

The Schwab story underscores the importance of planning. Any system is better than no system. Without a system, you may never decide on your priorities. Planning is the first step. It gives you more control over your time. Making a daily list, setting priorities, and completing them are integral to any time management system.

Pareto's Law

This law, sometimes called the 20–80 rule, is credited to Vilfredo Pareto, a 19th century Italian economist and sociologist. The law states that a small percentage of a group accounts for a large percentage of a particular characteristic. For example, a small number of authors may account for most of a publisher's sales, a few inventors may hold the largest number of a firm's patents, or a handful of students may represent a large percentage of absences. By altering the behavior of a few in the influential group, one can produce disproportionate results.

In terms of time management, this means that you should devote a major portion of your time and energy to major goals. Get someone else to do the more trivial things or don't bother with them at all. Individuals who allot too much time and energy to unimportant tasks will not only fail, but exhaust themselves in the process.

The key factor in this law is identifying the most valuable tasks, items, or objectives. Only you can make that decision. What is most important to you? To your company? For your family? What things bring the biggest payoff? Put these things on your priority list and mark them with a star.

The 20–80 rule applies to many business problems. For example, consider the Best Upholstery Co., which has 100 commercial accounts. Last year, 80 percent of Best's profits came from 20 accounts. A review of Best's management of time resources, however, determined that its employees were spending equal time on all accounts (i.e., 80 percent of their time was spent on the 80 less profitable accounts). One doesn't need to be a genius to realize this was inefficient and courted disaster. It is foolish to concentrate on trivial things, while neglecting essentials.

The Pareto rule is not infallible, but it emphasizes that the lion's share of the reward can be gained by concentrating on a relatively small number of things. So what if you don't get everything done? Do the things that matter most and you'll be successful.

Make a list of 10 things you want to do tomorrow. The chances are that two of them (20 percent) promise to reap the biggest benefits to you personally. Concentrate on those two things and experience the success this brings.

Murphy's Three Laws

Murphy's three laws are not just the punch lines to office jokes. They may be funny, but each has a significant message.

The first law is: "Nothing is as simple as it seems." This is a warning not to underestimate a task. Few of us can see all the obstacles ahead, especially in big projects. It is crucial to plan for the unexpected.

The second law is: "Everything takes longer than you think." This follows from the first, since underestimating the complexity of a job will lead to delays, broken deadlines, and possible failure.

The third law is the most famous: "If anything can go wrong, it will." This principle underscores the need for contingency planning, too often neglected in the rush to get a project under way. Plan for the unexpected and fall back on alternate plans when things go wrong.

Parkinson's Law

Parkinson's Law states that work will expand to fill the time allotted to its completion. Without specific planning, the time for small, minor tasks will expand and crowd out time for major priorities.

Schedule fixed amounts of time for specific activities to prevent Parkinson's Law from defeating your goals. Newspaper editors, who work against daily deadlines, know that reporters will take as much time (or as little time) as editors will give them to finish a story.

Applying Parkinson's law should help you accomplish more things in less time. By watching the clock, you should be able to increase efficiency. You may be pleasantly surprised to find that quality does not suffer, although it may at first as you adjust to the new time constraints.

PERSONAL STYLE AND TIME MANAGEMENT

Different personalities use time differently. Some people are naturally organized, while others are naturally disorganized. Recognizing strengths and weaknesses in our personal styles will help us manage our time better.

The bottom line in time management is: Are we accomplishing what we want to do in the time we want to do it? As we begin our day, a hundred distractions loom in our way. How we cope with these obstacles depends a lot on the type of person we are. Some people are tempted to do too much and fail to complete things. Others find it hard to make up their minds what to do. Let's look at a few different types.

Busyness

The old maxim that if you want something done, ask a busy person, is only partly true. Some people are too busy. They are like hummingbirds, buzzing from one thing to another in a blur of motion. Easily distracted by other things, they are likely to drop everything to pick up something else, never completing the thing left behind. They tend to be absent-minded and forget things. They live on the edge of panic. Constant anxiety and stress quickly lead this person to exhaustion.

The best advice for the too-busy person is to slow down, relax, and find some "quiet time" to restore a balance in competing priorities. Keep a detailed record of the day, hour by hour. Learn to eliminate interruptions. Don't be quick to pick up somebody else's crisis. Be tough and learn to say no! The daily list of objectives is crucial. Refer to it often and stick to the plan.

Indecisiveness

We all have attacks of indecisiveness from time to time, especially when we are tired. Faced with difficult choices, we can't make up our minds. This is fine if it happens once in a while, but we encounter trouble if we put off making *any* decisions. Worse, we may let someone else make our decisions for us. Our goals remain unfulfilled and we end up frustrated.

An effective way to combat indecisiveness is to list specific priorities. Analyze goals, desires, and needs, and then set your priorities. Work consistently on those few goals. Realize that nobody makes the right decision every time. Being wrong is sometimes better than not making the choice at all. Try to make your decisions one at a time.

Perfectionism

People who feel that anything short of perfection is failure impose many obstacles in their path to success. Perfectionists have such high expectations for themselves that failure is virtually inevitable.

To make matters worse, perfectionists take on too much and try to do it all, expecting superhuman achievements from their efforts. Perfectionists exhaust themselves by striving to succeed against impossible self-imposed odds. Sometimes they become so discouraged, they stop trying altogether. Either way, they risk a life of frustration and exhaustion.

The seeds of perfectionism are usually sown in childhood, when the person may have sought to please a parent or other role model who set high and possibly unrealistic standards.

The friendly reminder for perfectionism is simple: Set realistic goals! Sort through your list of goals, throw out the unrealistic ones, and identify those you can attain. This concentrates your energy on fewer tasks and provides early success. Learn to accept the best you can do. It may be better than you think.

Brinkmanship

Some people thrive on stress and push deadlines to the brink before completing tasks. They wait until the last minute, then make an eleventh hour effort powered by an adrenalin rush that typically leaves them exhausted once it passes. Frequently, these people need this type of pressure to get moving. They feel they work well under pressure. This may be true, but in the long term the anxiety, stress, and exhaustion caused by the hectic pace will produce unfavorable results.

In a sense, brinkmanship is a product of procrastination. Reduce procrastination by setting early deadlines. Break projects up into smaller parts and set different deadlines for each, working toward them step by step. Better planning is the key to overcoming the disasters of brinkmanship.

PLANNING—SETTING GOALS AND PRIORITIES

Goals are the key to planning. Without them, we are travelers rushing headlong into nowhere. We must set a destination to bring sense and order to our trip. Where are we going? How are we to get there? These are critical questions for the manager of time.

Our goals fall into two broad categories—short term and long term. The short-term goals might involve a variety of daily or weekly tasks. These account for most of the things on the daily to-do list and are relatively unimportant. The things we hold most dear are our lifetime goals.

Lifetime goals are our dreams of success—a college education, a new career, retirement to Florida, a new home, a trip to Europe. These lifetime goals are what we live and work for. We can achieve all our short-term objectives and still be discouraged, frustrated, and unfulfilled. For happiness, we must make progress toward our dreams.

Other long-term objectives have nothing to do with money or careers, but revolve on what type of life we want to live. These goals embrace our personal relationships, religious beliefs, social commitments, and family life. Such intangible things are the fabric of our lives and deserve as much of our time as possible.

In the rush of making it through the day, few people stop to ask themselves what they've done to work toward their lifetime goals. What was done to strengthen a marriage or friendship? What activity brings that college graduation nearer? These top-priority goals too often become victims of expediency, put off to accomplish short-term objectives.

Make a list of your lifetime goals. These are your top priorities. Resolve to do something each day to work toward them. Schedule time every day for these activities.

Short-term goals are significant, too, but there are many more of them and they must be sorted out into their own hierarchy of priorities. In going over this list, ask yourself a number of questions:

1. Does this help in achieving a lifetime goal?
2. Can this item be eliminated or can someone else do it for me?
3. When does this need to be done?
4. How much time will it take?
5. What priority does it deserve?
6. What is the best time to do this during the week? During the day?

Only you know what the top priorities are in your life and only you can set the agenda for the things you want to accomplish. Scrutinize the daily list. Analyze each item. Be ruthless in tossing things out that conflict with your highest goals.

WHERE DOES YOUR TIME GO? DAILY TIME LOG

Most people have never sat down to figure out where each minute of their day has gone. If they did, they might be surprised at how much free time they have. Others might be surprised they have any free time at all!

Before setting out on your new time-managed life, it may be useful to reflect on the old one. A detailed time log of your daily routine can be a great tool in reevaluating your allocation of time. Keep track of your activities throughout the day, writing them down in a notebook every hour on the hour. Maintain the log for at least a week to see what patterns emerge.

People are often amazed to find how much time they waste every day. A lucky few may luxuriate in the discovery of large blocks of time, such as two or three hours each night spent watching television. Reclaiming these blocks for higher priority items usually results in a wealth of rewards. Unfortunately, most people realize that their free time is a mere fraction of their waking day—perhaps an hour and a half or two hours. These people quickly realize how precious this time is and redouble their efforts to make the most of it.

The time log is useful in demonstrating the variety of activities we encounter throughout the day. Every day is different, presenting new crises and new challenges. The effective time manager takes this into account and plans for the unexpected.

When writing the time log, note whether the activity was planned or not. Rate the activity from 1 to 10 in terms of importance and the amount of satisfaction it gives you. Make a special note for interruptions in your schedule, such as unexpected phone calls, drop-in visitors, or family emergencies. Be on the lookout for any consistent interruptions.

Review the time log periodically to find out where you can save time. Could some things be delegated? Could some be eliminated altogether? Can you increase your discretionary time? What share of time was planned? Can you increase the amount of planned time? Finally, determine which goals were accomplished. Once you have analyzed the log carefully, make the necessary adjustments to your schedule.

DAILY TO-DO LIST

Once your goals and priorities are set, put Ivy Lee's lesson to work for you. The daily "to-do" list is the most essential of all time management tools. Write the list each night during a quiet moment alone before going to bed. At this time, review your long- and short-term goals, add any new priorities to your goals, then write down the things you want to accomplish tomorrow. Set up a system of notation to flag the items for priority. Number them or give them letters from A to Z. You might circle those that have to be done or underline those with the lowest priority.

Once the priorities on the daily list are marked, estimate the amount of time each will take to complete. If a project will be on-going for many days, estimate the time to complete one part of it. Finally, schedule time slots the next day for each of the items, taking into account their priority and estimated completion time.

In the beginning, you may find the available time for these things is terribly short. The bulk of your schedule has already been blocked out with meetings, appointments, and commitments that are unmovable—a dental appointment, piano lesson, sales meeting. After you become a veteran of this type of planning, however, you will find ways to expand this discretionary time.

Before making up the schedule, identify your high productivity hours and plan your day accordingly. Everybody has peak energy periods during the day. Some people are barrels of energy the first thing in the morning. Others hit their peak after sunset. Schedule your high priority activities for your best hours, leaving lower priorities for when you are in a slump.

Making a list and checking it twice is only the first step. Next comes the hard part—accomplishing the objectives. In the course of a day, a dozen interruptions and distractions will tempt you from your path. Whatever happens, keep to the plan. Depart from your list only in case of emergencies and unexpected developments that change your priorities.

The to-do list isn't sacred, but nearly so. Don't let it rule your life, however. Stay flexible so you can respond to the events of the day. The thing is to get back on track when you stray.

At the end of the day, perhaps when you are preparing the next day's list, evaluate how things went. What sidetracked your efforts? How can this be avoided in the future? Are there any chronic problems that come up over and over again?

It is hard to understate the importance of the daily list, but it is only one tool and it is only as useful as you make it. Keep your lists on file and review them to see the progress you are making towards your goals.

PROCRASTINATION

Procrastination is the king of time wasters. It drains energy and leaves a person tired before anything has been done. Thinking about doing something instead of doing it is no way to succeed. The best antidote is action. Force yourself to break through the barrier of inertia and do what needs to be done.

Why do people procrastinate? Three factors seem to contribute most to this problem. First, avoiding unpleasant things is part of human nature. Second, putting off difficult tasks is a temptation most people can't ignore. Third, making tough choices is difficult because it involves risk.

Effective planning with detailed objectives and a schedule for completing them is the best weapon against procrastination. A variety of strategies have proved effective in fighting this insidious time waster.

Set Deadlines

Deadlines concentrate the mind wonderfully on a given task. A moderate amount of pressure is all it takes to get something off square-1. Deadlines might involve setting meetings to review progress or simply marking the calendar.

Break big jobs down into small ones and schedule the different parts with different deadlines. Remember that a trip of a thousand miles begins with a single step. Looking at the entire task as a whole may be overwhelming and frightening, which will encourage you to put the task off.

Do the Difficult First

Review your list of goals and sort out the tough ones to concentrate on first. If you work on the easy ones first, you may fall victim to Parkinson's Law, allowing the time for these activities to expand and crowd out time for the tough ones. Again, break the complex tasks into smaller parts, working on each of them systematically. This makes the tough jobs easier to manage. It also builds confidence as you complete each separate phase of the project.

Reward Yourself

Nothing motivates people like a little reward. Promise to buy yourself something after you have finished a project. This helps take some of the pain out of the unpleasant things we need to do and provides incentive to get them done. Positive reinforcement is a staple of behavioral psychology. Choose your rewards carefully. They need not be expensive or elaborate. The positive feeling of accomplishment is what counts.

Make a Decision

Indecision is at the heart of procrastination. A perfectionist will find dozens of reasons to put off a decision. Many times, fear is the cause of the delay. Accept the fact that any decision is fraught with inherent risks. A timely choice allows time to correct any problems and offers some insurance for success. Sometimes it helps to make a decision with others. Your spouse or co-workers can offer valuable input to make tough decisions easier.

Look at the Downside

The risks of moving ahead often pale in comparison with the risks of not doing anything. Have you been putting off that roof repair? Think of the downside—ruined furniture, water-damaged walls, rotted wood. The result is more costly repairs later. Looking at the downside should spur the procrastinator to action.

Procrastination is a bad habit and can be overcome only with self-determination. It is primarily a psychological problem and requires a change in behavior, but don't try to change overnight. Slow, gradual change offers the best chance of success. Identify the things you tend to put off regularly and then work on one thing at a time. Once you've mastered one, take up another.

TIME MANAGEMENT AT THE OFFICE

Unfortunately, for many of us work is associated with stress, frustration, and exhaustion. Anything that can reduce stress in the work place would be welcome and, fortunately, time management for business has become something of a science.

The incentive for business is money. In the business world, time is money. Lawyers bill clients in 6-minute blocks. Most workers are paid on an hourly basis. Management of workers' time is in the essence of business management itself.

Your own time and energy are the most valuable assets you possess, so anything that wastes either must be dealt with ruthlessly. All the time management techniques—the daily list, time log, goal setting—apply to your work day, but three areas of office operations are especially notorious for wasting time. Analyze the way you handle paperwork, telephone calls, and meetings for big time savings.

Paperwork

If you are drowning in paperwork, you probably aren't screening the mail carefully enough. Most mail can be thrown out. Make it a habit to handle a piece of paper just once. Either toss it, file it, delegate it, or answer it. Don't keep moving it around on top of your desk.

One helpful tip is to answer letters with quick notes in longhand on the original. This saves time and paper! A lot of replies may be done with a form letter on file in your office computer. Simply make notes on the boilerplate and print out your reply.

Paper creates work and drains time and energy. It must be read, sorted, filed, and some of it must be answered. Make it a point to cut down on the amount of paper coming into your office at every opportunity.

Telephones

The telephone can be an office tyrant. You can waste a lot of time on the phone. Whenever you think of calling someone, ask yourself if a brief note might save time.

If you have a secretary, make sure you block all telephone calls at least part of your working day so that you can concentrate on your list of priorities. Have your staff screen the calls more effectively. It may surprise you how many calls can be handled completely by your secretary or other subordinates. If you have no secretary, you might want to use an answering machine to screen your calls.

Adopt a "telephone style" to keep conversations shorter and to the point. Speak to the heart of the matter, keep small talk to a minimum, and stick to the point. It helps to plan your call. Make a note of the points you want to make or information you need, cover them quickly, and then end the conversation.

Meetings

Of all the office time wasters, meetings top the list. Meetings are essential, but they can also be dull, inefficient, and unproductive. The first question to ask before scheduling a meeting is: Is this meeting necessary? If it isn't, don't meet.

Long meetings—those that take more than an hour—are almost always the most unproductive. Few meetings should run more than an hour. If certain meetings tend to run long, schedule them an hour before lunch or quitting time.

Here are more suggestions to make meetings more productive:

1. Have a clear agenda and stick to it. Make sure people attending the meeting have a copy so they arrive prepared.
2. Don't let people talk about anything they choose. Keep discussion focused on the issues outlined on the agenda.
3. Keep the size of the meeting at a manageable level—certainly less than a dozen members. Any more and you are asking for trouble.
4. Look for alternatives to the meeting, such as electronic mail, memoranda, or conference telephone calls.
5. To get an idea of the relative monetary value of a meeting, add up all of the salaries for those attending and find out what it's costing the company. This may encourage more effective, if not fewer, meetings.

TIME MANAGEMENT FOR THE BUSY HOMEMAKER

Most homemakers are models of efficiency by necessity. They wouldn't survive long if they weren't. Any woman raising a family, taking care of her husband, paying the bills, doing the shopping, and keeping the household on track deserves an honorary degree in time management.

The key for survival is control. As any good homemaker knows, control comes with organization. The daily to-do list is critical. A desk, calendar, bulletin board, and a place to hang keys are handy, too. An updated address book, a posted list of telephone numbers, and delegation of chores can save time.

Space can be the battlefield on which time is won or lost. Closets, shelves, filing cabinets, drawers, and cupboards should be neat and organized. This saves countless hours of fruitless searches for things later.

Make sure you have time for yourself every day. Everyone needs time alone, especially the mother of small children. Take a break whenever you can. Try to get out for a date with your spouse or a friend at least once a week.

FITTING IT INTO YOUR LIFESTYLE

Time management is a wonderful tool that can help boost morale and motivation simply by providing a "to-do" list of fun, exciting things to do. When people are tired, they don't feel like doing anything and time management skills help defeat that attitude.

For others, time management may be a lifesaver. Caught up in the hectic workaday world, these people are struggling against intense pressures, pushing themselves to exhaustion. Time management may help these too-busy people regain control of their lives. Human beings can only stand so much wear and tear before chronic, unremitting fatigue strikes home.

Saving time is only one objective. The real goal is to make the most of the hours available in our lives by planning more effectively. Time is a luxury. It is a precious and nonrenewable resource.

In the chaos of daily life, it is often too easy to lose sight of our moral objectives—our religious beliefs, family values, and personal philosophies—that help us cope with the difficulties we face. Time management gives us a chance to review these essential ideals every day.

Time management can ease the stress and fatigue that comes as we each work toward our goals by providing the energy to revitalize our lives.

Time Management Tips

1. Make a daily list of objectives you want to accomplish, set priorities, and schedule time for each.
2. Write down your lifetime goals, then list specific activities that will help you reach them.
3. End procrastination by identifying its cause and working toward change.
4. Work on the most important things first.
5. Keep a time log of your activities and use it to analyze what you do, when you do it, and where you do it.
6. Finish everything you start. Don't let a streak of perfectionism prevent you from finishing a task because it doesn't live up to unrealistic standards.
7. Make good time management techniques a habit in your daily life.
8. Delegate as many tasks to others as possible.
9. Block interruptions during the day. For example, develop a plan to handle phone calls.
10. Make it one of your goals to seek out and destroy the time wasters in your life. For instance, cut back on television for an hour a day.
11. Be more assertive in saying no to others. Don't work on the to-do lists of others until you finish your own!
12. Break down the big jobs into little ones and set deadlines for the different parts.
13. Don't let your subordinates dictate your use of time. Manage them, don't let them manage you!
14. Set aside your most productive time for your highest priorities.
15. Keep track of where your time is going with a daily time log.
16. Move fast on reversible decisions, but slower on the ones you can't take back.
17. Tackle the tough jobs first.
18. Clean out your desk at least once a week. Throw out everything you don't need.
19. Make time for yourself to relax with friends and family. You need this time to recharge your batteries and renew creative juices.
20. Prepare an agenda for meetings and stick to it.
21. Give yourself a pat on the back when you reach an important goal. Buy yourself a special gift you have really wanted.

CHAPTER FOURTEEN

PUTTING IT ALL TOGETHER

Everyone faces change at some point during a lifetime. It comes to different people at different times and in different ways. It may mean breaking off a romantic attachment, switching jobs, or any number of things. To beat fatigue, change is inevitable. One must change to eliminate the cause of the fatigue, whether its source is alcoholism, smoking, overeating, or insomnia.

Significant lifestyle changes may be necessary. Giving up old habits will not be easy. People instinctively seek security in familiar patterns. Any change poses risks because something will be lost. At such times, doubts are normal. Will life really be better? Will I really change? What are the other, safer options?

These doubts arise from a fear of change, even if the outcome promises a better life. Self-change might be compared to passing another car on the road. The initial decision to pass is made once the road ahead is carefully inspected. Anxiety rises as the driver pulls out to pass. The fear is replaced by relief only after he has safely returned to his lane, but the driver continues with confidence that he will be able to overcome future obstacles in the road ahead.

There are many opportunities to "pass" or change in everyone's life. The problem, whether it is fatigue or something else, has forced the point of decision. In a sense, reading this book indicates that you may have already reached this decisive point.

HOW DOES A PERSON CHANGE?

A prescription for change may seem simple at first, but behind the common sense solutions are some formidable challenges. Resistance is a normal part of human nature. Letting go of the familiar things in our lives requires faith, not only in the remedy, but also in our own capacity to change.

As we have learned, fatigue has many causes. Rarely is one cause the sole culprit. A matrix of intermingling factors is more likely at the heart of the issue. To put things right, people must assess the overall situation, gain insight and knowledge about their individual problem, then plot an effective strategy, summon the necessary motivation, and commit themselves to action. Finally, once they are fully prepared, they must act.

The first step is a visit to your family doctor for a complete medical examination. Your physician will help you eliminate many possible causes of fatigue, especially those linked to organic disease. You can best help your doctor by providing a careful assessment of your medical history and personal habits. How much coffee do you drink? Do you smoke cigarettes, drink alcoholic beverages?

Once physical disease has been discounted, don't be lulled into complacency by the apparent simplicity of the doctor's advice. He may attribute the fatigue to a combination of a sedentary lifestyle, insomnia, and emotional stress. He might suggest that you exercise more, avoid stressful situations, and cut down on caffeine before bedtime. Although this sounds easy enough, putting it into practice may require fundamental changes in your lifestyle. Reducing stress, for example, may require a change of jobs. Finding time to exercise may force a complete reorganization of your daily schedule. And giving up coffee may not be easy, either.

Only after careful analysis, by the individual and the family doctor, can the diverse factors causing fatigue be whittled down to a short list. We must concentrate all our efforts on this short list of possible causes.

Any military man knows that a fundamental battle strategy is to divide the enemy. The divide and conquer stratagem is a good one in the battle against the causes of fatigue. Pick one target—smoking,

10 Tips to End Fatigue

These are some of the factors that will help alleviate fatigue.
1. **Proper Nutrition.** Eat a well-balanced diet that includes the major food groups—meat, fish, fruits, grains, vegetables, and dairy products.
2. **Comfortable Environment.** Review your environment, especially your sleeping quarters, for noise, poor ventilation, high or low temperatures, and inadequate lighting.
3. **Exercise Regularly.** If you spend much of the day sitting, plan an exercise program to build your stamina. Poor physical conditioning may be the problem.
4. **Improve Sleep.** Insomnia is a common complaint, but it can often be resolved. Experiment by sleeping more or less, going to bed earlier or later, to discover proper sleep time.
5. **Reduce Excess Weight.** The excess pounds you carry around all day may be responsible for your fatigue. Resolve to lose a certain amount of weight over a set period.
6. **Time Management.** Stop running around trying to do too much too soon. Take advantage of time management techniques to gain control over your life.
7. **Relax More.** Use some of the proven relaxation techniques to reduce stress. Biofeedback, meditation, autogenic training, and others can ease tension, promote sleep, and reduce emotional stress.
8. **Reduce Caffeine.** Caffeine is a drug that may overstimulate the body and mind, interfering with sleep and increasing anxiety. Try cutting back to no more than a couple of cups a day to see if it helps reduce fatigue.
9. **Quit Smoking.** Nicotine is a drug that creates dependence and is incompatible with health. Effects of tobacco smoke have been linked to many of the diseases that cause fatigue.
10. **Avoid Alcohol.** Alcohol is another drug that depresses bodily functions, causing fatigue and lethargy. Alcohol disturbs sleep, especially when taken near bedtime, and causes emotional turmoil that contributes to fatigue.

depression, stress, or whatever—and focus all your firepower on that one cause, win the battle, then turn to the next thing on your list. With each successive victory, you will become stronger for the next battle.

THE ABC MODEL

Although the number of causes of fatigue is great, a single method can be used effectively against most of them. The method, known as the ABC modality, is widely used by behavioral scientists to treat a range of difficulties, including smoking, alcoholism, obesity, stress, depression, and insomnia. The ABC model involves the affective (A), behavioral (B), and cognitive (C) aspects of a person's life. The method concentrates on control and management of human emotions, behavior, and thinking.

The affective mode is comprised of our feelings and emotions. When feelings get out of balance, they can overwhelm a person, causing intense anxiety or depression. Some people may have trouble expressing feelings, such as anger or fear, which can later emerge in unpredictable ways.

The behavior component of the ABC model refers to actions and patterns of actions that can be easily identified. Because behavior is overt, it can usually be managed effectively. A person who has trouble controlling eating behavior, smoking, or drinking can use the ABC method to reassert control.

Cognitive function, the third aspect of the ABC method, represents the perceptual faculties, such as reasoning and planning. The thinking that occurs in our minds affects our actions as well as our emotions. Some people carry negative attitudes or distorted perceptions, which adversely impact on their lives. Illogical thinking or poor problem-solving abilities also cause individual problems.

Healthy individuals maintain a balance of the three modes—affective, behavioral, and cognitive functioning. None of these modes exist independently of the others, since all must work together to form a well-integrated personality. At the same time, change in any one aspect, emotions, for example, may or may not affect change in the other two modes.

It was once thought that changing the way a person feels or thinks must precede a change in behavior, but a growing body of scientific evidence suggests that insight and understanding actually follow a change in behavior. This increasingly influential theory emphasizes modification in behavior and believes that our actions affect our moods and the way we perceive ourselves.

APPLYING THE THEORY

The three modes of the ABC model are constantly shifting and changing. At any moment, one may dominate, then give way to another. For example, a person who is obese may feel depressed about their weight (affective), think of themselves as ugly and hopeless (cognitive), and turn to eating for solace (behavioral). This sets up a vicious cycle that may be repeated over and over again. By concentrating on behavior and imposing weight control measures such as diet and exercise, the person should begin to feel better and develop a better self-concept. Review the Panel on page 204 in Chapter Nine for a detailed list of behavioral techniques used in weight reduction programs.

A destructive cycle like this one can be replaced by a beneficial cycle. For example, an employee who has a poor self-image (cognitive) may experience apprehension on the job (affective), leading to poor performance (behavioral). The worker can break this negative cycle and turn the pattern around. An accomplishment on the job may result in satisfaction and pride (affective), which then leads to improved self-confidence (cognitive), and finally to new and decisive action on the job (behavioral). This healthier cycle replaces the old and gains strength as it continues.

Although we have not specifically referred to the ABC method in the chapters of this book, we have discussed many of its key elements. Dysfunction in any of the three modes—emotions, thinking, and behavior—can contribute to fatigue. To change the affective or emotional causes one can employ relaxation techniques, meditation, hypnosis, insight, or self-awareness.

Distorted cognitive processes, such as poor self-concept, might require specific forms of psychotherapy, such as those discussed in the chapter on depression. Insight and knowledge gained through reading about various causes of fatigue will also help in cognitive restructuring by altering illogical or distorted thinking.

The behavioral techniques are the most commonly employed, since it is usually some sort of action that is causing the fatigue. Specific types of behavioral change are suggested in the chapters on smoking, alcoholism, insomnia, diet, relaxation, stress, and time management. Eliminating negative behaviors and replacing them with positive, reinforcing habits comprises the heart of behavior modification theory.

Once the dominant aspects of the ABC model are identified in relation to the causes of your fatigue, it will be much easier to decide on a course of action. Time management skills are helpful in charting a strategy, since planning and scheduling are crucial to any effective plan. It does little good to resolve to exercise every day, for example, but then provide no time to do it. Furthermore, specific goals that are accomplished by scheduled actions will boost confidence in one's ability to change.

Finally, self-change requires sacrifice. One may need to give something up that represents a significant investment, either emotionally or financially. There may be a sense of loss, a nostalgic longing to return to the old and familiar, but this will surrender after time to a new sense of confidence and self-control.

NEW ENERGY FOR NEW CHALLENGES

As fatigue lifts, a surge of new-found energy can revitalize all aspects of your life. This energy provides new strength for new challenges. Like anything else, success begets success. The energy rich get energy richer.

We know there is no single solution for everybody. Everyone has a unique set of situations in their lives. The ABC method works for many people, but not everyone. The important thing is to design a plan and work at it every day. Put the pieces of the puzzle together until you have a clear picture, then decide on a specific course of action.

People change in leaps and bounds, not by incremental steps. There is no slow and painless way to change, because an abrupt break with something in our past is necessary. Putting an end to the offending behavior is like walking through a door. Behind you lies the safe and familiar, in front awaits the unknown.

Fear accompanies any risk that threatens to change our lives. Human nature resists anything that throws the body and mind off balance. For some people, fatigue is a refuge of safety, a protective cloak used to avoid unpleasant things. These people may genuinely fear loss of this protection. What will it be like to live without fatigue? How will I cope with the new feelings?

A certain amount of apprehension is normal. It helps at such times to remember the alternative. Fatigue exacts a terrible price. A tired life is an unhappy life. Prolonged fatigue is a form of living death. The fatigue drains the sustenance from our lives, leaving our bodies listless and weak. A tired person drags himself joylessly through the day, while the person filled with energy is full of life itself. For these energetic people, vitality enriches every living moment.

Ending fatigue must, therefore, become a top priority, because fatigue affects every aspect of our lives—family, friends, hobbies, and career. Nothing escapes its debilitating effects.

Can we summon what energy remains to put up the good fight? As long as we live and breathe the answer must be yes. Anything else denies life itself. Change means we are growing, reaching for the higher rung of the ladder, stretching our human talents to the limit.

The goal we seek—a life free of fatigue—can be reached, but we deceive ourselves if we think it will come easily. Nothing this valuable is gained easily, but there are solutions out there waiting for us. The road is paved with the success of others. You can do it, too. Planning, persistence, sacrifice, and common sense will see you through.

The challenge is to walk through the door. In time, you will find your bearings in a new, brighter world that is free of the tired shackles that have bound you. You will do it. In fact, you have already begun.

REFERENCES AND FURTHER READINGS

INTRODUCTION

References

1. Halberstam, Michael J. "Fatigue," in *Current Diagnosis*, ed. Rex B. Conn. (Philadelphia, Pa.: W. B. Saunders, 1985), pp. 80–82.
2. Minden, Sarah and Peter Reich. "Nervousness and Fatigue," *MacBryde's Signs and Symptoms*, ed. Robert S. Blacklow. 6th edition. (Philadelphia, Pa.: J. P. Lippincott, 1983), pp. 591–621.
3. Chen, Martin. "The Epidemiology of Self-Perceived Fatigue among Adults," *Preventive Medicine* 15 (1986), pp. 74–81.
4. Morrison, John D. "Fatigue as a Presenting Complaint in Family Practice," *The Journal of Family Practice* 10 (1980), pp. 795–801.
5. Ibid.
6. Havard, C. W. H. "Lassitude," *British Medical Journal* 290 (April 20, 1985), pp. 1161–1162.
7. Morrison, John D. "Fatigue as a Presenting Complaint in Family Practice," *The Journal of Family Practice* 10 (1980), pp. 795–801.
8. Jerret, W. A. "Lethargy in General Practice," *The Practitioner* 225 (May, 1981), pp. 731–737.
9. Holmes, Gary P. and Jonathan E. Kaplan, et al. "Chronic Fatigue Syndrome: A Working Case Definition," *Annals of Internal Medicine* 108 (1988), pp. 387–389.

Further Reading

Atkinson, Holly. *Women and Fatigue*. (New York: G. P. Putnam, 1987.)

Clark, Marguerite. *Why So Tired?: The Whys of Fatigue and the Ways of Energy*. (New York: Duell, Sloan and Pearce, 1962.)

Hilliard, Marion. *Women and Fatigue: A Woman Doctor's Answer*. (Garden City, N.Y.: Doubleday, 1960.)

Laird, Donald A. and Eleanor C. Laird. *Tired Feelings and How to Master Them*. (New York: McGraw-Hill, 1960.)

Miller, Donald B. *Personal Vitality*. (Reading, Mass.: Addison-Wesley, 1974.)

Podell, Richard N. *Doctor, Why Am I So Tired?* (New York: Pharos Books, 1987.)

CHAPTER ONE

References

1. FDA Consumer, 1988.
2. Bunker, Mary Louise and Margaret McWilliams. "Caffeine Content of Common Beverages," *Journal of The American Dietetic Association*, 74 (January, 1974), pp. 28–31.
3. Ibid. p. 30.

Further Reading

MacMahon, Brian and Takashi Sugimura. *Coffee and Health Banbury Report 17*. (Cold Spring Harbor Laboratory, 1984.)

Dews, P. B., ed. *Caffeine: Perspectives from Recent Research* (Berlin: Springer-Verlag, 1984.)

Goulart, Frances Sheridan. *The Caffeine Book* (New York: Dodd, Mead & Co., 1984.)

CHAPTER TWO

References

1. For a complete evaluation of nicotine gum please refer to *Review and Evaluation of Smoking Cessation Methods: The United States and Canada, 1978–1985*, published by the U.S. Department of Health and Human Services, April 1986, pp. 35–42.
2. For more information on relief of symptoms and various studies on nicotine gum, please refer to *The Health Consequences of Smoking: Nicotine, A Report of the Surgeon General 1988* published by the U.S. Department of Health and Human Services.

Further Reading

Ferguson, Tom. *The Smoker's Book of Health*. (New York: Putnam, 1987.)

Schwartz, Jerome. *Review and Evaluation of Smoking Cessation Methods: The United States and Canada, 1978–1985*. (Washington, D.C.: National Cancer Institute, 1987.)

Smoking and Health: A Report of the Surgeon General (Washington, D.C.: U.S. Department of Health, Education, and Welfare, 1979.)

CHAPTER THREE

References

1. Jellinek, E. M. *The Disease Concept of Alcoholism*. (New Haven, Conn.: Hillhouse, 1960.)
2. Selzer, M. L. "The Michigan Alcoholism Screening Test: The quest for a new diagnostic instrument," *American Journal of Psychiatry*, (1971) 127:1653–1658.
3. Blum, Kenneth. *Handbook of Abusable Drugs*. (New York: Gardner Press, 1984), p. 241.
4. Royce, James E. *Alcohol Problems and Alcoholism*. (New York: Free Press, 1989), p. 107.
5. Cox, W. Miles. "The Addictive Personality," *Encyclopedia of Psychoactive Drugs*. (New York: Chelsea House, 1986.)
6. Mendelson, Wallace. *Human Sleep: Research and Clinical Care*. (New York: Plenum, 1987.)
7. Light, William J. Haugen. *Alcoholism: Its Natural History, Chemistry, and General Metabolism*. (Springfield, Ill.: Charles Thomas, 1985), pp. 55–56.
8. Royce, James E. *Alcohol Problems and Alcoholism: A Comprehensive Survey*. (New York: Free Press, 1989), p. 172.
9. Hennecke, Lynne and Vernell Fox. "The Woman and Alcoholism," in *Alcoholism: A Practical Treatment Guide*, eds. Stanley E. Gitlow and Herbert Peyser. (Philadelphia, Pa.: Grune and Stratton, 1988), pp. 172–189.
10. Vaillant, George E. "The Alcohol-Dependent and Drug-Dependent Person," in *The New Harvard Guide to Psychiatry*, ed. Armand M. Nicholi, Jr. (Cambridge, Mass.: Belknap Press, 1988), p. 705.
11. Ibid. pp. 706–707.
12. Fishman, Ross. "Alcohol and Alcoholism," *Encyclopedia of Psychoactive Drugs*. (New York: Chelsea House, 1987), p. 93.
13. Royce, James E. *Alcohol Problems and Alcoholism* (New York: Free Press, 1989), p. 273.

Further Reading

Beattie, Melody. *Codependent No More: How to Stop Controlling Others and Start Caring for Yourself*. (San Francisco, Calif.: Harper/Hazelden, 1987.)
Blum, Kenneth. *Handbook of Abusable Drugs*. (New York: Gardner Press, 1984.)
Cahn, Sidney. *The Treatment of Alcoholics: An Evaluative Study*. (New York: Oxford University Press, 1970.)

Cox, W. Miles. "The Addictive Personality," *Encyclopedia of Psychoactive Drugs*, Solomon H. Snyder, ed. (New York: Chelsea House, 1986.)

Fishman, Ross. "Alcohol and Alcoholism," *Encyclopedia of Psychoactive Drugs*, Solomon H. Snyder, ed. (New York: Chelsea House, 1987.)

Fort, Joe. *Alcohol: Our Biggest Drug Problem.* (New York: McGraw-Hill, 1973.)

Gallant, Donald M. *Alcoholism: A Guide to Diagnosis, Intervention, and Treatment.* (New York: W. W. Norton & Co., 1987.)

Gitlow, Stanley, and Herbert S. Peyser, eds. *Alcoholism: A Practical Treatment Guide.* (Philadelphia: Grune & Stratton, 1988.)

Goodwin, Donald W. *Alcohol and the Writer.* (Kansas City, Mo.: Andrews and McMeel, 1988.)

Light, William J. Haugen. *Alcoholism: Its Natural History, Chemistry and General Metabolism.* (Springfield, Ill.: Charles C. Thomas, 1985.)

Nicholi, Armand M., Jr., ed. *The New Harvard Guide to Psychiatry.* (Cambridge, Mass.: Belknap Press, 1988.)

Royce, James E. *Alcohol Problems and Alcoholism: A Comprehensive Survey.* (New York: Free Press, 1989.)

Tarter, Ralph E., and A. Arthur, eds. *Alcoholism: Interdisciplinary Approaches to an Enduring Problem.* (Reading, Mass.: Addison-Wesley, 1976.)

CHAPTER FOUR

References

1. Nicholson, A. N. and J. Marks. *Insomnia: A Guide for Medical Practitioners.* (Boston: MTP Press, 1983), p. 22.

2. Karacan, Ismet and James W. Howell. "Narcolepsy," in *Sleep Disorders: Diagnosis and Treatment.* Robert L. Williams, Ismet Karacan, and Constance Moore, eds. (New York: John Wiley, 1988), p. 87–105.

3. Mendelson, Wallace. *Human Sleep: Research and Clinical Care.* (New York: Plenum, 1987), pp. 303–304.

4. Moore-Ede, M. *Shiftwork and Your Health.* (New York: Circadian Technologies, Inc., 1986.)

5. Blum, Kenneth. *Handbook of Abusable Drugs.* (New York: Gardner Press, 1984), p. 371.

6. Refer to *Handbook of Abusable Drugs* by Kenneth Blum for a comprehensive review of benzodiazepines, barbiturates, and alcohol.

Further Reading

Dotto, Lydia. *Losing Sleep.* (New York: William Morrow & Co., 1990.)

Goldberg, Philip and Daniel Kaufman. *Natural Sleep: How to Get Your Share.* (Emmaus, Pa.: Rodale Press, 1978.)

Hales, Dianne. *The Complete Book of Sleep: How Your Nights Affect Your Days.* (Reading, Mass.: Addison-Wesley, 1981.)

Hartman, Ernest. *The Sleep Book: Understanding and Preventing Sleep Problems in People Over 50.* (Washington, D.C.: Scott, Foresman & Co., 1987.)

Hindmarch, I. ed. *Sleep, Benzodiazepines and Performance.* (Berlin: Springer-Verlag, 1984.)

Kales, Anthony, and Joyce D. Kales. *Evaluation and Treatment of Insomnia.* (New York: Oxford University Press, 1984.)

Nicholson, A. N., and J. Marks. *Insomnia: A Guide for Medical Practitioners.* (Boston, Mass.: MTP Press, 1983.)

Parkes, J. D. *Sleep and Its Disorders.* (Philadelphia, Pa.: W. B. Saunders Co., 1985.)

Paupst, James C., and Toni Robinson. *The Sleep Book.* (New York: Collier Books, 1975.)

Phillips, Elliot R. *Get a Good Night's Sleep.* (Englewood Cliffs, N.J.: Prentice-Hall, Inc., 1983.)

Regestein, Quentin R., and James R. Rechs. *Sound Sleep.* (New York: Simon and Schuster, 1980.)

Riley, Terrence L., ed. *Clinical Aspects of Sleep and Sleep Disturbance.* (Boston, Mass.: Butterworth, 1985.)

Sweeney, Donald R. *Overcoming Insomnia: A Medical Program for Problem Sleepers.* (New York: G. P. Putnam, 1989.)

CHAPTER FIVE

References

1. Morrison, John D. "Fatigue as a Presenting Complaint in Family Practice," *Journal of Family Practice* 10:5 (1980), pp. 795–801.

2. Beck, Aaron T. *Depression: Cases and Treatment.* (Philadelphia, Pa.: University of Pennsylvania Press, 1967), p. 40.

3. *The Diagnostic and Statistical Manual of Mental Disorders* (*DSM-III-R*). (Washington, D.C.: American Psychiatric Association, 1987), p. 222.

4. Adapted from the appendix of "Diagnostic Criteria for Depression" in *The Handbook of Depression*, eds. William R. Leber and Ernest E. Beckham. (Homewood, Ill.: Dorsey Press, 1985), pp. 362–366.

5. Mathew, Roy J., Maxine Weinman and Hohsen Mirabi. "Physical Symptoms of Depression." *British Journal of Psychiatry* 139 (1981), p. 292.

6. *Diagnostic and Statistical Manual of Mental Disorders* (*DSM-III-R*). (Washington, D.C., American Psychiatric Association, 1987), p. 229.

7. Rosenthal, Norman E. and Thomas A. Wehr. *Psychiatric Annals* 17 (October, 1987), p. 10.

8. Bowlby, J. "The Making and Breaking of Affectional Bonds," *British Journal of Psychiatry*, 130 (197), pp. 201–210.

9. Arieti, Silvano and Jules Bemporad. *Severe and Mild Depression.* (New York: Basic Books, 1978), pp. 143–154.

10. Beck, Aaron T. *Depression: Causes and Treatment*. (Philadelphia, Pa.: University of Pennsylvania Press, 1967), p. 212.
11. Seligman, Martin. *Helplessness: On Depression, Development, and Death*. (San Francisco: Freeman, 1975), pp. 93–106.
12. Klerman, Gerald. "Depression and Related Disorders of Mood," in *The New Harvard Guide to Psychiatry*, ed. Armand M. Nicholi. (Boston: Belknap Press, 1988), p. 323.
13. Mendelwicz, J. "Genetic Research in Depressive Disorders," in *Handbook of Depression: Treatment, Assessment and Research*, eds. Ernest Beckham and William Leber. (Homewood, Ill.: Dorsey Press, 1985), p. 798.
14. Green, Alan I., John J. Mooney, and Joseph J. Schildkraut. "The Biochemistry of Affective Disorders: An Overview," in *The New Harvard Guide to Psychiatry*, ed. Armand M. Nicholi. (Cambridge, Mass.: Belknap Press, 1988), p. 135.
15. Mendels, Joseph and Doris Chernik. "Sleep Changes and Affective Illness," in *The Nature and Treatment of Depression*. (New York: Wiley, 1975), pp. 309–333.
16. Hartmann, Ernest. "Sleep," in *The New Harvard Guide to Psychiatry*, Armand M. Nicholi, ed. (Cambridge, Mass.: Belknap Press, 1988), p. 161.
17. Elkin, Irene et al. "National Institute of Mental Health Treatment of Depression Collaborative Research Program," *Archives of General Psychiatry*, 46 (November, 1989), pp. 971–984.
18. Shuchman, Miriam and Michael S. Wilkes. "Dramatic Progress Against Depression," *The New York Times Magazine*, Part 2. (October 7, 1990), p. 30.

Further Reading

Arieti, Silvano and Jules Bemporad. *Severe and Mild Depression: The Psychotherapeutic Approach*. (New York: Basic Books, 1978.)
Badal, Daniel W. *Treatment of Depression and Related Moods: A Manual for Psychotherapists*. (Northvale, N.J.: Jason Aronson, Inc., 1988.)
Beck, Aaron, T. *Cognitive Therapy and the Emotional Disorders*. (New York: New American Library, 1979.)
———. *The Diagnosis and Management of Depression*. (Philadelphia, Pa.: University of Pennsylvania Press, 1967.)
Beck, Aaron T., Brian F. Shaw, Gary Emery A., and John Rush. *Cognitive Therapy of Depression*. (New York: Guilford Press, 1979.)
Beckham, Ernest and William R. Leber, eds. *Handbook of Depression: Treatment, Assessment, and Research*. (Homewood, Ill.: Dorsey Press, 1985.)
Burns, David D. *Feeling Good: The New Mood Therapy*. (New York: New American Library, 1980.)
Byck, Robert, ed. "Treating Mental Illness," *Encyclopedia of Psychoactive Drugs*. (New York, N.Y.: Chelsea House, 1986.)
Clayton, Paula J. and James E. Barrett, eds. *Treatment of Depression: Old Controversies and New Approaches*. (New York, N.Y.: Raven, 1983.)
Corsini, Raymond J. *Current Psychotherapies*. (Itasca, Ill.: F. E. Peacock Publishers, 1984.)

Diagnostic and Statistical Manual of Mental Disorders (DSM-III-R), 3rd ed. (Washington, D.C.: American Psychiatric Association, 1987.)

Georgotas, Anastasios, and Robert Cancro, eds. *Depression and Mania*. (New York: Elsevier, 1988.)

Gilbert, Paul. *Depression: From Psychology to Brain State*. (Hillsdale, N.J.: Lawrence Erlbaum Associates, 1984.)

Kovel, Joel. *A Complete Guide to Therapy: From Psychoanalysis to Behavior Modification*. (New York: Pantheon, 1976.)

Nicholi, Armand M., Jr., ed. *The New Harvard Guide to Psychiatry*. (Cambridge, Mass.: Belknap Press, 1988.)

Priest, Robert. *Anxiety and Depression: A Practical Guide to Recovery*. (New York: Arco, 1983.)

Rush, John, ed. *Short-Term Psychotherapies for Depression: Behavioral, Interpersonal, Cognitive, and Psychodynamic Approaches*. (New York: Guilford Press, 1982.)

Seligman, Martin E. *Helplessness: On Depression, Development and Death*. (San Francisco: W. H. Freeman, 1975.)

Striano, Judi. *How to Find a Good Psychotherapist: A Consumer Guide*. (Santa Barbara, Calif.: Professional Press, 1987.)

Williams, J. Mark. *The Psychological Treatment of Depression*. (New York: The Free Press, 1984.)

CHAPTER SIX

References

1. Selye, Hans. *Stress without Distress* (Philadelphia, Pa.: Lippincott, 1974), passim.

2. Selye, Hans. "The Stress Concept Today," in *Handbook on Stress and Anxiety*, eds. Irwin L. Kutash and Louis B. Schlesinger. (San Francisco, Calif.: Jossey-Bass Publishers, 1980), p. 129.

3. Holmes, Thomas and Richard Rahe. "The Social Readjustment Rating Scale." *Journal of Psychosomatic Research* 11 (1967), p. 213.

4. Friedman, M. and R. Rosenman. *Type A Behavior and Your Heart*. (New York: Knopf, 1974.)

5. Kobasa, Suzanne C. "Stressful Life Events, Personality, and Health," *Journal of Personality and Social Psychology* 37 (January, 1979), pp. 1–11.

6. Hamilton, M. "The assessment of anxiety states by rating," *The British Journal of Medical Psychology* 32 (1959), p. 50.

7. Ware, J. Catesby. "Sleep and Anxiety," in *Sleep Disorders: Diagnosis and Treatment*, ed. Robert L. Williams et al. (New York: Wiley, 1988), pp. 189–214.

8. Grossman, P. and J. C. G. De Swart. "Diagnosis of Hyperventilation Syndrome on the Basis of Reported Complaints," *Journal of Psychosomatic Research* 28 (1984), pp. 97–104.

9. Lum, L. C. "The Syndrome of Habitual Chronic Hyperventilation," in *Modern*

Trends in Psychosomatic Medicine. Vol. 3. ed. Oscar Hill. (London: Butterworth, 1976), pp. 196–383.

10. Rice, Raymond L. "Symptom Patterns of Hyperventilation Syndrome," *American Journal of Medicine* (June, 1950), p. 691.

11. Lum, L. C. "Hyperventilation: The Tip of the Iceberg," *Journal of Psychosomatic Research* 19 (1975), pp. 375–383.

12. Grossman, P. and J. C. G. de Swart "Diagnosis of Hyperventilation Syndrome on the Basis of Reported Complaints," *Journal of Psychosomatic Research* 28 (1984), pp. 97–104.

13. Blum, Kenneth. *Handbook of Abusable Drugs* (New York: Gardner Press, 1984), p. 167.

14. Rosenfeld, Robert and George S. Everly, Jr. "The Pharmacological Treatment of Excessive Stress," in *A Clinical Guide to the Treatment of Human Stress Response* ed. George S. Everly (New York: Plenum, 1989), p. 254.

Further Reading

Cooper, Cary L., ed. *Stress Research: Issues for the Eighties.* (New York: Wiley & Sons, 1983.)

Beech, H. R., L. E. Burns, and B. F. Sheffield. *A Behavioral Approach to Management of Stress.* (New York: Wiley & Sons, 1982.)

Benson, Herbert, and Miriam Z. Klipper. *The Relaxation Response.* (New York: Avon, 1976.)

Everly, George S., ed. *A Clinical Guide to the Treatment of Human Stress Response.* (New York: Plenum, 1989.)

Folkard, Simon and Timothy Folkard, eds. *Hours of Work: Temporal Factors in Work-Scheduling.* (New York: John Wiley, 1985.)

Girdano, Daniel A., and George S. Everly, Jr. *Controlling Stress and Tension: A Holistic Approach.* (Englewood Cliffs, N.J.: Prentice-Hall, 1979.)

Hockey, Robert, ed. *Stress and Fatigue in Human Performance.* (New York: John Wiley, 1933.)

Kutash, Irwin L., Louis B. Schlesinger and Associates, eds. *Handbook on Stress and Anxiety.* (San Francisco, Calif.: Jossey-Bass, 1980.)

Jacobson, Edmund. *Progressive Relaxation.* 1929. Midway Reprint. (Chicago: University of Chicago Press, 1974.)

Maslach, Christina. *Burnout: The Cost of Caring.* (Englewood Cliffs, N.J.: Prentice-Hall, 1982.)

Morse, Donald R., and M. Lawrence Furst. *Stress for Success: A Holistic Approach to Stress and Its Management.* (New York: Van Nostrand Reinhold, 1979.)

Nucho, Aina O. *Stress Management: The Quest for Zest.* (Springfield, Ill.: Charles C. Thomas, 1988.)

Potter, Beverly. *Beating Job Burnout: How to Transform Work Pressure Into Productivity.* (Berkeley, Calif.: Ronin Publishing, 1980.)

Riggar, T. F. *Stress Burnout: An Annotated Bibliography.* (Carbondale, Ill.: Southern Illinois University Press, 1985.)

Selye, Hans, ed. *Selye's Guide to Stress Research. Vol. 1.* (New York: Van Nostrand Reinhold, 1980.)

———. *Selye's Guide to Stress Research. Vol. 2.* (New York: Van Nostrand Reinhold, 1983.)

Shaffer, Martin. *Life After Stress.* (New York: Plenum, 1982.)

Simonson, Ernst and Philip C. Weiser. *Psychological Aspects of Physiological Correlates of Work and Fatigue.* (Springfield, Ill.: Charles C. Thomas, 1976.)

Woolfolk, Robert L., and Paul M. Lehrer, eds. *Principles and Practice of Stress Management.* (New York: Guilford Press, 1984.)

CHAPTER SEVEN

References

1. Jacobson, Edmund. *Progressive Relaxation.* 1938. (Chicago: University of Chicago, 1974), p. 419.

2. Morse, Donald Roy. *Stress for Success: A Holistic Approach to Stress and Its Management.* (New York: Van Nostrand Reinhold, 1979), pp. 227–240.

3. Shaffer, Martin. *Life After Stress.* (New York: Plenum, 1982), pp. 64–67.

4. Luthe, W. and Schutz, J. H., eds. *Autogenic Therapy* (vols. 1–6) (New York: Grune and Stratton, 1969.)

5. Benson, Herbert. *The Relaxation Response.* (New York: Avon Books, 1975), pp. 159–61.

6. *Stress Management.* Tactical Air Command Medical Services, United States Air Force. U.S. Government Printing Office, 1989, pp. 32–33.

7. Schwartz, Mark Stephen. *Biofeedback: A Practitioner's Guide.* (New York: Guilford Press, 1987), pp. 163–172.

8. Lehrer, Paul M. and Robert L. Woolfolk. "Are Stress Reduction Techniques Interchangeable, or Do They Have Specific Effects?" in *Principles and Practice of Stress Management* (New York: Guilford Press, 1984), pp. 404–77.

Further Reading

Powers, Melvin. *A Practical Guide to Self-Hypnosis.* (North Hollywood, Calif.: Wilshire Book Co., 1961.)

Rosa, Karl Robert. *You and AT.* (New York: Saturday Review Press, 1973.)

Schwartz, Mark S. and Associates. *Biofeedback: A Practitioner's Guide.* (New York: Guilford Press, 1987.)

Soskis, David A. *Teaching Self-Hypnosis: The Complete Guide for Clinicians.* (New York: Norton, 1986.)

Yates, John M., and Elizabeth S. Wallace. *The Complete Book of Self-Hypnosis.* (Chicago: Nelson-Hall, 1984.)

CHAPTER EIGHT

References

1. National Center for Health Statistics, C.A. Schoenborn, 1988. Health Promotion and Disease Prevention: United States, 1985. Vital and Health Statistics. Series 10, No. 163. Public Health Service. (Washington, D.C.: U.S. Government Office, 1988.)
2. President's Council on Physical Fitness and Sports. Physical Fitness Research Digest. Series 1, No. 1. (Washington, D.C., 1971.)
3. Chen, Martin K. "The Epidemiology of Self-Perceived Fatigue among Adults," *Preventive Medicine* 15 (1986), pp. 74–81.
4. Ledwidge, Barry. "Run for your mind: Aerobic Exercise as a means of alleviating anxiety and depression," *Canadian Journal of Behavioral Science* 12 (1980), pp. 126–140.
5. Hughes, John R. "Psychological Effects of Habitual Aerobic Exercise: A Critical Review," *Preventive Medicine* 13 (1984), pp. 66–78.
6. Stephens, Thomas. "Physical Activity and Mental Health in the United States and Canada: Evidence from Four Population Surveys," *Preventive Medicine* 17 (1989), pp. 35–47.
7. Greist, John H., et al. "Running as Treatment for Depression," *Comprehensive Psychiatry* 20 (Jan.-Feb. 1979), pp. 41–53.
8. Blumenthal, J. et al. "Psychological Changes Accompany Aerobic Exercise in Healthy Middle-Aged Adults," *Psychosomatic Medicine* 44 (1976), pp. 529–536, 1976.
9. Brown, Robert S., Donald E. Ramirez and John M. Taub. "The Prescription for Depression," *The Physician and Sports Medicine* (December, 1978), pp. 35–45.
10. Ibid.
11. Nieman, David C. *Fitness and Sports Medicine* (Palo Alto, Calif.: Bull Publishing Co., 1990), p. 395.
12. Ribisl, Paul M. "Developing An Exercise Prescription for Health," Ohio State University Libraries, Microfiche (October 4, 1975).
13. Karvonen M., K. Kental and O. Muslala. "The effects of training heart rate: A longitudinal study," *Annales Medicinae Experimentalis et Biologiae Fennaie* 35 (1957), pp. 307–315.

CHAPTER NINE

References

1. Chen, Martin. "The Epidemiology of Self-Perceived Fatigue among Adults," 15 *Preventive Medicine* (1986), pp. 74–81.
2. Ibid.
3. Altschul, Aaron. "Energy Balance," in *Weight Control: A Guide for Counselors and Therapists*, ed. Aaron Altschul. (Westport, Conn.: Praeger, 1987), pp. 45–46.

4. Buckmaster, Lisa and Kelly D. Brownell. *Behavior Modification: The State of the Art.* (Rockville, Md.: Aspen, 1988), pp. 225–240.

5. Stunkard, Albert J., Jennifer R. Harris, Nancy Pederson, and Gerald E. McClearn. "The Body-Mass Index of Twins Who Have Been Reared Apart," *The New England Journal of Medicine* 322:21, pp. 1483–1487.

6. Foreman, L. "The Fat Fallacy," 15:9 *Health* (1983), p. 23.

7. Altschul, Aaron. "The Complexity of Obesity and Its Treatment," in *Weight Control: A Guide for Counselors and Therapists,* ed. Aaron M. Altschul. (Westport, Conn.: Praeger, 1987), pp. 54–55.

8. Bouchard, Claude et al. "The Response to Long-Term Overfeeding in Identical Twins," *The New England Journal of Medicine,* 322:21 (May 24, 1990), pp. 1477–1482.

9. Coburn, Kerry L. "Physiological Controls for Energy Balance: A Historical View," in *Weight Control: A Guide for Counselors and Therapists,* ed. Aaron M. Altschul. (Westport, Conn.: Praeger, 1987), p. 29.

10. Wadden, Thomas A. and Albert J. Stunkard. "Social and Psychological Consequences of Obesity," *Annals of Internal Medicine,* 103 (1985), pp. 1062–1067.

11. Ibid.

12. Ibid.

13. Stunkard, Albert J. and Berthold, Howard C. "What is behavior therapy? A very short description of behavioral weight control," *The American Journal of Clinical Nutrition,* 41 (April 1985), p. 822.

14. Prout, T. E. "The Myth of the Usefulness of Amphetamines in the Long-Term Management of Obesity," in *Controversies in Therapeutics,* ed. L. Lasagna. (Philadelphia, Pa.: W. B. Saunders, 1980), pp. 184–190.

15. Franklin, Barry A. "Myths and Misconceptions in Exercise for Weight Control," in *Nutrition and Exercise in Obesity Management,* eds. J. Storlie and H. A. Jordan. (New York: Spectrum, 1984), pp. 53–92.

Further Reading

Abramson, Edward E. ed., *Behavioral Approaches to Weight Control.* Springer Series in Behavior Modification Vol. 3. (New York: Springer, 1977.)

Altschul, Aaron M., ed. *Weight Control: A Guide for Counselors and Therapists.* (Westport, Conn.: Praeger, 1987.)

Frankle, Reva T., ed. *Obesity and Weight Control: The Health Professional's Guide to Understanding and Treatment.* (Rockville, Md.: Aspen, 1988.)

Powers, Pauline S. *Obesity: The Regulation of Weight.* (Baltimore, Md.: Williams & Wilkins, 1980.)

Storlie, Jean and Henry A. Jordan, eds. *Evaluation and Treatment of Obesity,* Sports Medicine and Health Science. (New York: Spectrum, 1984.)

Storlie, Jean and Henry A. Jordan, eds. *Nutrition and Exercise in Obesity Management.* Sports Medicine and Health Science. (New York: Spectrum, 1984.)

Stunkard, Albert J. *Obesity.* (Philadelphia, Pa.: W. B. Saunders Co., 1980.)

CHAPTER TEN

References

1. Recommended Dietary Allowances. 10th edition. (Washington, D.C.: National Academy Press, 1989), p. 87.

Further Reading

Aero, Rita, and Stephanie Rick. *Vitamin Power: A User's Guide to Nutritional Supplements and Botanical Substances That Can Change Your Life*. (New York: Harmony Books, 1987.)

Bosco, Dominick. *The People's Guide to Vitamins and Minerals from A to Zinc*. 1980 (Chicago: Contemporary Books, 1989.)

Cheraskin, Emanuel, and W. Marshall Ringsdorf and Emily L. Sisley. *The Vitamin C Connection*. (New York: Harper & Row, 1983.)

Complete Book of Vitamins. Editors of Prevention Magazine, eds. (Emmaus, Pa.: Rodale Press, 1984.)

DeMoss, Virginia. *Runner's World Vitamin Book*. (Mountain View, Calif.: Runner's World Books, 1982.)

Faelten, Sharon, and Editors of Prevention Magazine. *The Complete Book of Minerals for Health*. (Emmaus, Pa.: Rodale Press, 1981.)

Gaby, Alan. *The Doctor's Guide to Vitamin B6*. (Emmaus, Pa.: Rodale Press, 1984.)

Handbook of Clinical Dietetics 5th edition. (Salt Lake City, Utah: Utah Dietetic Association, 1986.)

Hausman, Patricia. *The Right Dose*. (Emmaus, Pa.: Rodale, 1987.)

Mindell, Earl. *Vitamin Bible for Your Kids*. (New York: Rawson, Wade, 1981.)

Recommended Dietary Allowances 10th ed. Food and Nutrition Board. (Washington, D.C.: National Academy Press, 1989.)

Robinson, Corinne H., Wanda L. Chenoweth, Ann E. Garwick, and Marilyn Lawler. *Normal and Therapeutic Nutrition* 17th ed. (New York: MacMillan, 1986.)

"Some Facts and Myths of Vitamins." (FDA Consumer, July, 1988.)

"Vitamins and Megavitamins." *NASA Health Bulletin* No. 45 (1986.)

Whitney, Eleanor N. and Corrine B. Cataldo. *Understanding Normal and Clinical Nutrition*. (New York: West Publishing, 1983.)

Williams, Sue R. *Nutrition and Diet Therapy*. 5th ed. (St. Louis: Times Mirror/Mosby, 1985.)

CHAPTER ELEVEN

References

1. Holmes, Gary and Jonathan Kaplan, John Stewart et al. "A Cluster of Patients with a Chronic Mononucleosis-like Syndrome." *Journal of the American Medical Association* 257 (May 1, 1987), pp. 2297–2302.

2. Holmes, Gary P., Jonathan Kaplan et al. "Chronic Fatigue Syndrome: A Working Case Definition," *Annals of Internal Medicine* 108 (March, 1988), pp. 387–389.
3. Gold, Deborah and Raleigh Bowden et al. "Chronic Fatigue: A Prospective Clinical and Virologic Study," *Journal of the American Medical Association* 264:1 (July 4, 1990), pp. 48–53.
4. Buchwald, Dedra, John L. Sullivan, and Anthony Komaroff, "Frequency of 'Chronic Active Epstein-Barr Virus Infection,' in a General Medical Practice." 257:17 *Journal of the American Medical Association* 257:17 (May 1, 1987), pp. 2303–2307.
5. Gold, Deborah and Raleigh Bowden et al. "Chronic Fatigue: A Prospective Clinical and Virologic Study," *Journal of the American Medical Association* 264:1 (July 4, 1990), pp. 48–53.
6. Holmes, Gary P., Jonathan Kaplan et al. "Chronic Fatigue Syndrome: A Working Case Definition," *Annals of Internal Medicine* 108 (March, 1988), pp. 387–389.
7. Manu, Peter and Thomas J. Lane, and Dale A. Matthews. "The Frequency of Chronic Fatigue Syndrome in Patients with Symptoms of Persistent Fatigue," *The Annals of Internal Medicine* (109) (Oct. 1, 1988), pp. 554–556.
8. Ibid, pp. 555.
9. Mathew, Roy, Maxine Weinman and Mohsen Mirabi. "Physical Symptoms of Depression," *British Journal of Psychiatry* 139 (1981), pp. 292–296.
10. Cox, I. M., M. J. Campbell, and D. Dowson. "Red blood cell magnesium and chronic fatigue syndrome," *The Lancet* (337) (March 30, 1991), pp. 757–760.
11. Gold, Deborah, and Raleigh Bowden, John Sixbey et al. "Chronic Fatigue: A Prospective Clinical and Virologic Study," *Journal of the American Medical Association* 264:1 (July 4, 1990), pp. 48–53.

CHAPTER TWELVE

References

1. See "Candidiasis: Reports of an 'epidemic' are premature," *The Mayo Clinic Health Letter*, April, 1988.
2. Quoted from the statement of the practice standards committee of the American Academy of Allergy and Immunology issued in the summer of 1985.
3. Trowbridge, John Parks and Morton Walker. *The Yeast Syndrome*. New York, Bantam: 1986. Preface.
4. Truss, C. Orian. *The Missing Diagnosis* (1983), p. 169. Also appeared as an article in *Journal of Orthomolecular Psychiatry*. 10:4 (1981), pp. 228–238.
5. Used with permission from William G. Crook, *The Yeast Connection*. (Jackson, Tenn.: Professional Books, 1983), p. viii.
6. Truss, C. Orian. *The Missing Diagnosis*. (1983), p. 6.
7. Staver, Sari. "Meeting Sheds Light on Chronic Fatigue." *American Medical News*. (May 28, 1989), p. 1–2.

Further Reading

Bodey, Gerald P., and Victor Fainstein. *Candidiasis.* (New York: Raven Press, 1985.)

Burton, Gail. *The Candida Control Cookbook.* (New York: New American Library, 1989.)

Crook, William G. *The Yeast Connection: A Medical Breakthrough.* (Jackson, Tenn.: Professional Books, 1983.)

Lorenzani, Shirley S. *Candida: A Twentieth Century Disease.* (New Canaan, Conn.: Keats Publishing Inc., 1986.)

Odds, F. C. *Candida and Candidosis.* (Baltimore: University Park Press, 1989.)

Saltarelli, Cora G. *Candida Albicans: The Pathogenic Fungus* (New York, N.Y.: Hemisphere Publishing Corp., 1989.)

Trowbridge, John P., and Morton Walker. *The Yeast Syndrome.* (New York, N.Y.: Bantam, 1986.)

——. *Yeast Related Illnesses.* (Greenwich, Conn.: Devin-Adair, 1987.)

Truss, C. Orian. *The Missing Diagnosis.* (Birmingham, Ala.: C. Orian Truss, 1982.)

Wunderlich, Ray C., and Dwight K. Kalita. *Candida Albicans: How to Fight an Exploding Epidemic of Yeast-related Diseases.* (New Canaan, Conn.: Keats Publishing, Inc., 1984.)

INDEX